People and the Hotel and Catering Industry

NDREW LOCKWOOD, BSc (Hons), CERT. ED., MHCIMA
*Senior Lecturer in Hotel and Catering Administration,
Guildford County College of Technology*

PETER JONES, BA (Hons), CERT. ED., MHCIMA
*Lecturer in Food and Beverage Service Systems,
Brighton Polytechnic*

HOLT, RINEHART AND WINSTON
LONDON · NEW YORK · SYDNEY · TORONTO

Holt, Rinehart and Winston Ltd: 1 St Anne's Road,
Eastbourne, East Sussex BN21 3UN

British Library Cataloguing in Publication Data

Lockwood, A.
  People and the hotel and catering industry.
  1. Hotel management
  I. Title   II. Jones, Peter, 1951–
  647'.9'068   TX911.3.M27

ISBN 0–03–910523–7

Typesetting and artwork by Multiplex medway ltd

Printed in Great Britain by Mackays of Chatham Ltd, Chatham, Kent.

Last digit is print no: 9 8 7 6 5 4 3 2 1

Contents

Acknowledgements

Acknowledgements go to the following people and organisations for their help and assistance:

Victor Amaranayake; Berni Inns; Richard Booth; *British Business* magazine; Burford Bridge Hotel; Catering Education Research Institute; *Catering and Hotel Management*; Consumer Industries Press; Lucy Dabbs; Juliet Dean; Michael Flagle; John Henwood; Her Majesty's Stationery Office; Holt, Rinehart and Winston; Hotel and Catering Industry Training Board; *International Journal of Hospitality Management*; Simon Jack; P.J. Johnson Esq.; Simon Lake; Fiona Lamming; Peter Lockwood; Wendy Lockwood; McGraw-Hill Book Company; Betty Major; Keith Mercer; Paul Merricks; Methuen and Co. Ltd; John Murray (Publishers) Ltd; Prof. P. Nailon; NOP Market Research Ltd; Kevin O'Leary; Penguin Books Ltd; Pergamon Press Ltd; Greg Ridout; Royal Garden Hotel; Matthew Salomonson; Scientific Methods Inc.; Helen Taylor; Ann Townsend; Travellers Fare; Rowena Ward.

Preface

THE success of any hotel and catering operation is dependent upon the satisfaction of the needs of two different groups of people — the million or so employees of the industry and the millions of customers catered for each year. The aim of this book is to help managers and supervisors to become more successful by developing their understanding of people in as straightforward a manner as possible and relating this to the special needs of the hotel and catering industry. It is not intended to be an academic treatment of the behavioural sciences, but a simple introduction to this field of study concentrating on those concepts relevant to the industry.

The book is aimed primarily at students studying for BTEC National and Higher Diplomas in Hotel and Catering Operations, Hotel Administration and Travel and Tourism to cover elements of Behavioural Studies, Introduction to Supervision, People and Communication and People in Organisations. It will also be found useful for HCIMA Parts A and B covering aspects of A100 Business and Supervisory studies and B206 Manpower Studies. Students studying on degree courses will find the book a useful introduction to their studies and the source of many references for further development. It is also hoped that practising supervisors and managers in industry will find it relevant to the problems facing them in the industrial situation and helpful in finding some solutions.

There are many different approaches to the behavioural sciences. This book, after an introduction to the special features of the hotel and catering industry, looks first at the individual in his or her own right, then in communication with others, as a member of a small group and of large groups, the behaviour of customers and finally the special problems facing individuals who supervise or manage other individuals. Each chapter can be read in isolation but the interrelated nature of the subject matter has been stressed by the use of cross references and the series of case studies which cover topics from a variety of chapters.

Each chapter consists of the main text interspersed with a number of tasks to be completed either individually or with one or two others, along with case examples which provide illustrations of how a particular concept applies in an industrial situation and with case exercises which require the consideration of particular situations and the proposal of solutions. At the end of each chapter is a list of the sources of references quoted during the chapter. This provides an opportunity for further reading and consultation of the original texts used for more detailed analysis. Many of the tasks and exercises can be extended for group work and lecturers should find that this book provides the theoretical background to allow the use of experiential/practical learning situations.

Dealing with people is fundamental to the work of almost every employee in the hotel and catering industry. We hope this book makes that experience more understandable, more successful and, above all, more enjoyable.

ANDREW LOCKWOOD
PETER JONES

For Wendy, Anna and Nicola; and Christopher

1 The People Business

OBJECTIVES: to define 'human relations' . . . to explain the role of human relations in the hotel and catering industry . . . to identify the contribution of human relations to hospitality management . . . to identify the need for a conceptual framework to deal with human relations experiences

1.1 INTRODUCTION

'IT is a very well-known and undeniable fact that human relations have a special importance in the field of all service related activities'. Such is the view expressed by the Association Internationale des Directeurs d'Écoles Hôtelières in their manifesto published following their international congress in 1982. But is this need for an understanding of human relations identified by people working in the industry, as well as educationalists in the hotel and catering field? According to the research carried out by Dr Paul Johnson for the HCIMA's 'Corpus of Knowledge', management personnel currently working in the industry were aware of the need for human relations skills. Of 259 managers interviewed, 81 per cent stated that they used such skills frequently, to the extent that it was identified as being the skill most often needed and utilised in day-to-day management. Dr Johnson states that whilst the response requires careful interpretation, there is a deficiency in the present level of knowledge of human relations in relation to managers' needs in their current jobs.

1.2 DEFINING HUMAN RELATIONS

Terry Morgan writes,[1] 'Human relations — the oil that keeps the organisational wheels turning — or, more often it seems, the grit that makes the machine shudder'.

This definition, although not very precise, does highlight the great importance of human relations in any organisation, suggesting that successful management of human relations will aid the smooth running of the business. However, it is our opinion that human relations is *the* most important aspect of management, particularly in the hotel and catering industry. For human relations is quite simply an understanding of people — who they are; why they behave the way that they do; how to deal with them effectively in a wide variety of situations. Examples of human relations at work are 'boss dealing with subordinates', 'members of a team dealing with each other', and 'employees dealing with clients'; any situation, in fact, where one person comes into contact, directly or indirectly, with another. The ability to deal with the human 'resource' is both vital and stimulating.

> The only resources within an organisation capable of transformation are human resources. Money and materials are depleted. Meals are consumed, beds are slept in. Equipment is subject to wear and tear; it can be used well or badly but can never perform more efficiently than it was originally designed to do. Humans alone can grow and develop. Therefore, it is this resource in industry which is both the most complex to deal with and the most rewarding . . . The successful incorporation of the human factor into management at all levels seems to be something that is desired by employees, many managements and society at large.[2]

It is relatively recently that the term human relations has been used to encompass all aspects of understanding people. We must make it clear that we are dealing with far more than was originally intended in the development of the human relations school of management thought originating in the 1930s. This approach arose from the Hawthorne Study conducted by Elton Mayo (see Chapter 7) which stressed the importance of treating employees as people and not just another factor of production. It emphasised the importance of the informal group within any organisation and of relationships in the work situation. However, its limitations were that it tended to concentrate on the welfare of employees and on keeping people happy, ignoring the economic realities of efficiency and productivity.

The resurgence of human relations as a major area of management concern has been associated with the application of the behavioural sciences, such as psychology and sociology, to the industrial situation and the adoption of an inter-disciplinary approach to management problems. This is exemplified by the increase in research dealing with human aspects of management, the findings of some of which we cite in this book, and the inclusion of a human relations element on courses in management approved by the Business and Technician Education Councils.

1.3 RELEVANCE TO THE HOTEL AND CATERING INDUSTRY

If we agree that human relations is basically the study of people, it is immediately apparent how relevant this is to the hotel and catering industry, simply by looking at the number and nature of people involved in the industry. The total market for catering in 1981 was estimated to be nearly £20 000 million in 1981[3] with over 220 000 catering outlets.[4]

The industry in the United Kingdom is a large employer. According to official figures there are at least 850 000 full-time workers[5] but this is very much an underestimation as shown in Table 1.1 which breaks down the number of people employed into different sectors of the industry.

Table 1.1 *Number of staff in sectors of the hotel and catering industry.*

Sector	Male			Female			TOTAL
	Part time	Full time	TOTAL	Part time	Full time	TOTAL	
Hotels	32 000	153 000	185 000	133 000	167 000	300 000	485 000
Guest houses	3 000	9 000	12 000	19 000	17 000	36 000	48 000
Restaurants	16 000	66 000	82 000	77 000	50 000	127 000	209 000
Cafes	10 000	25 000	35 000	58 000	39 000	97 000	132 000
Industrial	7 000	34 000	41 000	77 000	124 000	201 000	242 000
Pubs	69 000	86 000	155 000	230 000	75 000	305 000	460 000
Clubs	24 000	23 000	47 000	69 000	17 000	86 000	133 000
Local authority	2 000	3 000	5 000	243 000	92 000	335 000	340 000
							2 049 000

Source: HCITB 'Manpower in the Hotel and Catering Industry—Tier 1' (1977)

It is possible from these figures to identify a wide variety of both employees and customers in the various sectors of the industry. For instance, it is unlikely that a food service operative working in an industrial canteen will seek employment in a luxury hotel, whilst a customer in a seaside guest house will have very different needs and expectations to a patient in a hospital bed.

The complexity of human relationships even within each sector is heightened by the many different occupational categories and further exacerbated by full-time and part-time working. Table 1.2 is an occupational breakdown of staff in the public house and licensed clubs sector.

Table 1.2 *Staffing in licensed premises.*

Occupation	Numbers employed	
	Full time	Part time
Managers and working proprietors	117 000	10 000
Assistant managers	4 600	800
Management trainees	1 100	—
Porters, etc.	1 000	5 300
Housekeeping staff	200	700
Cleaners	11 900	88 400
Head waiters	1 200	700
Waiting staff	4 900	19 000
Head chefs	3 100	800
Other chefs	7 500	8 300
Counter assistants	1 300	4 000
Head bar staff	8 500	12 600
Other bar staff	34 500	236 300
Non-catering staff	3 900	4 000
Total	200 700	391 800

Source: HCITB 'Manpower in the Hotel and Catering Industry — Tier 1' (1977)

Occupational differences will express themselves with regards to human relations in a variety of ways, such as expectations of reward, level of involvement with customers, intellectual ability, and even physical characteristics. The implications of this for management are shown in such aspects as the recruitment and selection of personnel, the way staff are addressed, discipline, determining pay structure, promotion prospects, and so on. An example of this can be seen in Fig. 1.1 which compares the recruitment advertisements for two different jobs in the catering industry.

Deputy Catering Manager

is required with special responsibility for the Restaurant.

Applicants must have at least two years' general catering experience and a good knowledge of restaurant and kitchen routines. Preference will be given to applicants who have completed OND or HND in Hotel and Catering Administration or equivalent, and who are aged between 22 and 28.

The salary offered will be in the range of £4,900 to £5,500.

The hours of work will be:

Tuesday to Friday 9 a.m. to 5.45 p.m., Saturday 8.55 a.m. to 6.10 p.m.

Staff benefits include:

● Profit-sharing scheme

● Four weeks' holiday

● Discount in our stores

Please apply to: Staff Office,
          Russel's of Bain Park,
          97 Lockwood Road,
          Bain Park,
          London SW7.
          Tel: 01-000 0000 ext 111.
                              HM9

 Royal Garden Hotel

Senior Receptionist

Do you like meeting people of all nationalities?
Do you fancy working in London's finest full service 5 star Hotels, which is proud of its efficient and friendly staff teams?
We're looking for someone with a bright personality to work at our reception desk (if you're a mouse we're not interested) someone who can make a guest feel welcome. You'll need at least one other language as well as English, some experience of office procedures and previous reception experience would be an advantage.
We can offer free meals on duty, free uniform, free weekly visit to our hairdressing salon and our system of alternate early and late duties means you've time to shop in comfort and travel outside the rush hour.
If you fancy a job that's different contact Personnel Department at the Royal Garden Hotel, High Street, Kensington W8, or phone 937 8000 extension 802.
                                    (107)A

Rank Hotels

Source: *Caterer and Hotelkeeper.*

Figure 1.1   *Recruitment advertising.*

Furthermore, management must recognise that there are many more differences between employees than simply the job they do, in the first instance the most obvious of these being such things as sex, age and ethnic origin.

So far, we have been introspective in evaluating the role of human relations in the catering industry, concentrating on the employer–employee relationship and ignoring the interaction between the industry and its customers, but quite obviously customers are as diverse in their characteristics as employees.

This means that people of every race and creed, from great wealth to straitened circumstances, and of every size and shape have been either fed, supplied with drink or provided with accommodation. Thus in 1982, 11 682 000 overseas visitors came to the UK, in addition to all those British people who used hotel and catering facilities during the same year (see Table 1.3).

Table 1.3 *Overseas visitors to the UK (000s)*

	Total all visits	North America	European Community	Other W. Europe	Other areas
			Area of Residence		
1979	12 486	2196	6249	1624	2417
1980	12 421	2082	6411	1499	2429
1981	11 452	2105	5696	1359	2291
1982	11 682	2150	5695	1400	2438

Source: *British Business* (11–17 March 1983)

We have left customers until now because it must be recognised that we have less opportunity to apply our human relations techniques to them in comparison with the impact we can make on employees. Moreover, by concentrating our efforts upon employees and their customer approach we should improve the service that customers receive. If we examine the characteristics of the service that the hotel and catering industry attempts to provide, it will give us an insight into the value of human considerations of customers' needs.

1. The service provided caters for the customers' basic physiological needs i.e. food, drink, shelter and sleep, and is a home substitute. But we must also be aware of the customers' psychological needs in terms of security, status and social contact. Research[6] has indicated that 65 per cent of hotel guests expect a hotel to be compatible with their home environment.
2. Customers are individuals and as such will have different perceptions of the service they receive and therefore different levels of satisfaction which are totally personal to them.
3. The satisfactions received have a very short time span; hunger, for instance, is only satisfied by a meal for five or six hours before it needs to be satisfied again. It also seems likely that the pleasure derived from one meal is altered by the pleasure derived from each subsequent meal.
4. Once customers have selected a hotel or restaurant they expect their needs to be met almost immediately and any delay is likely to cause antagonism, whereas in other industries it is quite usual for customers to wait for delivery and thereby defer the satisfaction of their needs for a considerable period of time.

5. Every customer who enters a hotel or catering etablishment considers himself or herself an expert in what constitutes a good meal or a good night's sleep, since they have been eating and sleeping since the day they were born. It is unlikely, however, that the customer's interpretation will match exactly that of the hotelier or caterer.

6. The needs of the individual customer will vary according to the circumstances of the need for a hospitality experience; for example, conference delegates who during the week are staying in a hotel will have different requirements when staying in the same hotel with their families for a weekend break.

7. The customer is an integral part of the atmosphere of the establishment and contributes to the enjoyment of other participants in the overall experience. Therefore for everybody concerned there is a degree of unpredictability about the event.

8. The relationship between customers and members of staff is a very personal one and interactions between them are mainly unsupervised.

9. Customers can on occasions come to believe that they are personally 'employing' the member of staff serving them and this can result in a conflict of interests for everybody concerned. It can also present problems for the management of staff. Hotel and catering workers can be divided into two groups (see Fig. 1.2). Diadic workers have little or no contact with the customer, i.e. chefs, chambermaids, storekeepers, whereas triadic workers work front of house, i.e. receptionists, waiting staff, porters.

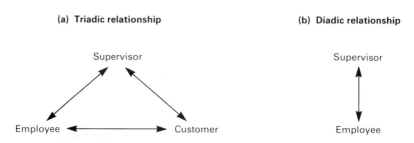

Figure 1.2   *Triadic and diadic relationships.*

Research[7] has indicated that 'triadic workers often see themselves as working for the customer. . . and have entrepreneurial attitudes as opposed to employee attitudes', whilst diadic workers are more likely to be trade union members.

10. If the service provided fails to meet the expected standard, it cannot be put right in the same way that a faulty part on a machine can be replaced. The opportunity to please customers on that occasion has gone forever, and it is extremely unlikely that they will return at a later date.

11. The hotel and catering industry is operating twenty-four hours a day throughout the year, and the customer expects to be able to enjoy a meal or a stay at any time.

Consideration of these several points illustrates that a knowledge of people and how they behave is essential in order to prevent possible conflict and enhance customers' and employees' satisfaction. Successful hoteliers and restaurateurs have an innate understanding of these human relations factors which they would probably describe as providing 'hospitality'.

1.4 HOSPITALITY MANAGEMENT

Hospitality is defined as 'the act of behaving in a warm and friendly manner',[8] but the term hospitality management has made an impact in recent years due to two publications. Firstly, by the decision of the HCIMA to change the title of its monthly magazine to *Hospitality*. In December 1979 the Editor, Jan Berger, wrote 'hospitality is the people business of providing security, physical and psychological comfort for reward'[9], so that all sectors of the hotel and catering industry are to be included in the definition but emphasising the stress to be placed on people in the industry. Secondly, by the introduction of the *International Journal of Hospitality Management*.

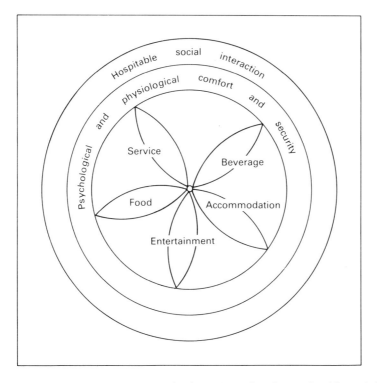

Figure 1.3   *The elements of hospitality. Reprinted with permission from* International Journal of Hospitality Management, *1 (1). Oxford: Pergamon.*

This does not mean to say that hoteliers and caterers had not been aware of hospitality before 1979. Walter Bachman published *Professional Knowledge* in 1951 which included a section on 'The service knowledge' written by two Swiss hoteliers, P. Ruch and C. Tuor. They write 'anyone who follows this profession of selling food and drink without being a real host to the guests is on the wrong tack'.[10] They go on to say that 'pleasant relations between head and staff infuse hotel and restaurant with a friendly spirit and the staff do their task with a feeling of inner satisfaction; thus creating a friendly pleasant atmosphere in which the guest feels at home'. Interestingly enough they too recognised the differences between potential customers—'members of different nations have different characteristics. But they have one thing in common — they love good food and accommodation'.

Today, the industry has moved away from these down-to-earth homilies, towards a more systematic approach to hospitality.

John Burgess[11] represents the elements of hospitality as a package (see Fig. 1.3). The outer, primary interacting element is that of the social relationships fostered by the warm, friendly, welcoming, courteous, open, generous behaviour of the host, creating the hospitable environment. This supports and promotes the positive feeling of security and comfort created by the physical structure, design, decor and location of the facility. Finally, the provision of accommodation facilities in which to sleep, eat, relax and wash, together with the supply of food, beverage, service and entertainment.

Another approach to the concept of hospitality management has been developed by Philip Nailon,[12] which emphasises the position of human resources and their management.

As can be seen in Fig. 1.4 human resources are regarded as being one of four major areas of management concern in a hospitality situation. In addition, it is important to consider human resources not in isolation, but in the way they interact with the other

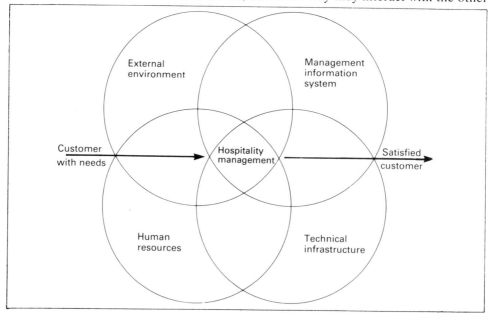

Figure 1.4   *Model of hospitality.*

three factors individually and collectively. As Nailon has stated 'hospitality manage-ment can therefore be seen as the active co-ordination and balancing of the inter-relationship of the four systems represented by the external environment, the human resources, the technical infra-structure and the management information systems. Its purpose is to provide physiological and psychological comfort and security as a busi-ness activity at a defined standard of service through provision of facilitating goods.' The role of this book is to examine in some depth this human resource in order to understand fully its capabilities, behaviour and limitations.

1.5 CONCLUSION

We have seen in this chapter the great diversity of people in the hotel and catering industry, both in terms of the different employees with whom managers must work and the customers whose needs they must satisfy. It is all too easy to assume that the human relations approach will provide a solution to all organisational problems and social conflict, but of course, no one technique can be totally successful. It must be used in conjunction with other management techniques of accounting, marketing, work study, and so on. No one human interaction is exactly like any other, they are all unique. But we can provide a framework of understanding about human relations within which to analyse our personal experience about human relationships and thereby guide our actions and make us more effective, more caring and more success-ful in dealing with people, whoever they may be. Our approach will therefore not be a prescription for success but a description of how success may be achieved. Perhaps one of the most important results of studying human relations is that as knowledge of how other people behave increases, so does self-awareness, and thus the individual is developed as a person as well as a manager.

Case example 1.1 A change in reception

This recent development is only one example of the ever-present awareness of the importance of people in the hospitality industry.

The Burford Bridge Hotel near Dorking was the first hotel in the Trusthouse Forte group to undergo a radical change to their reception area. The old high traditional reception desk in this 52-bedroom 4-star hotel which used to pro-vide a physical and psychological barrier between the receptionist and the newly arrived guest has been replaced by an elegant pedestal desk in an open plan lounge area. When guests arrive, the receptionist can help them to register either at this desk or in any other part of the lounge as there is com-pletely free access. After registering the receptionist takes the guests to their room showing the hotel's other facilities on the way and providing an oppor-tunity to get to know the guests a little better. None of the clerical work of reception is done on the desk in the lounge, it is all done in the back office so that the telephone switchboard, billing machine and reservations computer are kept out of sight, once again stressing the personal nature of the service. If a receptionist is working in the back office they can keep an eye on the lounge at all times through the doorways and a series of strategically placed mirrors, so that no guest can go unnoticed. Helen Taylor, the head recep-tionist who was directly involved in the change, said that at first staff felt strange and ill at ease in such an open environment. Very soon though, they get used to the new system and indeed find it more rewarding as they feel more involved with the guests on a one-to-one basis and more involved with the rest of the hotel, not being isolated behind a desk. Trusthouse Forte are now in the process of changing all the reception areas in their hotels and inns to this new system where possible and are considering how to adapt this principle to their Post Houses as well.

REFERENCES

1. Rackham, N., Honey, P. & Colbert, M. (eds) (1971) *Developing Interactive Skills*. Northampton: Wellens.
2. Mercer, K. (1978) Psychology at work in the hotel and catering industry. *HCIMA Review*, **4**.
3. Euromonitor (1982) *The Hotel and Catering Industry*. London: Euromonitor.
4. *Catering Prospects 1981*, BIS Marketing Research.
5. *Employment Gazette* (1983) April.
6. Shamir, B. (1978) Some organisational characteristics of hotels. *Journal of Management Studies*.
7. Lowe, A. (1979) *New Methods of Decision-making*. Birmingham: University of Aston.
8. *Webster's Dictionary*.
9. *HCIMA Journal* (1979) December.
10. Bachman, W. (1951) *Professional Knowledge* Vol. III. London: MacLaren.
11. Burgess, J. (1982) Perspectives on gift exchange and hospitable behaviour. *International Journal of Hospitality Management*, **1** (1).
12. Nailon, P. (1982) Theory in hospitality management. *International Journal of Hospitality Management*, **1** (3).

2 Looking at Individuals

Mad dogs and Englishmen go out in the midday sun, The Japanese don't care to, the Chinese wouldn't dare to; Hindus and Argentines sleep firmly from twelve to one

Noël Coward

OBJECTIVES: to identify the factors that contribute to differences between individuals . . . to analyse the role of physique, intelligence, personality and sociocultural heritage in individuals . . . to relate the study of individual differences to the hotel and catering industry

2.1 INTRODUCTION

'INDIVIDUAL *adj.* single; particular; special; having distinct character — *n.* single member of a class, group, or number; single human being (opp. to society, the family, etc.)'

The above dictionary definition of what it means to be an individual highlights that although part of a larger group, every person is unique in some way or another. But there are various dimensions to this uniqueness and it is these that we shall be examining in this chapter. A point to be stressed, however, is that no one dimension is more important than another, although some are more relevant in particular situations than others; for instance an individual's weight is unimportant if driving a train, but may be crucial if riding in the Derby.

We have identifed four major dimensions of individual differences, shown below.

(1) Physical

This dimension is concerned with all aspects of an individual's physical characteristics, and includes factors such as size, shape, appearance, colour and sex.

(2) Intellectual

This is a general term for abilities underlying thought and reasoning. These have probably been the most extensively investigated of the areas of differences between individuals and are primarily concerned with what is commonly known as intelligence.

(3) Personality

This dimension has been defined by H.J. Eysenck as 'the more or less stable and enduring organisation of a person's character, temperament, intellect and physique which determines his unique adjustment to the environment.'

(4) Sociocultural

Each society has its own attitudes, beliefs, and accepted standards of behaviour and these obviously will have a profound effect on the behaviour patterns of the individual. This process is generally known as socialisation.

Before we examine in more detail each of these dimensions, it should be pointed out that one of the great dangers of such an examination is the tendency to stress the extremes. This is because most of the dimensions can be described as a continuum, that is to say a range of possible attributes between one clearly definable limit to the opposite extreme. For instance, people's heights range from very short to very tall. However, in any given population it would be wrong to assume that each of the possibilities along the range is equally represented; in fact the distribution tends to follow what is known as a normal distribution curve, so there may be a relatively small number of very short and very tall people and a very large number of people around average height as illustrated in Fig. 2.1.

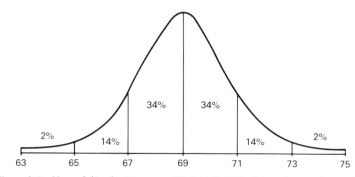

Figure 2.1 *Normal distribution curve of height (in inches) in a given male population.*

Task 2.1 Self-rating guide

For each of the factors in Fig. 2.2 rate yourself on a scale from 0 to 10. A score of 5 represents the average, more than 5 is above average up to the superlative score of 10, and less than 5 is below average.
  Complete only column A (the other three columns will be completed later).

Factors	A	B	C	D
Physical fitness				
Appearance				
Intelligence				
Numerical ability				
Creativity				
Judgement				
Outgoingness				
Emotional stability				
Persuasiveness				
Dominance over others				
Respect for authority				

Figure 2.2 *A self-rating guide.*

2.2 PHYSICAL DIFFERENCES

Human beings differ from each other physically in as many ways as there are parts of the human body.

The major differences include height, weight, shape, colour of hair, eyes and skin, facial features, tone of voice, size of limbs, and posture. Such characteristics are primarily hereditary, but they can be affected by upbringing, illness, accident or training. Let us look at some of these differences in more detail, before discussing implications of these to the hotel and catering manager.

Sex

Not only is sex one of the most obvious and basic differences between individuals in the population, it is also one of the most controversial. The purpose of the Sex Discrimination Act 1975 was to try to eliminate discrimination against anybody on the basis of their sex, particularly in the field of selection, promotion and employment of personnel. Even so the Act does recognise that there may be exceptions where there may be some special characteristics of a job which make it suitable only for someone of a particular sex, for instance lavatory attendant, or actor or actress. Just as the Act recognises these differences, so it is relatively easy to contrast the purely physical attributes of men and women.

(a) Height

The average height of females in the UK population is approximately 65 inches, whereas the average male height is 69 inches. This will obviously prevent a large percentage of the female population taking jobs which have a height requirement as a genuine occupational qualification (GOQ); for instance the Fire Service stipulates a minimum height requirement for its personnel of 66 inches (168 cm).

(b) Body structure

Apart from the obvious differences in the physical form of males and females, men tend to have a larger bone structure, less fatty tissue, straighter legs, and a narrower pelvis than women, since the female body is adapted to cope with child-bearing.

(c) Strength

Since strength is directly related to stature, it is obvious that *on average* females are not as strong as males. It is therefore true to say that there are some occupations which involve heavy physical effort which are *on average* more suitable for men, for instance, manual labourer, or docker.

(d) Rate of growth

Girls tend to grow most rapidly between the ages of ten and fifteen, whereas boys experience a growth acceleration between fourteen and eighteen, so that women are physically mature at an earlier age than men.

(e) Life expectancy

In the United Kingdom the average life expectancy of males in the population is 70.2 years, and that of females is 76.3 years (*United Kingdom in Figures*, 1980). It is for this reason that females in the UK outnumber males by 1.4 million.

Race

A second major physical difference between individuals is their racial origin, the most obvious sign being the colour of a person's skin. However, as well as the obvious differences of such things as hair type and colour, dental structure, head and nose shape, and average height, there are less obvious differences in terms of frequency of blood groups, fingerprints, susceptibility to certain diseases, and reaction to certain chemicals. People can basically be divided into three racial groups.

(a) Caucasoid

Characterised by a light skin colour, hair is usually straight or wavy and abundant on the body; facial profile is straight, the nose usually high and narrow; blood group A predominates over B. These people are found in Europe, the Americas, the Middle East, India and Australasia.

(b) Mongoloid

The classic mongoloid is found in Central Asia and North China. They have straight, coarse black hair with very fine bodily hair, yellow-brown skin, a flat, broad face with a low bridged nose and a fold of skin over the eye.

(c) Negroid

These people originate in Africa and have a dark brown to black skin colour; a broad nose, thick everted lips and a marked projection of the lower face; hair is woolly and scarce on the body; arms and legs are long in relation to the trunk.

   The above characteristics only identify the three major racial groups, but a number of authorities in this field such as Garn[1] and Baker[2], and so on would further sub-divide these into other groupings such as capoid, australoid, melanesian and polynesian.

Age

Finally, there are obvious physical differences between persons of different ages, notably between children and adults. The most obvious physical differences associated with ageing are that the skin becomes more wrinkled and loses its youthful bloom, teeth may fall out and gums recede, hair may change its colour or fall out, blood circulation slows down and so on. In reality the differences are not as great as may at first be thought. Research has indicated[3] that 'compared with a person aged twenty an eighty year old loses on average only fifteen to twenty per cent of brain weight and only twenty-five per cent of muscle strength'. Whilst older people may still perform satisfactorily at work, they will be working nearer to the limits of their abilities than they did when younger. A.T. Welford[4] suggests that the decline with age of short-term memory and speed of decision-making has a great influence on the performance of older people. Reaction time tests in which people are asked to respond to a given stimulus and their response time is measured, have shown that older people are only slightly slower than younger people, but that as the complexity of the task increases so does the older person's response time.

Ergonomics

In a pioneering booklet in 1971, R.H.D. Strank[5] discusses the role of 'ergonomics' in the catering industry. He writes that the word ergonomics 'will be unfamiliar to many readers. It is a new word coined to describe a new subject . . . It seeks to design better tools, better equipment, better procedures and better environments'. The basis of such developments and new designs is related very closely to an understanding of the human physique. 'The starting point for the ergonomic design of any article is that it should allow the person using it to adopt a natural and unstrained position'. In this context many, if not all items, of catering equipment and furniture have been designed with this in view, usually on the basis of average dimensions although as Strank points out there are many instances where this will not produce acceptable results. The type of human dimensions considered are wide-ranging to include not only height, but also shoulder width (relevant, for instance, with regard to the width of aisles, corridors and gangways), eye height (which has implications for the siting of notices and instructions), elbow height (which is important in regard to the height of work surfaces), maximum upward reach, normal forward reach, and other dimensions with regard to the seated posture of human beings.

Task 2.2

Strank was writing in 1971. He recommended that seats suitable for use in restaurants should have the following dimensions:

Seat height	41 – 43 cm
Seat width	50 cm
Seat depth	40 – 45 cm
Gap between seat and backrest	20 cm
Backrest	10 – 20 cm
Seat arms above seat	20 – 25 cm

Measure the seats in restaurants you have access to. Do they meet these criteria? If not, why might they be bigger or smaller than Strank recommends?

2.3 INTELLECTUAL DIFFERENCES

It is manifestly obvious that people display different levels of intellectual competence, the two extremes of which are moron and genius. Amongst social scientists there is considerable debate about the nature and development of these intellectual abilities, some taking the view that they are derived from heredity, others stressing the importance of the environment. However, we are less concerned with the origins of intellectual ability, than the performance of persons with different intellectual abilities and how these may affect the work situation. For example, the suitability of a person for a particular job may well depend upon their intellectual ability, which is often measured on the basis of educational achievement (see Fig. 1.1) but can also be measured by specific testing designed to test different abilities, the most notable of which is the intelligence test.

In order to understand the intellectual differences between individuals, we must review the research that has been undertaken in this field. But in view of the very great number of investigations and theories, we shall confine ourselves to a brief survey of theories that have been developed since 1900.

The simplest theory is that developed by Spearman[6] and is usually called the 'two factor' theory. This suggests that each individual has a general level of ability which he called the 'g' factor, accounting for the major differences in human performance. In addition, he identified the 's' factor, or specific factor, which accounts for an individual's ability in certain areas such as an individual's flair for music, writing or mathematics. Another view of intelligence is the 'hierarchical group-factor' theory, proposed by Burt and others[7] which is a much more complex and sophisticated concept as illustrated in Fig. 2.3. This shows abilities arranged into three levels — general ability, group abilities, and special abilities.

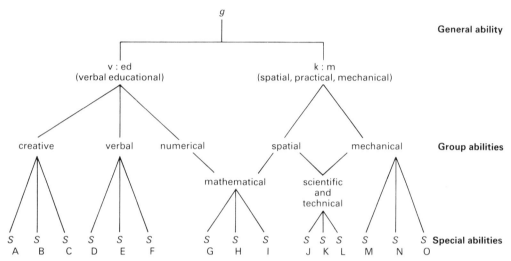

Figure 2.3 *Diagrammatic representation of the hierarchical group-factor theory of intelligence. Adapted from Vernon, P.E. (1969)* Intelligence and Cultural Environment. *London: Methuen.*

This theory takes Spearman's general factor and divides it into a verbal educational component (v:ed) and a spatial, practical, mechanical component (k:m). These two are then sub-divided into different groups which are then further sub-divided into specific abilities. A third expert in this field, Thurstone,[8] refutes the view that such a thing as general ability of 'g' can be identified. Using a different analytical procedure he suggests that intelligence is composed of a number of separate and specific factors which he called 'primary mental abilities'. These include verbal comprehension (v), verbal fluency or word power (w), numerical ability (n), spatial ability (s), memory (m), reasoning (r) and perceptual speed (p). In view of this approach he believed that it was more appropriate to look at a profile of an individual's intellectual ability rather than attempt to identify a single, general level in absolute terms. This idea may be more helpful than others in the context of personnel selection as it enables us to isolate those abilities which are appropriate to a specific job and therefore match up applicants most suited to the work. Finally, one theory is that proposed by Guildford[9] who suggests that there as many as 120 different component factors in an individual's intellectual make-up and although this may do justice to the complexity of human intelligence its diversity makes it difficult to apply in any practical situation.

   Whichever theory of intelligence one subscribes to, Hebb has suggested that every individual has an intelligence 'A' and an intelligence 'B'. The former is the potential intelligence of a person, determined genetically by the structure of the brain, and whatever happens after birth can either help to realise that potential or hinder it, but it cannot affect the potential itself. Intelligence 'B' is the extent to which this in-built potential has been achieved by the interaction of a person's genetic make-up and the environment in which they are raised. Thus from the moment of conception, external factors are affecting the development of the individual, so that it is impossible to measure intelligence 'A'. It does seem possible to measure intelligence 'B' until it is pointed out, as Vernon has done,[10] that tests can only measure a sample of human intelligence. Vernon goes so far as to suggest that there is such a thing as intelligence 'C' which is that part of 'B' that can effectively be measured by a test.
   This brings us to the whole question of intelligence testing and its value to the potential manager. Intelligence tests generally are used to establish an individual's IQ or intelligence quotient. This originally was calculated by using the following formula:

$$IQ = \frac{\text{mental age}}{\text{chronological age}} \times 100$$

This, however, has been superseded by a statistical technique which sets the mean score for an age group at 100 and then compares the individual with that mean, so that someone with a score higher than 100 is of above average intelligence for that particular age group. Since intelligence follows a normal distribution curve, over two-thirds of the population have an IQ of between 85 and 115. To be classified as a 'genius' according to MENSA, a person must score 140 or more. Such tests tend to measure three main areas, verbal ability, numerical ability and spatial ability as illustrated in the sample questions in Table 2.1 and owe a great deal to the developmental work of Binet which began in the 1900s.

Table 2.1   *Examples of typical intelligence test questions.*[11]

VERBAL   Find the odd one out: NIROY   LEEST   PORPEC   NOBREZ

Insert a word that completes the first word and begins the second: SHR(. . .)ALE

Choose the correct alternative:
Male is to female as dog is to:
(a) cat (b) vixen (c) canine (d) bitch

NUMERICAL
Insert the missing number: 5   8   12
                                   7   12   18
                                   3   4   ?

Insert the missing number:

                                   ?   2

                  73   6

                       34   15

SPATIAL Find the odd one out:

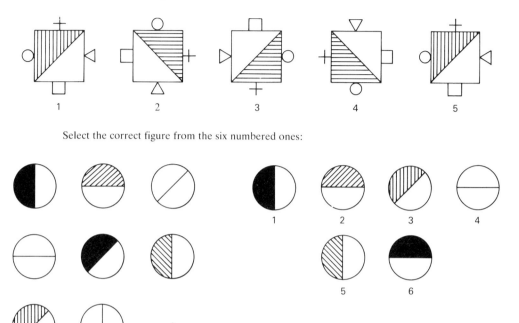

Select the correct figure from the six numbered ones:

(Reprinted by permission of Penguin Books Ltd.)

There have been many criticisms levelled at intelligence testing:

1. Only specialised skills are tested, ignoring such factors as creativity, business acumen, musical ability and so on.
2. Overemphasis is placed on verbal ability.
3. Since the tests have been developed by and sampling is based on the performance of mainly European and North American population samples, they are said to be culturally biased.
4. Only a sample of abilities is tested at a particular moment in time.
5. It is possible to coach individuals in the skills needed to do well in tests and thereby improve their test score.

Another aspect of intellectual ability is the thinking style a person adopts in the solution of problems. This can be divided into divergent and convergent thinking. Convergent thinkers are best in dealing with problems requiring one correct solution clearly definable from the available information; most of the items found in intelligence tests, for instance. They tend to adopt a logical and conservative approach to problem solving, which we examine in more detail in Chapter 8. Divergent thinkers are best in dealing with problems requiring the creation of a number of alternative solutions, where the emphasis is upon originality and variety; for instance a sample question from a test designed to measure divergent thinking might be 'how many uses are there for a house brick?' It is important to realise that both thinking styles are equally valid but may be more applicable to some situations than others. Intelligence tests tend to favour the use of convergent thinking and people such as de Bono are anxious to correct what they see as an imbalance by developing tests and routines designed to encourage divergent thinking.

Task 2.3

The diagram in Fig. 2.4 shows a training board for fault-finding in electrical work. The trainee is given such a board and must discover where the break in the circuit has occurred by inserting the testing plug into any one of the twenty-five sockets. If the circuit is complete the bell will ring. Imagine you are the trainee and write down the sequence of socket numbers that you would test in order to find the fault.

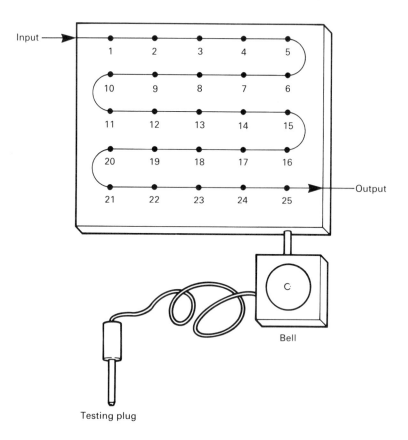

Figure 2.4 *Training board for fault finding.*

2.4 PERSONALITY DIFFERENCES

Since early civilisation people have attempted to categorise one another on the basis of their character and temperament. In the second century AD Galen proposed four personality types based on the distribution of 'body fluids' or 'humours' first suggested by Hippocrates in the fifth century BC as illustrated in Table 2.2.

Table 2.2   *Galen's four personality types.*

Humours	Black bile	Blood	Phlegm	Yellow bile
Personality type	Melancholic	Sanguine	Phlegmatic	Choleric
Typical behaviour	Pessimistic, suspicious, depressed	Optimistic, sociable, easy-going	Calm, controlled, lethargic	Active, irritable, egocentric

It is interesting to note, as we shall see, that this classification accords with current thinking with regard to personality types in many respects, although there is obviously no physiological basis for this as the Greeks believed.

At the end of the nineteenth century the work of Sigmund Freud formed the basis of much of modern psychology. Unfortunately, it is difficult to draw many conclusions from his work as his theories are extensive and open to many different interpretations. For these reasons his theories have limited practical value in an industrial situation, but as he has had such a profound effect on psychology we must consider the basic principles which he developed. He proposed that experiences in early childhood, especially to do with the development of sexual behaviour, have a critical impact on behaviour patterns in later life. He differentiated between the conscious actions and the unconscious thoughts of the individual and believed the former, the normal operating state of the mind, could be affected by the unconscious, which largely consisted of previous, probably unpleasant experiences. Freud also put forward three different types of behaviour which he called the 'id', 'ego' and 'superego'. The 'id' is the product of heredity and is the basic level of instinctive response, being mainly concerned with self-preservation, reproduction, and aggression. The 'ego' is the part of the person which rationalises the demands of the 'id' into intelligent action and socially acceptable behaviour. The 'superego' represents the moral values which are developed throughout childhood. Human behaviour therefore consists of a balance between the instinct of the 'id', the repression of the 'superego', and the intellectual control of the 'ego'.

Perhaps the most significant contributions to the study of the personality in relation to the work environment are those of Eysenck and Cattell. These theorists have adopted the trait or psychometric approach. This is based on an analysis of adjectives describing people's behaviour, such as shy, outgoing, brave, serious and so on. These adjectives can be analysed and categorised to arrive at a number of characteristic styles of behaviour. Eysenck, for instance, identifies three basic dimensions, whereas Cattell has identified 16 different personality factors. Once these major characteristics have been established, it is then possible to place an individual on a personality scale according to their responses to certain tests, rather like the process of intelligence testing.

Eysenck's three personality types are extraversion–introversion; emotional stability–neuroticism; and masculinity–femininity. Each of these types is made up of a number of personality traits.

A person can therefore be identified as tending towards one end of the continuum or the other in each of the three types according to their observable behaviour and test responses. Extraverts display such traits as being sociable, impulsive, and uninhibited, enjoying social gatherings, craving excitement and danger, seeking variety and are generally carefree and optimistic, whereas introverts are quiet, retiring, tending towards introspection and reserved, planning carefully ahead, keeping their feelings under tight control, ethical, reliable and generally pessimistic. Emotionally unstable individuals show a low level of self-esteem and wide variations in mood, they are easily upset and suffer from anxiety which may well lead to such symptoms as headaches, digestive disorders, and insomnia; whereas emotionally stable individuals are able to cope with stress and remain calm and controlled in most situations.

Task 2.4

The diagram below shows the continua mentioned above at right angles to each other dividing personality types into four broad areas (somewhat like Galen). Place the words from the list below into the most appropriate quadrant, for instance moody should be placed in the top left quadrant.

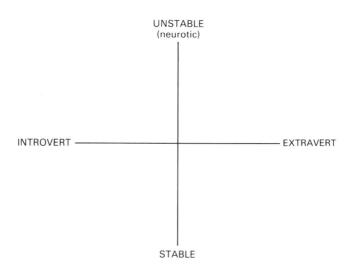

ACTIVE; AGGRESSIVE; ANXIOUS; CALM; CAREFREE; CAREFUL; CHANGE-ABLE; CONTROLLED; EASY-GOING; EVEN-TEMPERED; EXCITABLE; IMPULSIVE; LEADING; LIVELY; MOODY; OPTIMISTIC; OUTGOING; PAS-SIVE; PEACEFUL; PESSIMISTIC; QUIET; RELIABLE; RESERVED; RESPON-SIVE; RESTLESS; RIGID; SOBER; SOCIABLE; THOUGHTFUL; TOUCHY; UNSOCIABLE.

Cattell's analysis is similar to that of Eysenck, but he has identified sixteen distinguishable personality factors, as shown in Table 2.3.

Table 2.3 *Cattell's 16 primary factors.*

High-score description	Factor	Low-score description
Outgoing, warmhearted, easy-going, participating (Cyclothymia)	A	*Reserved*, detached, critical, cool (Schizothymia)
More intelligent, abstract thinking, bright (Higher scholastic mental capacity)	B	*Less intelligent*, concrete thinking (Lower scholastic mental capacity)
Emotionally stable, faces reality, calm (Higher ego strength)	C	*Affected by feelings, emotionally* less stable, easily upset (Lower ego strength)
Assertive, independent, aggressive, stubborn (Dominance)	E	*Humble*, mild, obedient, conforming (Submissiveness)
Happy-go-lucky, heedless, gay, enthusiastic (Surgency)	F	*Sober*, prudent, serious, taciturn (Desurgency)
Conscientious, persevering, staid, rule-bound (Stronger superego strength)	G	*Expedient*, a law to himself, by-passes obligations (Weaker superego strength)
Venturesome, socially bold, uninhibited, spontaneous (Parmia)	H	*Shy*, restrained, diffident, timid (Threctia)
Tender-minded, dependent, over-protected, sensitive (Premsia)	I	*Tough-minded*, self-reliant, realistic, no-nonsense (Harria)
Suspicious, self-opinionated, hard to fool (Protension)	L	*Thrusting*, adaptable, free of jealousy, easy to get on with (Alaxia)
Imaginative, wrapped up in inner urgencies, careless of practical matters, bohemian (Autia)	M	*Practical*, careful, conventional, regulated by external realities, proper (Praxernia)
Shrewd, calculating, worldly, penetrating (Shrewdness)	N	*Forthright*, natural, artless, sentimental (Artlessness)
Apprehensive, worrying, depressive, troubled (Guilt proneness)	O	*Placid*, self-assured, confident, serene (Untroubled adequacy)
Experimenting, critical, liberal, analytical, free-thinking (Radicalism)	Q_1	*Conservative*, respecting established ideas, tolerant of traditional difficulties (Conservatism)
Self-sufficient, prefers own decisions, resourceful (Self-sufficiency)	Q_2	*Group-dependent*, a 'joiner' and sound follower (Group adherence)
Controlled, socially precise, self-disciplined, compulsive (High self-concept control)	Q_3	*Casual*, careless of protocol, untidy, follows own urges (Low integration)
Tense, driven, overwrought, fretful (High ergic tension)	Q_4	*Relaxed*, tranquil, torpid, unfrustrated (Low ergic tension)

There are many different ways of attempting to test personality.

(a) The self-rating questionnaire

This includes tests developed by Cattell's '16 PF' questionnaire and the Minnesota Multiphasic Personality Test. The tests consist of a series of questions to which individuals must respond either yes, no or uncertain, true or false, or rate their agreement on a scale from 'strongly agree' to 'strongly disagree'. For instance:

Do you like playing practical jokes?   YES   NO   UNCERTAIN
I would rather fly an aeroplane than
    read a book   TRUE   FALSE
Dogs are more trustworthy than people STRONGLY   AGREE   DISAGREE   STRONGLY
                                                              AGREE   DISAGREE

The response to these questions is then analysed and a score for each of the personality variables is arrived at. This makes it possible to draw up a personality profile of the individual which compares their results with the average profile, as illustrated in Fig. 2.5.

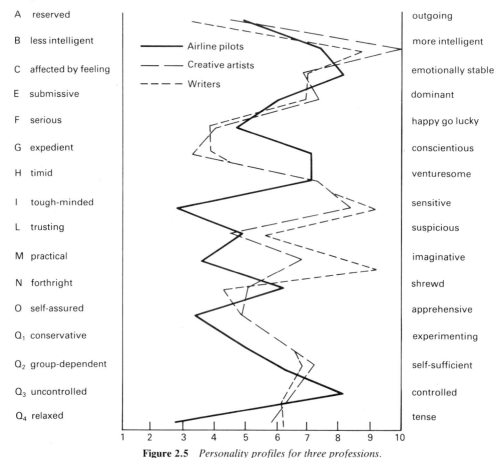

Figure 2.5 *Personality profiles for three professions.*

(b) Projective tests

These are loosely based on Freud's theories of the unconscious mind, and encourage subjects to provide a wide variety of responses to the ambiguous pictures, sentences or stories with which they are presented. For instance, the two most widely used tests are the Rorschach Blot Test (Fig. 2.6) which consists of a series of black and coloured ink blots on white card, and the Thematic Apperception Test, which consists of a series of black and white illustrations depicting people in a variety of situations. The interpretation of such tests is very difficult and must be carried out by a highly trained person.

Figure 2.6 *A design like those used in the Rorschach Blot Test.*

(c) Situational tests

These tests place people into a group and the group is then set a task to perform. This may be discussing a particular issue, or solving a practical problem. Throughout the process, trained observers record the activities engaged in and can then produce a profile of an individual's performance in relation to their ability to get on with people.

(d) Interviews

Probably one of the most widely used techniques for assessing personality is the face-to-face interview, although it is also probably the most unreliable means of assessing an individual's personality due mainly to the subjective nature of the assessment, the stressful environment in which it takes place, and the lack of training and skill of the interviewers.

Before leaving the question of personality, it should be pointed out that, unlike an individual's intelligence which tends to remain fixed throughout life, individuals may undergo quite sharp and major changes in the way in which they act and behave. Normally, an individual's personality will evolve slowly, being influenced by such factors as personal experience, peer group pressure, parental influence and the work environment. On some occasions, however, personality can change abruptly, usually due to trauma or illness, or biological reasons such as post-natal depression, pre-menstrual tension, and the menopause.

2.5 SOCIO-CULTURAL DIFFERENCES

Individual differences are also derived from the society or culture in which a person lives which will have a major impact on the formation of attitudes, values and beliefs and as a consequence upon behaviour. A good example of this is the dietary habits of different peoples — the Jew will eat a kosher diet, the Muslim will consume no alcohol, the Hindu will refuse to eat beef, and so on. It should be recognised that within the broad framework of cultures, there are an almost infinite number of sub-cultures acting upon the individual, notably the family group, the neighbourhood, the work organisation (or lack of employment), and an individual's friends and associates.

GUILDFORD SHOPPING STUDY —						
	TOTAL	**Age**				
		16-24	25-34	35-44	45-54	55+
TOTAL	1498	63	349	303	231	552
HYPERMARKET SELLING WIDE RANGE OF NON-FOOD PRODUCTS	25%	40%	42%	30%	26%	10%
DISCOUNT FURNITURE WAREHOUSE	8%	17%	13%	12%	5%	4%
LARGE CO-OP SUPERSTORE	11%	2%	8%	8%	11%	15%
SPECIAL HEALTH FOOD STORE	5%	2%	7%	4%	·3%	4%
MODERN FOOD SUPERMARKET WITH FREE SURFACE CAR PARKING	33%	35%	40%	39%	36%	23%
STORE SELLING FRESH FISH	35%	16%	23%	30%	39%	45%
DIY/HOME IMPROVEMENTS SUPERSTORE & GARDEN CENTRE	12%	14%	18%	12%	13%	9%
CHEMIST	4%	–	3%	3%	3%	7%
BUTCHERS	1%	–	#	1%	1%	1%
BRITISH HOME STORES	1%	2%	2%	3%	1%	1%
LITTLEWOODS	1%	2%	1%	1%	1%	#
SMALL SHOP OFFERING PERSONAL SERVICE	1%	–	#	#	1%	1%
OTHERS	8%	10%	11%	8%	5%	7%
NONE	15%	13%	8%	12%	16%	21%
DON'T KNOW	2%	6%	1%	1%	2%	2%

= Less than .5

Percentage figures include multiple answers.

Figure 2.7 *Sainsbury's survey in Guildford.*

Every individual holds a range of attitudes on a wide variety of subjects and if asked to comment on almost any topic will be able to provide an instantaneous response. Opinion polls which are conducted in town centres on an almost daily basis demonstrate this ability to provide positive or negative feedback to questioning, the number of 'don't knows' is invariably a very small proportion, as illustrated in Fig. 2.7 which was a comprehensive survey on additional shopping facilities in Guildford, Surrey.

It is therefore evident that people have a very real need to hold attitudes and opinions. One reason for this is that they provide a means of structuring the world and our experiences through life into an ordered system. Without attitudes each new experience would create a dilemma of how to respond. Attitudes provide a frame of reference against which to evaluate the external environment. Religious belief is one example of this. For instance, the Ten Commandments provide a rigid set of rules on how to conduct oneself in a given situation. Such a framework apart from making life less confusing, also provides pyschological security for the individual, removing some of the anxiety and concern about how to behave in social situations. To a certain extent this leads to conformity in a group of people who come into regular contact, as the holding of 'correct' attitudes leads to group approval. An example of this might be that an individual in a group of adolescent British males is likely to consume more alcohol than he really enjoys and to exaggerate his success with females. In certain circumstances when individuals do not conform with the norms of society, they may

FIELDWORK DATES: 22nd OCTOBER—7th NOVEMBER 1982

Class				Working Status of Housewife			Presence of Children		Household Size				
AB	C1	C2	DE	Full Time	Part Time	Not Work	None	1+	1	2	3	4	5+
434	385	337	342	145	439	914	821	677	151	443	272	416	216
21%	29%	32%	20%	29%	30%	23%	16%	37%	7%	16%	32%	36%	28%
5%	10%	11%	8%	12%	9%	8%	5%	12%	5%	5%	10%	11%	12%
6%	6%	16%	18%	9%	9%	12%	14%	8%	18%	14%	9%	8%	7%
6%	4%	5%	4%	5%	4%	5%	4%	5%	4%	4%	4%	5%	6%
39%	31%	35%	24%	34%	35%	31%	26%	40%	17%	26%	36%	41%	36%
40%	34%	28%	36%	33%	31%	37%	43%	25%	43%	42%	37%	27%	25%
15%	13%	11%	9%	18%	13%	11%	10%	15%	9%	10%	15%	16%	10%
2%	4%	3%	7%	5%	4%	4%	5%	3%	9%	5%	3%	2%	3%
1%	#	1%	#	—	1%	1%	1%	1%	—	1%	#	1%	1%
2%	1%	2%	1%	3%	#	2%	1%	2%	1%	1%	1%	2%	2%
1%	1%	1%	1%	3%	#	1%	1%	1%	—	1%	—	1%	2%
1%	1%	#	1%	1%	#	1%	1%	#	2%	1%	1%	1%	—
10%	6%	8%	7%	6%	10%	7%	7%	10%	6%	6%	13%	8%	7%
16%	16%	10%	18%	14%	14%	16%	19%	10%	24%	20%	13%	10%	12%
1%	3%	2%	1%	4%	1%	2%	2%	1%	—	3%	#	2%	2%

Source: NOP Market Research Ltd.
Interviews held throughout the Guildford local authority area.

justify their behaviour by adopting very strongly held but very personal views. An example of this is smokers who refute totally the medical evidence concerning the incidence of lung cancer amongst smokers.

This leads us to a definition of attitudes devised by Rokeach[12] — 'an attitude is a relatively enduring organisation of beliefs around an object or situation predisposing one to respond in some preferential manner'.

This definition stresses two important facets of attitudes, namely that they persist over a considerable period of time and are relatively difficult to change, as we shall examine later, and that they provide an almost automatic and sometimes ill-considered response to situations which arise.

It is possible to identify three component parts of attitudes.

1. The knowledge we have about a particular subject, a collection of facts, true or false, which we gather from a wide variety of sources, such as personal experience, the media, acquaintances, and so on. This is known as the cognitive component, or more commonly as 'belief'.
2. The affective component is composed of our emotions and feelings whether we like or dislike a particular topic. It is affected by our value system, that is our collection of beliefs about how people ought or ought not to behave.
3. The behavioural component consists of how we actually react to the stimulus, what we will say or do about a particular issue. It is important to note, however, that what we say is not always translated into action, we are merely providing a public expression of our attitude, merely giving our 'opinion'.

Normally, one would expect the three components of attitudes to work together but this is not always the case. Neither will a particular act necessarily be repeated on all occasions. For instance, in 1934 La Pierre conducted research in a number of hotels and restaurants in the USA by visiting these establishments accompanied by two smartly dressed Chinese at a time when there was considerable anti-Chinese feeling in the USA. On only one occasion were they refused service. However, when later he wrote to these establishments asking if they would accept Chinese clientele in their restaurant, over 90 per cent wrote back to say they would not. This apparent inconsistency may be explained by the fact that that hotel or restaurant managers may hold other conflicting attitudes such as not wanting to cause a scene in public or simply that although prepared to reject Chinese clientele in a letter their attitudes may not be strong enough to reject them face to face.

Just as tests have been devised to measure intelligence and personality it is also possible to measure attitudes by a variety of methods. If, for example, we are trying to establish a man's attitudes to children we could follow him and observe his behaviour with respect towards children. This would, however, be a rather time-consuming and probably inaccurate method. The most common method of estimating attitude is to use an attitude scale which consists of a series of statements about which individuals express their degree of agreement or disagreement. In the case of our example such statements might include 'children should be seen and not heard', 'spare the rod, spoil the child', and so on.

Task 2.5

Go back to p.13 and complete the column marked B on the self-rating scale, indicating what in your opinion the ideal supervisor should be like, making sure that you avoid any bias by covering up the previous scores so that your real attitudes are revealed.

2.6 IMPLICATIONS OF INDIVIDUAL DIFFERENCES FOR THE HOTEL AND CATERING INDUSTRY

So far we have seen how differences in physique have ergonomic consequences, but otherwise we have examined differences between individuals without reference to their implications for the management of hotel and catering operations. Managers in running their business will come into contact with a very large number of individuals and it is therefore impractical to identify all the occasions when an understanding of individual differences may be relevant. We have therefore concentrated on three main areas — personnel selection procedures, training of staff and management practices.

Selection

The selection procedure falls into three separate activities. First, a definition of the job to be carried out and the attributes of the ideal person for the job. Second, an attempt must be made to assess the abilities, characteristics and experience of the applicants for the position. Finally, each applicant must be matched against the ideal to evaluate their suitability for the job. In drawing up a personnel specification (a list of desirable and essential attributes) consideration must be given to such things as a person's intellectual capacity, personality, attitudes, and obviously physical characteristics, such as height or appearance. (See Fig. 2.8.)

JOB TITLE Chef de Cuisine

	Essential	Desirable
1. Physical make-up		
(a) Age	Over 25	28 – 50 years
(b) Height	(Not applicable)	(Not applicable)
(c) Health	No serious disability	Sound health record over past 5 years
2. Qualifications		
(a) Educational	Ability to express himself or herself clearly	CSE 1 or above in English/maths
(b) Technical	706/2 or equivalent	706/3 or NEBSS
(c) Other		HCITB instructor
3. Work experience	Five years as chef de partie Two years in à la carte work	Experience as sous-chef
4. Personal characteristics	Honesty as shown by previous references Ability to cope under stress Ability to control a mixed staff of various nationalities	Stable employment record Above average intelligence
5. Personal circumstances	Ability to work late Must live out	

Figure 2.8 *Personnel specification for a head chef of an à la carte restaurant in a four-star hotel.*

The next step is to make an assessment of the applicants for the position with regard to the stipulated criteria. A variety of techniques will be used including an analysis of the application form, a selection interview, and possibly a set of tests. These tests could include intelligence tests, personality tests, attitude tests, and even tests of skill achievement, such as the setting of a short typewriting exercise for applicants for a secretarial position. It should then be possible to match the ideal specification with the results of the various assessment techniques used in order to select the best candidate.

Case example 2.1   Officer selection for the Army Catering Corps

Selection to become an officer in the British Army is a two-stage process. First the applicant must obtain the sponsorship of a corps or a regiment before passing on to the Regular Commissions Board to assess general acceptability for officer training.

Applications are initially made to the Army Catering Corps who will invite those who comply with the academic requirements to attend for two to three days at the Catering Corps Training Centre in Aldershot. During this period, the applicants are provided with all relevant information about the corps and its work and are subjected to a number of tests. These tests include:

Physical aptitude tests	a series of problems
Individual leadership tasks	requiring physical and
Group leadership tasks	mental effort designed to
	test for leadership
	potential
Group discussions	

At the end of these tests the results are passed to an interview panel consisting of three senior officers who will make the decision as to whether the corps will sponsor the applicant or not. The success rate at this stage of the procedure is approximately 50 per cent of those invited for interview.

From here, applicants are invited to attend the Regular Commissions Board at Westbury in Wiltshire for three days of very intensive selection process following a similar pattern to the corps selection and including:

Intelligence tests
Oral communication tests
Group discussions
External tests
Leadership tests
Guts and brains tests (a series of obstacles which can be crossed by either guts and physical determination or a mixture of brains using aids and physical effort in a given time)
Interviews (both individual and panel)

Two or three days after attending this selection process applicants either receive a normal pass as acceptable for training, a deferred watch which means acceptable for training but lacking in personal experience which must be gained before entering training, or a fail. The success rate for this stage is only 30 per cent of those attending the RCB, so that of 100 people invited to attend for interview initially by the ACC, only 15 will in fact reach Sandhurst for 6 to 12 months of officer training. At each stage applicants are assessed against very rigorous and specific criteria and the Army is prepared to accept a shortfall in officer recruitment rather than lower these predetermined standards.

Training

In the previous section we identified that selection attempts to match the applicants for a position against the ideal, but it is unusual for the two to fit perfectly. These gaps are the areas where training is required. In addition to which, current employees will need updating and even retraining as conditions change, for instance with the introduction of computers in front of house operations. Once these needs have been identified, an appropriate training method must be selected, and consideration must be given to the individual trainee's intellectual and personal characteristics. Some examples of these problems are that a question and answer training session is likely to be ineffective with Chinese staff as they have a fear of losing face if they answer incorrectly and therefore will not answer at all even if they know the correct answer. It may take longer to train employees of low intellectual ability; it must be established that all staff actually understand the language in which the training session is conducted, for employees are likely to come from a wide variety of cultures; and older employees may find it difficult to adapt to new methods and techniques, and may actively resist change. It is therefore necessary to consider the trainee's individual requirements before designing a training programme.

The HCITB have identified three components that go to make up a job. They are the skill element, the manipulative ability to do a job; the knowledge element, the background facts and procedures; and the attitude element, the approach people adopt to their work. Although it is fairly straightforward to improve a person's skill and knowledge through training, the problem of changing a person's attitude is much more difficult. In fact, it could be argued that 'training programmes do not incorporate any activity which consciously sets out to make trainees aware of what is and what is not the most appropriate attitude to adopt to their work'.[13] There seems to be no simple method of changing a person's attitudes. Perhaps the only truly effective method is brainwashing through the use of sensory deprivation, severe shock, etc. but this is obviously out of the question; less extreme alternatives include the use of group pressure to make an individual adapt to the norms of behaviour, as for instance in T-groups (see also p.98); providing factual information to attempt to change the cognitive component of attitudes and so affect behaviour; or identifying with a highly respected individual who suggests by their example a more appropriate course of action. Whichever of these methods is attempted, attitude change must go through three distinct phases, called by Lewin 'the unfreeze, change and refreeze process'.

Management practices

A multitude of applications for individual differences arise when one considers the day-to-day work of hotel and catering managers. At all times they are confronted by a kaleidoscope of customers and employees all of whom require a slightly different approach. Some examples of this include the preparation of staff meals to account for different cultural and personal dietary needs, the provision of staff accommodation, the selection of appropriate uniforms, the ways of addressing staff, and the means of communicating and interacting with staff generally.

2.7 CONCLUSION

The overwhelming evidence from this chapter is that there are a great many ways in which people differ from each other. Some of these differences will be significant, whilst others are unimportant. The behaviour of managers towards individuals will be determined by their own prejudices, the policy of the organisation they work for and the statutory obligation placed upon them, particularly with regard to sexual and racial discrimination. The great danger with identifying dimensions of individual differences as we have done is that it becomes very easy then to label people — he is intelligent, she is extravert, they are black, and so on. So that by highlighting the differences, a very important consideration is lost, namely that we (i.e. human beings) are a lot more alike than we are different. The vast majority of people, whatever their colour, personality, intelligence or attitudes have similar hopes and fears, abilities and aptitudes, needs and wants. Of course, there are people who are raving lunatics or amazing geniuses, highly neurotic or wildly extravert, extremely prejudiced or unbelievably liberal, but such people are very much a minority. The purpose of identifying individual differences is twofold. First, it is usefully applied to certain areas of management practice where individuals of a specific type are needed to fulfil certain roles. But more importantly, the second reason is to help individuals to understand a little more about themselves and in so doing help them to recognise that whilst individuality helps to preserve a sense of identity, the overwhelming similarity between people helps to preserve one's sanity.

REFERENCES

1. Garn, S.M. (1971) *Human Races*. Springfield, IL: Thomas.
2. Baker, J.R. (1974) *Races*. London: Oxford University Press.
3. Hardy, M. & Heyes, S. (1979) *Beginning Psychology*. London: Weidenfeld & Nicholson.
4. Welford, A.A. (1965) *Performance, Biological Mechanism and Age*. Springfield, IL: Thomas.
5. Strank, R.H. (1971) *Ergonomics*. London: Edward Arnold (for the Luncheon Voucher CERI).
6. Spearman, C. (1927) *The Abilities of Man*. London: Macmillan.
7. Burt, C. (1949) The structure of the mind. *British Journal of Educational Psychology*.
8. Thurstone, L. (1949) *Primary Mental Abilities*. Henley: Science Research Associates.
9. Guildford, J.B. (1967) *The Nature of Human Intelligence*. London: McGraw-Hill.
10. Vernon, P.E. (1960) *Intelligence and Attainment Test*. London: University of London Press.
11. Eysenck, H.J. (1966) *Check Your Own IQ*, pp.47, 137, 159, 182. Harmondsworth: Penguin.
12. Rokeach, M. (1965) The nature of attitudes. *Encyclopedia of the Social Sciences*. London: Collier-Macmillan.
13. Chopping, B. (1974) Attitude training. *HCIMA Journal*.

3 Perceptions

All that is gold does not glitter,
Not all those who wander are lost;

J.R.R. Tolkien

OBJECTIVES: to explain the concept of perception . . . to identify the ways in which individual perception may vary ... to analyse the factors affecting our perception ... to identify the relevance of perception to the hotel and catering industry . . . to outline theories of how people learn

3.1 INTRODUCTION

HAVING identified individual differences in the last chapter, the whole operation of human relations is made more complex by how people perceive the world around them and how they perceive the people inhabiting that world.

Philosophers have for centuries pondered the question of our existence, and whilst we do not wish to philosophise, it is manifestly apparent that the world for each of us only exists inside our own head — we cannot ever know how another person sees or perceives the world. This is particularly illustrated by a consideration of our perception of colour. Something like 3 per cent of the male population suffers from some degree of colour blindness and their interpretation of the colours they see will be very different from those of 'normal' people. But who is to say which perception of the world is the right one?

What is perception?

An attempt to understand and interpret the wide variety of signals created by the senses. Our five senses are those of sight, hearing, smell, taste and touch. These have different importance, however (see Fig. 3.1).

We learn   2% with our sense of TASTE
                 3% with our sense of TOUCH
                 7% with our sense of SMELL
                 22% with our sense of HEARING
                 66% with our sense of SIGHT

Figure 3.1   *The use of our senses (from Industrial Audiovisual Association, USA).*

Should one be deprived of one sense, the other senses do compensate — for instance, a blind person's senses of smell and touch are much more highly developed than a sighted person's. But the important point, central to this chapter, is that even amongst human beings who have all their faculties intact, these may be used to arrive at different conclusions about signals from the outside world to those arrived at by other people.

3.2 PERCEPTIVE ILLUSIONS

The perception of depth is subjective as the real three-dimensional object is transmitted to the brain through the two-dimensional retina. The brain must, therefore, attempt to reconstruct reality from the stimulus patterns it receives. Unfortunately, these stimulus patterns can be both ambiguous and misleading, as some examples of optical illusions demonstrate.

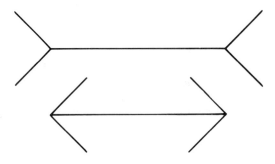

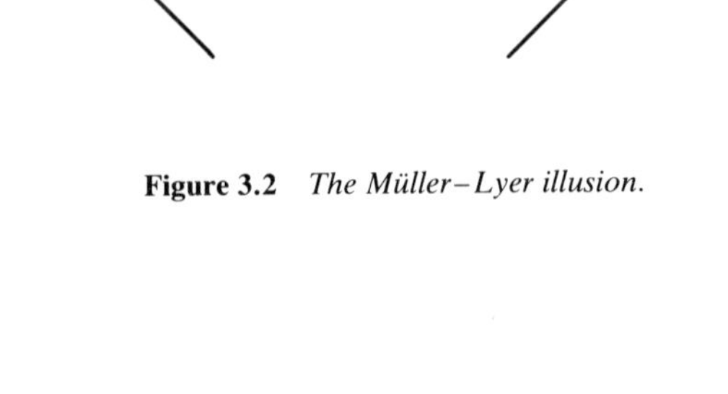

Figure 3.2   *The Müller–Lyer illusion.*

Figure 3.3 *'A new ambiguous figure' (from Boring 1930, American Journal of Psychology).*

Figure 3.4 *Figure–ground reversal.*

Figure 3.5 *Perceiving the whole object involves more than merely identifying the component features. (Photograph by R.C. James, taken from Thurston, J. & Carraher, R.G. (1966)* Optical Illusions and the Visual Arts. *New York: Litton Educational.*

The illustration in Fig. 3.6 shows a sequence of drawings generated by a group exercise based on 'Chinese whispers' but in visual form. The original drawing is shown to the first member of the group for five seconds who is then asked to reproduce the drawing on a piece of paper. This new drawing is then shown to the second member of the group for five seconds who draws it and this continues until all members of the group have had their turn. The exercise illustrates a number of interesting points:

1. Perception is selective. We cannot record all the information we receive and so tend to concentrate on some aspects and omit others.
2. Perception is constructive. If there are some items missing which we feel should be present then we will probably add them for ourselves. For example, the way eyebrows and talons appear from nowhere — and disappear just as quickly.
3. Memory is defective. The full sequence represents what can happen to our memory of an initial perception over time. The final memory of what happened or what we saw can be very different from the actual event or image as it actually occurred.
4. Perception is directed. The original drawing was entitled 'an owl' and the bird-like quality persists until the title is lost on the third drawing. From then on dramatic changes take place and any resemblance to an owl disappears. Using the same initial drawing but titled 'a cat', a completely different set of drawings is produced and tails and whiskers emerge from the same initial stimulus.

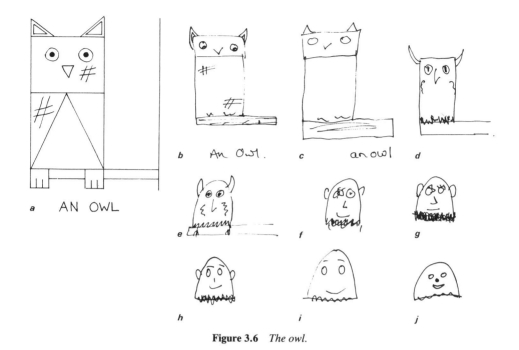

a AN OWL

b An Owl.

c an owl *d*

e *f* *g*

h *i* *j*

Figure 3.6 *The owl.*

Why is all this?

We have such a vast amount of stimuli from the world we must be selective and it is the subjective selection of what is important and unimportant that can lead to our different perceptions of reality. Although all our examples have been optical illusions (due to the nature of this medium, i.e. a book) it is possible to find examples of the unreliability of all our senses, for instance, a sound played in conjunction with a film of someone mounting steps is often perceived to be rising in pitch when in fact it is the same note repeated.

When faced with stimuli, particularly visual stimuli, that do not have apparent form or pattern, most individuals unconsciously impose a pattern or 'gestalt'. There are four ways in which this pattern is achieved.

1. Similarity — where similar elements such as shape, size and colour are present these tend to be grouped to form a pattern. Thus it is possible to see a Dalmatian dog in Fig. 3.5 out of an apparent random distribution of black and white.
2. Proximity — this occurs when separate elements that are close to each other are grouped together to form a coherent whole. For instance, morse code relies on the fact that we hear specific groups of dots and dashes as opposed to a random sequence.
3. Continuity and symmetry — certain aspects of visual stimuli, notably lines, tend to stand out and become conspicuous when they make up recognisable shapes. In the 'new ambiguous figure' (Fig. 3.3) we can see two different women as we perceptually shift from one set of conspicuous shapes to another. Our appreciation of

music is derived from our perception of its continuity rather than its being made up of a series of completely separate sounds.

4. Closure — where gaps in our perception arise we tend to complete the missing parts. Thus most visual stimuli depend upon picking out particular features known as the 'figure' against the background of their situation. For instance, at the beginning of a film we tend to look at titles rather than what is going on behind them. We look at the people posed in photographs and not their surroundings, and we pick out certain flavours against the background of other tastes. Fig. 3.4 is an example of figure–ground reversal where the arrows can be seen to point to the inside or the outside but not both at the same time.

3.3 PERCEPTION AND OUR SURROUNDINGS

One might think that such perceptual differences have little to do with the hotel and catering industry. In fact, with food in particular, a great deal of research, effort and understanding goes into the development of dishes suitable for sale to the public. The great French classical chefs such as Escoffier, may not have empirically been aware of the need for perceptual congruence but intuitively recognised the need for balance of colour, taste, texture and aroma. More recently, the emergence of nouvelle cuisine has shown a more avant-garde approach to the use of colour and texture in the preparation of dishes, for example, the use of gold leaf, which suggests that our modern perception of what is good to eat is different to our ancestors'. It is noticeable, however, even in nouvelle cuisine some colours do not appear, notably blue (have you ever seen a blue Smartie?). Another influence of perception is in the design of hotel accommodation and restaurants. The different colours, patterns and lighting effects have a profound effect upon the atmosphere that is generated.

> The colours used in the decor of the room can have several effects — dark colours make a room appear smaller than it is, while bright colours expand it. Blue is a cold colour, while red is warm. Research has shown that people placed in a room painted blue record that it feels colder than a room painted red, even though the actual temperature was the same in both rooms ... [and] generally speaking a clash of colours increases tension ...[1]

Task 3.1

> Visit three different types of catering establishments to identify their colour schemes. To what extent does this reflect the type of establishment and its clientele?

Interior designers also use our perception of patterns to create certain visual effects such as vertically striped wallpaper to 'add' height to a smaller room and large designs to make a room appear smaller. The type of lighting used will affect not only our perception of colours, note the effect this is likely to have on food in the different lighting of kitchens and restaurants, but also can be used to create pathways or segregated areas of a room, and to create sensations of intimacy or spaciousness.

Case example 3.1   Profiting from design

The following is adapted from an article by Malcolm Brocklesby who is Chairman of Group Northern Design.

. . . it is possible to create an atmosphere which makes an important contribution to the commercial success of the operation. Where the object is to use design to attract people and then encourage them to enjoy spending in that environment. It's all a subtle form of social engineering . . .

Three factors — Science, Art and Mystery — should be taken into account when designing successful leisure projects. Firstly, take the basic practical and technical factors: knowledge of the client's objectives; the selected market factors; financial constraints; health, safety and planning requirements. Not forgetting current technology. Then introduce creativity. We use art to create atmosphere, to hit on the ambience which will generate the right response from the selected market sector.

But it is the mystery Factor 'x' — the element of empathy with the future customer — and sensing how he will react to the imagined environment, which is so crucial.

Make a mistake here — in the mood and 'feeling' of the place — and the cost of putting it right can be crippling.

Design is more than just the creation of a backcloth against which the activities of an hotel are played out. It has a dynamic role to play in the marketing of the hotel, first to attract people as guests and then in encouraging them to make use of facilities and to 'spend . . . spend . . . spend'.

The whole character of the place must be friendly and welcoming. The Group Northern approach is to design hotels which 'smile at you', where the atmosphere radiates a 'glad you came' feeling, and not, as many interiors do today, a 'who are *you*?' image.

Each aspect of the hotel should be designed to enhance the guest's sense of individuality and esteem. Scale is important. 'Impressive' foyers only serve to impress the arrivals how big and important the hotel is, and how insignificant they are by comparison. The real need is to design a setting which creates the impression that the hotel has been waiting for the guest, and that his arrival is the most important thing that has happened today.

Corridors are a necessary evil. In an old hotel they can be ... a confusing labyrinth; in a modern building they can be deadly boring. Yet it's just a question of decor, lighting and dressing. An element of interest, surprise or humour can work wonders! Bars, like the restaurant, must be designed to the highest commercial standard. It must actively attract custom rather than provide a passive service to residents. It should have a dynamic role as the social focus of the hotel. So why not aim for a decor which caters for casual and family custom during the day, changing to a more sophisticated atmosphere in the evening? And control the mood by clever use of lighting and background music.

For bedrooms ambience is a priority. The room must feel individual and personal. The minute you open the door of some hotel bedrooms you sense that it is identical to every other room in the place. And it's equivalent to the manager telling you that you are no more than a number on his computerised business returns.

Although some standardisation is essential, it is neither expensive nor difficult to create a feel of individuality. All you need is a little imagination and a sense of hospitality.

We all want as an end product a relaxed and friendly environment.

3.4 PERCEPTION AND PEOPLE

Task 3.2

Match the occupations listed below with the photographs:

Barrister
Hairdresser
Nurse
Police constable
Managing director
Catering manager

Compare your answers with the answers at the end of the chapter.

   This exercise is designed to show the extent to which we have preconceived ideas
and how often our perception of people may be inaccurate. When encountering
another person, we go through a complex but largely automatic and very rapid assessment of that person.

Information processing

Our response to the person will first be affected by what we know about them already,
either from our memory of previous contact or what other people have told us or what
the other person looks and sounds like or the situation in which we find them. As we
have shown in the case of the owl exercise, our memory is both selective and faulty
especially with regard to the length of time since the previous event or encounter. The
same exercise shows what happens when messages are passed from person to person
and how easy it is for the message to become distorted. Likewise, the impression we
receive from other people must also contain distortions. The task at the beginning of
this section also shows how we ourselves distort the information we receive and how
difficult it is to make an accurate judgement of a person on the basis of their appearance alone. Finally, this judgement will be affected by the environment in which the
person is found. For instance, Dr David Carter of the University of Surrey has been
studying how the background against which people on television are seen can affect
what viewers think of them. His results showed that presenters standing in front of a
library-type background were seen as more pleasant, more powerful and more active
than the same presenter stating the same things in an office setting.

Interpretation

The information from these sources is then processed to establish our feelings towards
the other person, a forecast of their likely behaviour and a classification of what type
of person they are. This processing of information will be affected by our current mental and physical state and our values and attitudes. Research in New York has shown
that witnesses of an event differ in the type of things they remember largely on the

A

B

C

D

E

F

basis of their role. A mixture of police and the public were shown the film of an incident and statements were taken afterwards. These showed that the police noticed much more detail, but were more prone than the public to special types of errors, notably an inference of sinister intent when none was evident.

Response

It is only after going through this sequence of selection, processing and interpretation of information, that we begin to formulate our response to the other person. This response will also depend on our own interpersonal needs and the purpose of the interaction. We will leave consideration of this interaction until Chapter 6 when we look at 'Interpersonal Behaviour'.

As we have already shown, this perception process is open to considerable error, and we shall look at five specific types of error in our perception of people.

Stereotyping

All people have a tendency to make decisions about people based on the small amount of information they received during the first few minutes of an interaction. They will tend to classify the other person according to one or two dominant or easily identifiable characteristics, e.g. colour of skin, style of dress, sex, age and so on. From this we then generalise about how that person will behave in a number of different areas. For instance, there are some clubs and restaurants which will not admit male customers who are not wearing a tie, inferring that such people are not suitable clientele. This type of attitude is supported by research conducted by Haire.[2] Managers were given photographs of a middle-aged reasonably dressed man. Half were told he was a manager, the other half were told he was a union official. They were then asked to describe him. The first group described him as conscientious, dependable, conservative and so on, whereas the second group described him as argumentative, aggressive, opinionated and so on. The study was repeated with a group of union officials and completely contradictory results were obtained.

   This example stresses the negative aspect of stereotyping, but it can also be helpful in allowing people to reduce the stress of meeting others for the first time. It is important to be able to adapt and revise the stereotype by being open to additional evidence of other people's behaviour and attitudes. There has been research[3] which suggests that underlying stereotyping there may be a grain of truth. A good example is the stereotype of older workers which portrays them as more resistant to change, less creative, more cautious and less physically able, even though their actual performance is as good as young employees. Nevertheless, older managers have actually been shown to be more cautious than younger managers.[4]

Halo effect

In this case, our impression, either good or bad, in one area, for example, intelligence, or appearance, will colour our perceptions of the rest of the person. At an interview, for example, somebody with ten O Levels and dressed neatly and conservatively may be given preference because it is assumed they will perform the job well and work hard. This generalisation from one characteristic is based on our own implicit personality theory, that is basic assumptions about which characteristics go together and how people are likely to behave. For instance, someone whom we classify as ambitious we may also assume to be aggressive, hard-working and inconsiderate, and we will therefore respond to them accordingly.

At work, the halo effect has serious implications for supervisors or managers, who are likely to observe only a small part of their staff's work activity.

The manager who sees a member of staff performing some task particularly well, will tend to judge that employee as excellent in all areas, even if it is the only thing they have done right all day. Likewise a worker who in front of the manager has an accident or is incompetent will be thought of as a bad employee in other respects.

Selective perception

It is not possible for individuals to take account of all the information they are receiving and they must therefore be selective about which information they pay most attention to. This will be influenced by such factors as their past experience and present needs. A good example has been identified by Dearbom and Simon. In their research[5] a group of executives were given a factual case study about a steel company. Each executive was allocated to a particular department such as sales, production accounting, public relations and they were then asked to identify 12 major problems that the new president should tackle first. Each executive saw the major problems as being in their allocated area of responsibility.

Projection

This refers to a situation where people think of others as having the same feelings as themselves which are likely to consist of their own negative aspects. In this way a person who is obstinate or lazy will tend to see those same characteristics in other people, partly in an attempt to protect their own self-image (see Chapter 6) by suggesting that other people are as 'bad' as they are.

Pro-self bias

This perceptual error is found in two areas. First, we assume that anything good that happens to us is due to our efforts whereas anything bad is due to circumstances beyond our control. Second, if we are observing other people at work, we attribute their success or failure to their own efforts, whereas our actions are affected by the environment. The important implication of these biases for supervisors is that if subordinates are performing badly, supervisors will emphasise the individual's lack of ability and attach no blame to their own supervisory contribution, whilst employees will stress the circumstances rather than their own failings. For example, if a customer has complained to the head waiter about slow service, the head waiter is likely to blame the waiter for working too slowly. The waiter on the other hand will put it down to some other factor such as the kitchen being slow or there not being enough staff in the restaurant.

It is impossible to avoid completely the perceptual errors we have identified above and the implications for managers must be to increase their awareness of their own biases and guard against their misguidance as much as possible. This is especially important in such areas as the interviewing of prospective employees, dealing with customers, or handling subordinates where errors of perception can have critical, and sometimes even legal, repercussions. Certain techniques that have been developed to train people in social skills go some way towards reducing the likelihood of perceptual bias, and more of these will be reviewed in Chapter 6.

3.5 PERCEPTIONS OF THE HOTEL AND CATERING INDUSTRY

In 1980 the HCITB commissioned research[6] into perceptions of jobs in the hotel and catering industry. They did so following the Manpower Services Commission Report on hard-to-fill vacancies in September 1979 which identified hotel and catering jobs, both at the craft and sub-craft level, as being in this category. They investigated the images held by three different groups of people—the public, active jobseekers and school leavers. Their sample indicated that a little under 20 per cent of the UK population are likely to have had some experience of working in the industry on either a full-time or a part-time basis. Somewhat surprisingly, the image of the industry held by those with catering experience was very similar to those without any experiences. Women in particular regarded catering jobs as potentially suitable employment. But men, especially under 25, were less favourably disposed towards the industry. The overall image is very favourable, although most people thought of the industry in terms of cook/chef and waiter/waitress as typifying careers in the industry. The report highlights that the public adopt sex stereotypes towards certain jobs. Receptionists, room domestics, and kitchen or counter assistants were seen as suitable female jobs, whereas men predominate in management and portering. The largest single reason amongst seekers for rejecting a job was that it was seen as being suitable only for someone of the opposite sex.

The major criticisms of hotel and catering work were concerned with the unsociable hours and the 'dirtiness' of the jobs. It is interesting to compare this view with those of workers in the industry, who would agree that their hours are unsociable, but do not perceive their jobs as being 'dirty'. Workers in the industry tend to complain of low wages, but the public's view is that rates of pay are not too unsatisfactory and certainly do not deter people from looking for catering jobs. Low status and the servile nature of the work were not found to be as much of a disincentive as was expected. The most popular jobs among job applicants were bar steward, cashier and receptionist and the least popular housekeeper, porter and room maid.

With regard to school leavers, the Report stated 'it is clear that the interest, or lack of it, which school leavers have in jobs in the industry is based on incomplete or even erroneous information, on stereotypes and guesses rather than on fact'. For instance, 71 per cent of school leavers thought that a receptionist spent more of his or her time dealing with people than any other category of hotel worker; nearly half of those questioned did not know if an assistant manager would normally be someone who has worked for several years as a chef, waiter or receptionsist, and only a quarter realised that a housekeeper has few opportunites to move to other areas of hotel work.

3.6 PERCEPTION AND LEARNING

Our investigation of visual illusion has significance with regard to how people learn. As we have seen, the gestalt school of psychology hold that perceptual organisation is inborn and that we perceive and give meaning to objects by their total of character-istics rather than the individual parts of the object.

This view has several implications with regard to how best to structure new learning experiences, and in particular the training of new staff. First, learning should have structure and be clearly organised in the presentation of material. Second, the starting point for learning the new experience must enable the learner to call on previous experience and proceed from what they already know towards the unknown knowl-edge or skill they are acquiring. Third, in some cases whole learning is more valuable than bits of learning. It is more efficient for trainees to get the total picture rather than get the information piecemeal since trainees may misinterpret what they are meant to learn, by projecting understanding and meaning from any part of the new skill or con-cept they are acquiring. Lastly, it emphasises the need to avoid false perceptions which may arise from the lack of or the inadequacy of auditory or visual materials and from learners not paying full attention.

This view of learning (outlined above) is classified as a cognitive theory as opposed to the behaviourist view of learning. Behaviourist theory places much less importance on internal processes such as perception and attitude formation and believes that people learn by developing certain responses to given stimuli. This view has evolved over the last century through the work of Watson, Thorndike and Pavlov up to the operant conditioning model of B.F. Skinner. Skinner's view is that learning is a four-step process. First, the trainee must want to learn, he must have motivation (see Chapter 4). Second, the trainee is provided with a stimulus which is in effect the new concept or skill to be learnt. Third, the trainee should be given the opportunity to respond to this stimulus as soon as possible and fourth, an appropriate response must be reinforced by giving encouragement, praise, and reward. The implication for train-ing staff is that learning is a step-by-step process; each stimulus should be short so that it can be reinforced immediately, providing feedback for the trainee.

An appraisal of these two viewpoints shows similarities and some disagreement. There is no doubt that all learning theories argue explicitly or by implication that the trainee must be motivated. People will only learn if they want to learn and can see the relevance of what they are learning. Both viewpoints also agree that the trainee must receive feedback; for the behaviourists this feedback is provided by the trainer whereas for the Gestalt psychologists feedback arises out of the insightful experience — that is the 'penny dropping'. Where these two theories disagree is over the desir-ability of whole or part learning; whether or not the learning experience should be broken down into very small steps. In fact, for training purposes this is not usually a problem due to the nature of on-the-job training (see Chapter 9).

Learning and training

These learning theories have obvious implications for the training process. The differ-ence between training and learning is that training is concerned primarily with the acquisition of simple skills usually of a technical nature whilst learning is much broader and attempts to develop the ability to adopt behaviour to suit a variety of situ-ations. The role of training in the hotel and catering industry is therefore usually con-cerned with taking people with either few or none of the required skills and developing these individuals so that their standards of performance achieve the desirable level.

Such skills tend to be 'psychomotor' skills, that is concerned with the ability to physically do things such as make beds, polish glassware, carry plates and so on, although as we shall see in Chapter 6, training can also be applied to 'affective' or social skills. Most training also necessitates the acquisition of knowledge.

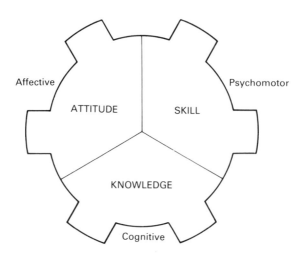

Figure 3.7   *Representation of the components of a task.*

3.7 RELEVANCE TO THE HOTEL AND CATERING INDUSTRY

Since we are selective in the information which we use to form responses to situations and people, the caterer and hotelkeeper must be aware of the stimuli that are the most influential in creating the 'right' impression on the customer. This can be seen in many instances.

1.   Most people's first impression of a McDonald's fast-food store or Granada's Country Kitchen will be their distinctive colour schemes, the intention of which is to create a bright and therefore cheerful atmosphere. The colour scheme is also designed to be distinctive and thereby imprinted on the consumer's memory, with the aim of generating repeat business.
2.   Uniforms are an importance influence on the way the customer relates to the staff and on the way in which the staff behave. Compare, for instance, the formal relationship typified by the traditional black-and-white uniforms used in restaurants, with the modern trend towards informality which is reflected in the style of dress adopted by contemporary restaurateurs. A good example of this approach is the Exchange restaurant chain, where staff wear a standard uniform but are encouraged to express their personality by wearing their own choice of badges and headgear. This approach takes advantage of the fact that a uniform implies to a

consumer certain standards of service and hygiene, but removes the impersonal and standardised impression a uniform can create.

3. As we have seen, the hotel and catering industry is a people business, and staff in the industry must be given guidance and training in the recognition of customers' needs and become more perceptually aware. To achieve this, staff could be provided with accurate information about customers and their requirements in advance; the staff's mental and physical well-being should be assured; staff could be encouraged to hold positive attitudes towards customers, and finally, staff should be rewarded for successful customer interactions. We shall examine in more detail some of the techniques used to develop social skills in Chapter 6.

4. As well as ensuring that the perception of staff is enhanced, managers too must realise that in many situations they are equally involved in the complexity of how they perceive the world and other people. This can be of particular relevance to situations such as dealing with customers' complaints, interviewing staff, selling and promoting their business, disciplining subordinates, training employees and discussing matters with colleagues.

3.8 CONCLUSION

Perception is something that everyone takes for granted. It rarely occurs to anyone to consider that what they see or hear or feel may be different to what someone else is seeing, hearing or feeling. What is interesting is that the usual reaction to such a perceptual disagreement is that the other person is mistaken or wrong. If the other person cannot see the beauty of a painting, or enjoy the music of a heavy metal band, or like a mutual acquaintance, then we naturally assume that they are 'blind', or have poor taste, or think badly of everybody. It is hoped that by explaining why we can, and often do, make mistakes about the world we live in and the people around us, we can attempt to improve the objective nature of what we see and feel. Just as perception is essential for effective learning, so learning is required before our perception is improved.

Case exercise 3.1   The selection interview

Ralph Johnson is the Assistant Personnel Manager of a large five-star London hotel. He has spent the afternoon interviewing candidates for the position of management trainee. He is conducting the preliminary interviews and four of the applicants will go forward to the final selection interview with the Personnel Manager and General Manager.

Johnson reads the application form of the last candidate whose name is Jane McBean. Ms McBean was graduating from the University of Surrey where Johnson had studied a few years earlier. She had spent her industrial release year working for an industrial catering organisation in the West Midlands. She had also worked during the vacations in a variety of jobs in several hotels near her home town of Buxton. The application form showed she was single and she enjoyed outdoor pursuits including pot-holing and the accompanying photograph showed an attractive and pleasant young lady. Johnson asked her to come into his office.

Johnson started the interview by saying that he too had studied at Surrey and asked Jane had she enjoyed it. Jane was very enthusiastic about the university and was particularly impressed by the expertise of some of the teaching staff. Johnson enquired after several of his old tutors and chatted for a few minutes about university life. They also discovered that they had both been at a social evening a few weeks earlier organised by Signet, the department's graduate society.

The interview then shifted to more specific questions about why Jane had applied for this particular management trainee position. Jane replied that it was extremely well paid, seemed to offer good opportunities for advancement and that she had been recommended to apply by one of the tutors they had just been discussing. He encouraged her to be more specific about her motivations and she seemed genuinely enthusiastic about the job. They then discussed exactly what the training programme involved and administrative aspects of the position such as salary, holiday entitlement and conditions of employment. At this point Johnson asked her if she had any questions for him. She only had one question which was to do with the number of female students that had applied for and were being interviewed for the position. Johnson replied that nearly 40% of applicants were women but that Jane was one of only two candidates out of a total of fifteen being interviewed. As Johnson was concluding the interview Jane noticed and commented upon an ornamental lump of rock which Johnson used as a paperweight, correctly identifying it as a fairly rare mineral. Johnson who was a keen amateur geologist found that Jane was quite interested in this field as a consequence of her pot-holing adventures. After a further brief chat Jane left and Johnson sat down to complete his notes about the interview. He decided almost straight away to put Jane on the short list of four candidates; she had been much more impressive than the other female candidate and seemed truly interested in the job.

1. Why do you think Johnson selected Jane for the short list?
2. From the examples of how we may wrongly perceive people, what type of error did Johnson make?
3. After reading Chapter 9 suggest ways in which Johnson could have improved the conduct of the interview to avoid his personal bias.

Answers to Task 3.2

A Managing director   D Barrister
B Nurse   E Catering manager
C Police constable   F Hairdresser

REFERENCES

1. Jones, P. (1983) *Food Service Operations*. Eastbourne: Holt, Rinehart and Winston.
2. Haire, M. (1955) Role perceptions in labour/management relations. *Industrial Labour Relations Review*, **8**.
3. Karlins, M., Coffman, T.L. & Walters, G. (1969) On the fadings of social stereotypes. *Journal of Personality and Social Psychology*, **13**.
4. Vroom, V.H. & Pahl, B. (1971) Relationships between age and risk-taking among managers. *Journal of Applied Psychology*.
5. Deerbom, D.C. & Simon, H.A. (1956) Selective perception. *Sociometry*, **21**.
6. Ellis, P. *The image of hotel and catering work: a report on three surveys*. London: HCITB.

4 Motivation

I like work: it fascinates me. I can sit and look at it for hours. I love to keep it by me: the idea of getting rid of it nearly breaks my heart.

Jerome K. Jerome *Three Men in a Boat*

OBJECTIVES: to identify a wide range of theoretical approaches to human motivation . . . to outline the concept of job satisfaction and job design . . . to discuss the application of theory to practical situations in the hotel and catering industry

4.1 INTRODUCTION

So far, we have seen how individuals differ from each other and perceive differently the world around them, but we have not looked at the question of why people behave in a certain way or do the things that they do. In general terms there must be many pressures and facts which are brought to bear to influence a person's behaviour. But over the years behavioural scientists have attempted to distinguish some common factors which explain this. These are generally referred to as theories of motivation and in this chapter we shall be looking specifically at those theories concerning the motivation of individuals at work.

Task 4.1 *Forced choice pairs grid* (see Fig. 4.1)

This grid attempts to identify the major factors in your motivational make-up by comparing each of a list of possible factors with each other. The factors under consideration are listed down the left-hand side.

Starting with pay, compare this factor with every other factor in turn working across the page. In the 11 boxes provided write down which of the two factors is more important to you in your work. Now move on to the next factor until all the boxes have been completed. To score count up the number of

49

times each factor occurs and enter this score in the total column. The column total must equal 66. Now compare the scores for the various factors and place them in rank order (the highest score being 1, and so on) thereby identifying the factors which are most influential for you.

Compare your scores with that of a test group of hotel and catering students of an average age of seventeen. The test results are given at the end of this chapter.

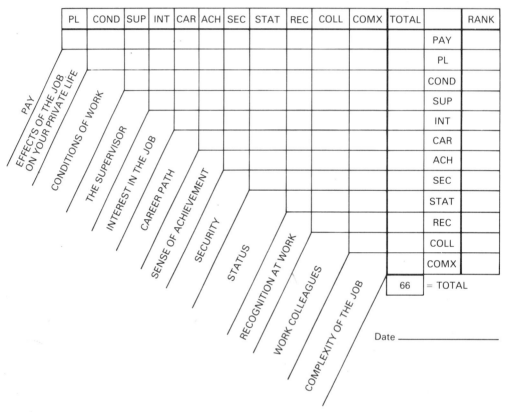

Figure 4.1 *Job motivating factors.*

4.2 THEORIES OF MOTIVATION

Basic physiological model

The simplest explanation of behaviour is based on the physiological model. In this model, human beings have a number of basic needs for such things as food, drink and sex, which if not met give rise to specific drives. These in turn lead to an activity designed to satisfy these needs. The satisfaction of the need leads to a reduction in the drive. An activity which results in satisfaction will be subject to positive reinforcement, that is to say the individual will be encouraged to repeat that activity at some time to satisfy the same need. Similarly, an activity resulting in dissatisfaction or even punishment will lead to negative reinforcement and thereby an inclination not to repeat that particular activity (Fig. 4.2).

Figure 4.2 *Physiological model of motivation.*

This model is easy to relate to our basic physiological needs but does not seem to explain the higher or psychological needs.

A.H. Maslow

There have been attempts to classify human needs, but one theory has been more influential than any other. This is the theory developed by A.H. Maslow.[1] He sees the human being as constantly wanting satisfaction of one need or another and that these needs could be classified into five major groups.

1. Physiological — the basic survival needs of the individual, such as the need for shelter, food, water, air and sleep, and also including such things as sex and sensing stimulation.
2. Safety — the need for a feeling of security and protection from danger and threat, the desire for stability.
3. Social — the need for a sense of belonging, the giving and receiving of friendship, an acceptance as a member of a group.
4. Esteem — the need for a high evaluation of oneself for a sense of achievement, recognition and respect from other people.
5. Self-actualisation — the need for self-fulfilment, personal growth and development, a sense of personal accomplishment and an opportunity for creativity and using one's talents to the full.

The second fundamental aspect of Maslow's theories is that this classification of needs follows a hierarchical pattern as shown in Fig. 4.3.

The activation of a higher level need can only occur if the low level need has been satisfied, e.g. if you are in the middle of a desert you will not be concerned with personal status or even safety when you are dying of thirst. Maslow did in fact identify two other sets of needs, namely the cognitive (the need for knowledge and understanding) and the aesthetic (the need for beauty and a sense of form). However, these needs do not fit easily into the hierarchy and have therefore been largely ignored by

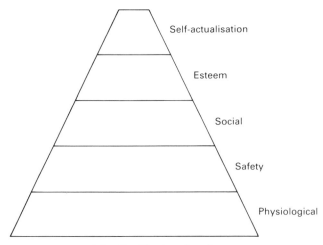

Figure 4.3   *Classification of needs.*

subsequent writers. It is also important to note that although influential, Maslow's theories have in fact not been supported by empirical research that can explain or refute his view.

F.W. Taylor

In the early part of this century, the prevailing theories of motivation saw man as a rational being motivated largely by incentives of which money was the most important. This view was adopted by F.W. Taylor according to whom 'what the workmen want from their employers more than anything else is high wages, and what employers want from their workmen is low labour cost'.[2] Taylor's approach was based on analysing work into its component parts, analysing these tasks to find the best way of carrying these out and then through measurement establishing production levels and financial incentives for standards of performance. This theory or concept was found in practice to be lacking.

McGregor — Theory *X* and Theory *Y*

The view of work adopted by F.W. Taylor was described by McGregor[3] as Theory *X*. This was based on the following assumptions. 'The average human being has an inherent dislike of work and will avoid it if he can'. 'Because of this human characteristic of dislike of work most people must be coerced, controlled, directed and threatened with punishment to get them to put forth adequate effort'. 'The average human being prefers to be directed, wishes to avoid responsibility, has relatively little ambition and wants security above all.'

For managers this implies close supervision of staff and the establishment of rigorous work routines and schedules, probably accompanied by repetitive tasks.

On the other hand, McGregor preferred to adopt what he called Theory *Y*, which has the following characteristics. There is no inherent dislike of work itself. Average humans will exercise self-direction and self-control towards objectives they are committed to. Commitment relates to rewards resulting from the achievement of the objective. The most significant rewards are the satisfaction of higher order needs. Individuals with encouragement will actively seek responsibility. A large percentage of the population can be creative in solving organisational problems, but these capacities are largely under-used.

'The essential task of management is to arrange organisational conditions and methods of operation so that people can achieve their own goals best by directing their own efforts toward organisational objectives.'

F. Herzberg — Motivation–hygiene theory

Whilst carrying out research into the factors which bring about job satisfaction, Herzberg discovered that they could be split into two groups, which he terms 'hygiene' factors and 'motivation' factors. The hygiene factors were those things which prevented someone from being dissatisfied with their work, but whose presence did not contribute directly to job satisfaction, i.e. salary, company policy and administration, style of supervision, working conditions, and other factors associated with the job environment. Herzberg called these hygiene factors because good hygiene cannot in itself generate good health but merely prevents an individual catching a disease. The other set of factors, he called 'motivators' as these contributed directly to job satisfaction and include a sense of achievement, recognition for work done, interest in the job itself, responsibility and career advancement. Thus it could be said that the hygiene factors explain why someone works in a particular place, but the motivators explain why they are prepared to work harder at their job.

Task 4.2

Look at the factors identified in Task 4.1 and determine whether they are motivation or hygiene factors. Herzberg's research would suggest that the motivator factors would be ranked more highly. Is this the case? See the end of this chapter for reference to test group.

D.C. McClelland — nAch, nAff, nPow

Taking a rather different approach, McClelland concentrates his attention on three needs in particular, namely the needs for achievement (nAch), the need for affiliation (nAff) and the need for power (nPow).

1. *nAch* — McClelland identified two types of people, those who welcome challenges and who are willing to work hard to achieve their goals, and those who have no need to do well. People with a high need for achievement like personal responsibility, like taking calculated risks, and like feedback on how they are performing. They may often be (or wish to be) in business for themselves in an entrepreneurial role.
2. *nAff* — the person with a high need for affiliation looks for social relationships, and are more concerned with popularity and friendship than with decision-making

or success. This may explain the score of the group in Task 4.1 who place colleagues highly. As a group of students they are in an environment and at an age
where social relationships are very important.
3. *nPow* — all successful managers seem to have a high need for power, that is a
    need to influence and direct people and this would be seen as more important
    than his need for affiliation.

Expectancy theory

This theory tends to concentrate more on the process of motivation rather than on
individuals' needs. It suggests that the amount of effort people will expend on a particular task is dependent upon the strength of the individual's needs as they see them
at that time and their expectation of the likely outcome of their efforts to satisfy those
needs. People's actual performance of the task is not only affected by the effort they
put into it, but also is affected by their own capabilities and by the environment in
which they carry out the task. For instance, a person may try very hard to decorate a
wedding cake, but not have the manual dexterity and artistic flair to complete the
task, whilst another person who has the ability may be employed in some other activity. The performance of a task will result in some reward, either intrinsic (in terms of
sense of achievement or self-fulfilment) or extrinsic (in terms of extra pay or congratu-
lations).

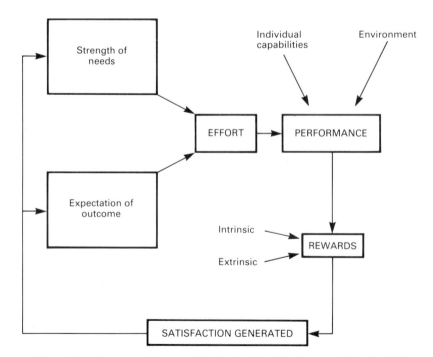

Figure 4.4   *Expectancy theory model of motivation (after Porter and Lawler 1968).*

The satisfaction generated by a good or poor performance will then affect and modify the person's needs and expectations (see Fig. 4.4).

Review of motivational theory

It may appear that different motivation theories have quickly superseded each other, but in fact all the theories have contributions to make to a fuller understanding of this area of human relations. Some, such as Taylor's view and the physiological theory, are seen as simplistic in their approach, although the ideas of scientific management that were developed by Taylor are still manifestly present in much of British industry today. From our point of view it does not matter which theorists are 'right' if indeed any of them are. In view of the emphasis we have placed on the difference between individuals in Chapter 2, it may well be that no general theory of motivation is possible. We are more concerned with how their theories will help us in our human relations approach to work and management.

The common strands of the theories are basically twofold. Human beings have *needs* which they strive to satisfy, and successful satisfaction positively *reinforces* an individual's behaviour. We shall now look in more detail at the areas that behavioural science has tended to ignore, namely the role of money and job design in motivating staff and enhancing job satisfaction.

4.3 FINANCIAL MOTIVATION

Motivation theorists have tended to avoid the question of money as a motivating force, primarily because it is difficult to define the exact nature of the need for money, since it can be used to satisfy all needs, from the very basic needs such as hunger through to higher needs, such as status and self-actualisation. Money can be seen to act in three separate ways. First, it gives people the opportunity to satisfy the needs that are most important to them at that moment in time, whether these are for food and shelter, or luxuries. Second, money provides a precise basis on which to make comparisons. It is therefore possible to compare one person's income from work against another to assess their relative worth. It is also true to say that it is not so much the absolute level of pay which is important, but more the relative level when compared with others, whether they are doing the same job or a different one, in the same firm or for another employer. For instance, the status of chefs de cuisine is partly based on the fact that in most hotels they are among the highest paid members of staff.

In the same way that money enables comparisons to be made between income levels, it also enables a person to 'rank' the relative cost of satisfying a wide variety of needs. Each person has an unlimited number of needs to satisfy, but limited resources with which to achieve them. Money is a valuable means of assessing which needs are to be left unsatisfied. For most people, the way in which they spend their money to satisfy needs tends to conform to a pattern, similar in structure to Maslow's hierarchy, as shown in Table 4.1.

Table 4.1   *Average weekly household expenditure of three income groups*

Commodity/Service	Disposable income of household per week		
	£40–£45	£80–£100	£200–£250
	£	£	£
Housing	12.37	16.41	26.01
Fuel, light and power	4.94	7.32	8.51
Food	11.23	23.08	37.71
Alcoholic drink	0.69	4.20	10.35
Tobacco	0.82	3.76	4.50
Clothing and footwear	1.96	6.19	14.71
Durable household goods	1.47	4.88	16.98
Other goods	2.64	6.99	14.31
Transport and vehicles	1.89	12.77	34.86
Services	3.86	8.81	22.98
Miscellaneous	0.03	0.41	1.05

Case example 4.1   job evaluation in the hotel and catering industry

Table 4.2   *A job grading system (using the Institute of Administrative Management method).*

Level definition	Example of jobs
1 Very simple tasks of largely physical nature	Porter* Cleaner
2 Simple tasks carried out in accordance with a small number of clearly defined rules, and which can be carried out after a short period of training of up to 2–3 weeks. The work is checked and closely supervised	Chambermaid* Life attendant Counter assistant Bar steward Hall porter
3 Straightforward tasks, but involving more complicated routines and requiring a degree of individual knowledge and alertness, as the work is subject to occasional check	Commis waiter* Clerk
4 Tasks calling for the independent arrangement of work and the exercise of some initiative where little supervision is needed. Detailed familiarity with one or more branches of established procedure required	Receptionist* Waiter Cashier Store keeper Florist
5 Routine work, but involving an individual degree of responsibility for answering non-routine queries and/or exercising some measure of control over a small group of staff	Head waiter* Senior receptionist Assistant housekeeper
6 Non-routine work, involving co-ordination of several lower grade functions, possibly some measure of control over small group of staff. Also non-routine work involving recognised individual knowledge and some responsibility without follow-up	Head housekeeper* Banqueting manager Restaurant manager
7 Work necessitating responsibility for sections involved on routine tasks and/or where there are also individual tasks to be undertaken, calling for specialist knowledge	Chef de cuisine* Front office manager

*Bench mark jobs
After: Boella, M.J. (1983) *Personnel Management in the Hotel and Catering Industry.*
London: Hutchinson.

However, for some people this normal pattern is disturbed and restructured; for instance alcoholics will spend their money on drink, ignoring the need for food and shelter, drug addicts will satisfy their drug need before all else, and so on. Between these extremes and the norm, people will have a wide range of options with regard to ranking the importance of such factors as their sustenance, residence, life style and so on which to a certain extent are socially and culturally based. For instance, the French place a high importance on food and drink, but a low importance upon the exterior appearance of their homes; young people spend a greater proportion of their income in public houses than do older people, and so on.

Task 4.3

Establish your weekly income and analyse one week's expenditure. Attempt to classify this under the headings determined by Maslow.

The third effect of money is its role as reinforcement for good performance. Employees who achieve their production targets or their required standard of performance may be rewarded financially with commissions, bonuses and notably in the catering industry, tipping.

In some cases where money is directly related to performance and effort, such as sellers of insurance and the self-employed, money is undoubtedly a motivating force in its own right.

4.4 JOB DESIGN

The importance of job design has been strongly influenced by the work of Herzberg, whose two-factor theory suggests which aspects of a job motivate the worker, despite the fact that Herzberg's original research has been challenged. The design of a job is based on its content and its context (see Fig. 4.5).

Job Content + Job Context = Job Satisfaction → Increased Productivity

Figure 4.5 *Model of Job Design.*

The *content* of a job is what the worker actually does. For instance, a waitress has tasks which include laying tables, carrying plates, serving food and so on. The job context is both the physical environment and social structure in which the work is undertaken, so that for the waitress this would include the interior design of the restaurant, her uniform, her co-workers and the customers she serves. The basic premise concerning the role of job design in motivation is that by improving the content and/or context of the job, satisfaction with the job is increased and consequently productivity is enhanced. Whilst this seems to be true in many instances, it should be pointed out that changing the content/context of a job does not necessarily increase job satisfaction and that the link between increased satisfaction and the level of output per worker is at best a tenuous one.

Despite these reservations many organisations in many different industries have redesigned the jobs that their workforce undertake. With job content, such changes are broadly divided into job enlargement and job enrichment. The former involves increasing the range of tasks that an employee carries out, without requiring changes in the level or type of skill involved, for instance the waitress may be given more tables to serve. Job enrichment involves expanding the types of task the worker is expected to do, so the waitress may be given the additional role of taking orders, greeting customers, preparing the bill. Herzberg has outlined seven principles that can lead to job enrichment.[4]

1.   Remove some controls while retaining accountability.
2.   Increase the accountability of individuals for their own work.
3.   Give people a complete natural unit of work.
4.   Grant additional authority to employees in their activity; job freedom.
5.   Make periodic reports directly available to workers themselves rather than to supervisors.
6.   Introduce new and more difficult tasks not previously handled.
7.   Assign individuals specific or specialised tasks, enabling them to become experts.

Research, such as Vroom (1964) and Carlson (1971), suggests that although job enrichment does not relate directly to level of output, it does have the effect of reducing voluntary absenteeism and labour turnover.

With regard to job *context*, one of the earliest and most famous studies was that by Elton Mayo in the experiments of the 1930s (see page 111). More recent programmes of job redesign carried out in industry, such as Volvo car production in South Africa (see Case Example 7.1) have supported the view that changing the physical environment and, perhaps more importantly, the social environment can have a profound effect upon productivity. Many modern industrial production techniques are still based on the principles of scientific management involving technical efficiency based on the division of labour and task repetition, with job satisfaction being derived primarily from monetary reward. Recent approaches to job redesign have shown that technical efficiency, due to the boring nature of the tasks involved, leads to job dissatisfaction, which can be overcome by increased emphasis on the social factors inherent in work organisation and a reduction in the amount of rigid control from superiors. Baker and Hansen state that 'workers in many jobs at different occupational levels have greatly negative reactions to those elements of their work roles which restrict freedom of movement, create monotonous conditions, limit opportunities for the use of skills and reduce the exercise of autonomy and control over task related activities.'[5]

4.5 IMPLICATIONS FOR THE HOTEL AND CATERING INDUSTRY

It is evident from our previous discussion that motivational theory and the concept of job satisfaction must be applicable to an industry which employs 2 million people. And yet, there is a dearth of research material related directly to the hotel and catering industry. Certainly in the larger established sectors of the industry, hotels in particular, the job that employees do and the way they are motivated appears to have changed very little since Escoffier's day. For instance, kitchens are staffed on the partie systems, chambermaids are employed to service a certain number of rooms in one shift, waiters have a commis to help them serve a 'station' and so on. One reason for this is that unlike other industries it provides a service and it is therefore difficult to establish productivity in terms of level of output per employee over a period of time. This is primarily because the industry is more concerned with customers' satisfaction, repeating business and level of turnover, than with the number of customers served. It is therefore very difficult to apply a quantitative measure to the effectiveness of motivating forces in affecting the provision of a quality-based service. A second complication arises from the nature of the tasks involved. Although hotel and catering employees do jobs that can be seen as repetitive, it is also true to say that in comparison with production-line industries they are much more highly skilled and have a wider variety of tasks to perform. We would argue in this respect that job enlargement has already existed in this industry for a long time, and that for those jobs involving contact with customers there is already a fairly high degree of job enrichment.

One recent study has looked at the question of job satisfaction and motivating factors in a typical large Midlands hotel[6]. Lowe found that the main sources of satisfaction were:

1. Being an employee of a successful company.
2. Enjoying comradeship at work.
3. Not being over-supervised.

On the other hand, the main sources of dissatisfaction were:

1. Uninteresting job.
2. Limited promotion prospects.
3. Shift work.
4. Not enough training.
5. Lack of responsibility.

This is broadly in agreement with those factors most employees identified as being good motivators.

1. Substantial increase in basic pay.
2. Improved working conditions.
3. Greater appreciation of individual effort.
4. Improved training facilities.
5. Better promotion prospects.

Task 4.4

Look back to Herzberg's seven principles of job enrichment and try to identify instances where these are intrinsic to the work of waiting staff.

This does not mean to say that theories of motivation have no place in the hotel and catering industry, not least because it has one of the highest levels of staff turnover in the country. In 1978–79 it was not unusual for hotels to have an annual staff

turnover of 125 per cent. In addition, traditional attitudes in the industry towards productivity and worker involvement are changing. The proportion of labour costs to
total costs in the industry has increased dramatically in the last thirty years and the
recent economic climate has forced companies to re-examine their staffing levels and
organisation structure. It seems likely that during the late 1980s, the concept of
productivity will be a key issue. Linked to this is the realisation that the social contact
between staff and customers and between the staff themselves can no longer be relied
upon to be intrinsically motivating, but that social skills require training and development if their full potential for improving staff effectiveness is to be fully realised.

It is also important to realise that there is considerable difference between the jobs
carried out in the industry and that therefore there is a need to approach motivation
of employees in a number of different ways. We have selected three areas to look at in
more detail which may have some significance in the industry in the future and which
illustrate the diversity and opportunities for development in this field.

4.6 ILLUSTRATIONS OF APPROACHES TO STAFF MOTIVATION IN THE INDUSTRY

The role of the chambermaid

Traditionally this job has to carry all service functions to a specified number of bedrooms, usually between 10 and 15. Analysing this structure from the viewpoint of
motivation it has the following advantages:

1. The chambermaid has responsibility for a particular section of rooms.
2. There is a wide variety of tasks to be completed.
3. There is some degree of customer contact and positive reinforcement.

However, we can identify some disadvantages.

1. Each chambermaid works alone and is therefore socially isolated.
2. It is technically inefficient to duplicate the tasks in this way.
3. Standards of performance appear to be poor due to the need for close supervision
   by floor housekeepers.

The job could therefore be redesigned to remove these disadvantages in the following
way: chambermaids organised into teams, each with a specific role within the team,
such as two making beds together, one cleaning bathrooms, one responsible for tidy-
ing, replenishing and polishing and the fifth responsible for finally vacuuming the floor
and checking that it was ready for occupation. These roles could be rotated to reduce
boredom and wherever possible teams would be allowed to select their own members.

Fast food operations

This sector of the industry is very different in its approach to food service in comparison with other sectors. It has applied the concept of the production line to preparing

food and retails a 'product' as a shop might do, rather than serve food as in a restaurant. Thus a worker in a fast food store will have one or two specific tasks — toast buns or fry chips or broil burgers or serve customers and so on. Such tasks are very simple and very repetitive but are technically efficient, hence the concept of fast food. To overcome the inherent lack of job satisfaction in such work, a crew member in a fast food store is expected to become proficient in as many as six or seven different skills and may well do two or three of these in one shift. The more skills that a worker acquires, the higher the level of pay and the greater prospects for promotion to floor supervisor and store manager. Most crew members will work during a week on the counter, thus promoting customer contact and their individual sales records are monitored, so that stores identify the 'crew member of the month' or the crew member who has achieved the highest turnover in a given sales period. Team identity and group cohesion is enhanced by all staff wearing the same uniform, but status is signified by the badges they may wear.

One would therefore expect this cohesiveness and motivational factors to reduce staff turnover. In fact it is reported in May 1982 that 'it is not uncommon for a fast food restaurant to experience 200–300 per cent employee turnover in one year'.[7]

Task 4.5

Suggest what other factors might cause such high levels of turnover.

Tipping as an incentive

During the 1970s the industry in general has moved away from the tradition of expecting staff to receive tips as a major part of their earnings, and some employers actively discourage it. Research undertaken in the USA suggests, however, that tipping is not necessarily inappropriate in a service situation.[8] Butler and Swizek suggest that staff whose income is in part directly derived from tipping have three possible ways of maximising the size of the tips. These are (i) cultivation, i.e. a sort of 'buttering up' process; (ii) increased ritualisation, i.e. overemphasis on service and a great deal of showmanship; (iii) increasing the consumer's average spend.

The latter (iii) appears from the waiting staff's point of view to be the most effective, as those consumers who are inclined to tip do so on the basis of a predetermined percentage of the bill. In the USA this is usually about 15 per cent whilst in Britain it is more like 10 per cent. For the employer, the conclusion appears to be that not only will the waitress be motivated due 'to exercising a measure of control of the reward structure governing her work', but will benefit from the fact that higher average spend is achieved.

4.7 CONCLUSION

It is difficult enough to try and define what makes oneself 'tick', without trying to understand other people's motivations. The fact that there are so many theories of motivation is an indication of the complexity of the issue. Perhaps the most important point for the potential manager to consider is that there is a very wide range of ways in which someone may be motivated. All too often it is assumed that the factor that motivates oneself will also get the best out of other people. It should be evident after reading this chapter and the chapter on individual differences that it is not as easy as that. However, by illustrating the possible motivating factors behind people's behaviour, it is hoped that the potential manager is more responsive to their needs and capable of dealing with them. It is essential that management at all levels has the ability to actively motivate subordinates, to get the best possible performance out of them, and create a happy and effective working environment. As well as identifying approaches and techniques to the question of staff motivation, it should also help to establish what motivates oneself, so that it may be possible to gain a clearer insight into what one wants out of life, especially with regard to career development. The diversity of the hotel and catering industry allows individuals the widest possible scope with regard to job, status, salary, and the sort of company they work for, so that all prospective managers should seek advice and give a great deal of thought to selecting a career that will suit them.

Test results for a group of TEC diploma students studying hotel and catering (1983) (see Fig. 4.1).

Year: 1983 Rank	Group: TEC1 Motivation factor	No. of students: 38 Total score	Mean
1	Job interest	333	8.76
2	Colleagues	302	7.94
3	Career path	299	7.86
4	Security	248	6.52
5	Achievement	207	5.44
6	Private life	194	5.10
7	Job complexity	181	4.76
8	Recognition	177	4.65
9	Supervisor	164	4.31
10	Conditions	153	4.02
11	Pay	137	3:60
12	Status	114	3.00

REFERENCES

1. Maslow, A.H. (1945) *Motivation and Personality*. New York: Harper.
2. Taylor, F.W. (1947) *Scientific Management*. New York: Harper.
3. McGregor, D. (1980) *The Human Side of Enterprise*. London: McGraw-Hill.
4. Herzberg, F. (1968) One more time: how do you motivate employees? *Harvard Business Review*, **46**.
5. Baker, S.H. & Housen, R.A. (1975) Job design and worker satisfaction: challenge to assumptions. *Journal of Occupational Psychology*.
6. Lowe, A. (1979) *New Methods of Decision-making*. Birmingham: University of Aston.
7. Kubarycz, N. (1982) *Fast Food*, May.
8. Butler, S.R. & Swizek, W.E. (1976) The waitress/diner relationship. *Sociology of Work and Occupations*.

5 Communication

You ain't heard nothin' yet, folks

Al Jolson

OBJECTIVES: to explain the process of communication . . . to analyse the role of verbal and non-verbal communication . . . to outline strategies for successful communication . . . to identify possible barriers to communication

5.1 INTRODUCTION

SO far, we have tended to emphasise the differences between people — their physical appearance, personality, perception of the world, what makes them tick. But individuals do not act in isolation from one another; in most cases there is a high degree of personal interaction, which in order to be effective necessitates the ability to communicate. Communication is all the processes of gathering, understanding and transmitting information and feelings from one person to another (Fig. 5.1). The person wishing to communicate first of all identifies what it is they wish to communicate. This may be an emotional state such as a feeling of anger, pleasure and so on; it may be information, i.e. a fact, or it may be opinion about factual information. It is very difficult for individuals to separate these three elements and communication will normally be made up of a combination of them. These elements are then put together to form a message which is then transmitted through the selected channel, which may be the spoken word, the written word, gesture and so on. Recipients of the message then interpret the meaning according to their own information, opinions and feelings, and respond to it on the basis of what they knew or felt previously. The process of communication is incomplete without feedback from the receiver to the transmitter to ensure that the message has been received and understood. However, at all stages in this process there may be 'interference' which affects the quality of the communication and which can lead to misunderstanding between the two parties. We have already looked at how

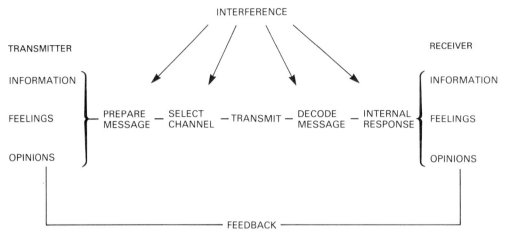

Figure 5.1   *Model of the communication process.*

individuals are affected by their opinions and feelings and how their perception of the
world may vary from one to another. In this chapter we will concentrate on those
aspects of communication concerning encoding the message and selecting the most
appropriate channel to transmit it. In doing so we will identify certain barriers to communication and the skills necessary to overcome them and reduce 'interference'.

5.2 STAGES IN THE COMMUNICATION PROCESS

Information gathering

The first stage in any communication process must be the gathering together of relevant information. This information will be derived from the five senses and interpreted by the individual's attitude of mind. The information can either be gathered
specifically for this communication event or it can be based on the individual's memory of past events and experiences. Not all the information that a person needs in
order to make an effective communication will be at hand and therefore an important
tool in communication is knowing where such information may be found. It is also
important at this stage to have an open mind and curiosity about the topic under
review as unless all relevant information is available the communication must be
deficient.

Understanding the information

It is not sufficient to simply gather information together; before communicating, it
must be thoroughly understood. This understanding derives from a person's thinking
skills and their in-built wisdom or common sense.

Task 5.1

I'm sorry I'll read that again.

Extract from the Wages Council Act 1959, Licensed Residential and Licensed Restaurant Wages Council.

Licensed restaurant does not include any place which forms part of a licensed residential establishment or which constitutes or forms part of a railway refreshment establishment or any place at which intoxicating liquor can legally be sold or supplied for consumption on the premises by reason only of the fact that in relation to that place an occasional licence is for the time being in force being a licence granted to some person other than the person carrying on, or a person in the employ-ment of the person carrying on the activities (other than the supply of intoxicating liquor) of a catering undertaking at that place; but, save as aforesaid, means any place which is used either regularly or occasion-ally as, or for the purposes of, a restaurant, dining-room, cafe or similar place at which it is lawful to sell (or supply in the case of a restaurant, dining-room or cafe of a club) intoxicating liquor for consumption on the premises and includes any bar or other place wholly or mainly used for the sale (or supply in the case of a club) and consumption on the premises of intoxicating liquor if the bar is situate on the same prem-ises as any such restaurant, dining-room, cafe or similar place as aforesaid and the activities of such restaurant, dining-room, cafe or similar place constitute the main catering activities carried on at the premises.

Now answer the following questions.

1. Which of the following would be classed as a 'licensed restaurant'?
    (a) A hotel restaurant.
    (b) A restaurant in a marquee.
    (c) A restaurant on a train.
    (d) A restaurant on a boat.
    (e) A working men's club.
    (f) A restaurant in a supermarket with an off-licence.
    (g) A restaurant in the stables of a country pub.
2. Define an occasional licence.

   This exercise illustrates how important it is to completely understand the information that has been gathered in order to communicate (as well as the importance of communicating it in a form that can be easily understood by others). The skills required for understanding include the mental skills of interpreting analysis and synthesis of data.

Transmitting the information

Once the information has been gathered and understood it is possible to select the most appropriate method of communication for the message you wish to transmit and the audience for which it is intended. This part of the process involves not only the correct choice of media but also the effective use of technical, personal and inter-personal skills. Technical skills include such things as the organisation and presentation of information, the production and/or use of audio-visual aids, clarity of speech and the use of appropriate language. Personal skills include confidence, self-expression, liveliness, creativity, and enjoyment of the communication process. Interpersonal skills include self-presentation, a sensitivity to other people, the ability to cooperate and perhaps most importantly an ability to adapt the message to the audience it is intended for.

Case example 5.1   The readability of union contracts[1]

Compare the two following extracts with regard to their effectiveness as a piece of communiction for their intended audience.

(1)   The Employer shall not discharge any employee without just cause and shall give at least one warning notice of the complaint in writing to the employee and to the Union, except that no warning notice need be given to an employee before he is discharged if the cause of such discharge is dishonesty, major violation of company rules that do not conflict with this agreement, or drinking while on duty.

(2)   The Employer cannot fire an employee without just cause. He has to write the employee and the Union and warn them at least once about the fault. No warning has to be given to an employee before he is fired for these causes:
(a)   He is dishonest
(b)   He commits a major violation of company rules which do not conflict with this agreement
(c)   He drinks while on duty.

5.3 METHODS OF COMMUNICATION

Communication can be divided into either verbal or non-verbal. The former is based on the concept of language — that is basically the spoken or written word — and because of its precision, versatility and adaptability, it tends to be regarded as the most important means of communication. There are, however, occasions when due to national or cultural differences such language has to be replaced by signs and symbols such as mathematical expressions or road signs. Non-verbal communication is sometimes called 'body language' and is all those activities, both unconscious and deliberate, that accompany any social interaction. Therefore in attempting to communicate there is usually an element of choice with regard to the most appropriate method of transmitting the information.

Selection of the appropriate 'channel'

In most cases the choice of appropriate method will be between oral or written verbal communication, basically because language is more comprehensive and precise than non-verbal communication. Written communication includes this book, memoranda, letters, newspapers, handbooks, posters, instruction manuals and questionnaires. It has the following advantages:

1. Authority — people tend to believe what they read.
2. Accuracy — more thought, time and effort tends to go into preparing the written word so as to avoid misinterpretation and inaccuracy of data.
3. Permanence — it provides an unchanging record of the substance of the communication which can be referred back to.
4. Coverage — can be tailored to the right length and duplicated for distribution to many recipients.
5. Retention. There is an old saying, 'I hear — I forget; I see — I remember'.
6. Economical — particularly in communicating with large numbers of people.

Verbal communication includes speeches, telephone conversations, meetings, interviews and person-to-person contact at all levels. It has the following advantages:

1. Personal — people learn to talk to each other long before they learn to write to each other.
2. Flexible — verbal communication can be adapted more easily to the individual receiver.
3. Two-way — feedback about the communication is instantaneous.
4. Easy, simple and fast — assuming the recipient is in close proximity to the communicator or a telephone, you can say more in a given period of time than you can write down.

Task 5.1

Select the most appropriate communication technique for the following situations:

1. Informing all staff about details of statutory sick pay regulations.
2. Promoting sales of the dish of the day.
3. Disciplining a member of staff for a serious breach of company regulations.
4. Accepting a reservation for accommodation a month hence.
5. Advertising a weekend food festival.

As we can see from the above task, the communicator's role would be much simpler if a single channel was obviously and specifically appropriate. In fact, in many cases for communication to be as effective as possible, both oral and written methods should be combined in some way either by a verbal exposition supported later by a handout as in a company training session, or a telephone call supported by a confirmatory letter, and so on. This combination recognises the fact that memory retention of verbal communication is limited.

Research supports[2] the view that a combination of oral and written methods in most business circumstances is the most effective means.

The role of non-verbal communication

People may be in one another's physical presence and not have spoken a word to each other, but still have communicated a great deal about themselves and their feelings

towards the other person. Non-verbal communication is this ability to convey information and feelings through the use of so-called 'body language'.

Task 5.2

Describe the meaning of a selection of gestures and facial expressions.

The main elements of non-verbal communication include the following.

(a) Appearance

As we have seen in the chapter on perception, appearance has a profound effect upon
the image that a person presents to the outside world and therefore will affect the way
others will relate to her or him.

For instance, the very formal pinstripe suit of the traditional hotel manager conveys
the image of respectability, responsibility and seniority, whereas the jeans and t-shirts
worn by staff in a bistro present a friendly, informal and youthful image. The impact
of appearance on others applies to all aspects of an individual's physical characteristics
(see p.13).

(b) Actions and gestures

These include all movements of the body, particularly the hands, arms and feet. They
have three main effects—first, an action can support and emphasise the spoken word,
such gestures tending to be unconscious, continuous and closely co-ordinated with
each utterance; second, they strongly communicate a person's emotional state, for
instance touching the face indicates anxiety, clenching the fist is aggressive, and so
on; third, in situations where speech is impossible for some reason, gestures can
replace the spoken word, for instance the sign language of the deaf, semaphore, and
the signs used in television and on film sets.

(c) Direction of gaze

Eye contact can have an extremely powerful effect upon interpersonal communication. It plays an important role in managing the conversational flow, establishing
the dominance of the speaker, communicating attention, affection, curiosity or aggression, and the aversion of gaze has the effect of isolating an individual.

(d) Facial expression

The face is one of the most communicative parts of the body and is used to display emotion and attitudes to others (refer to Task 5.2) and it is possible to distinguish a person's general emotional state from their facial expression alone. However, the face is subject to conscious control and therefore may not be a reliable indicator as less controlled signals such as fear may not show on a person's face, but their heart rate will increase.

(e) Head nods

These are similar to gestures and have two specific roles. First they help to control the synchronisation of speech between two people. Second, they act as reinforcers and encourage the speaker to say more.

(f) Posture

The way that a person holds their body is a largely involuntary act, but it does provide important social signals. For instance, somebody who stands very erect with their head tilted backwards and hands on hips is adopting a dominant attitude, whilst other postures can signify impatience, modesty, relaxation, and so on.

(g) Proximity

Allied to posture is the physical proximity that a person adopts when communicating. This can be a cue for intimacy, friendship or aggression and varies dramatically between different cultures. People from Middle Eastern cultures stand very close to each other when talking, whereas Scandinavians prefer to be at least arm's length away. People have around them an imaginary space which they would prefer others not to enter according to whether someone is a stranger, friend or intimate partner. When this 'space' is invaded due to circumstances, such as a crowded train or in a lift, other non-verbal signals are used to compensate for this such as averting gaze, non-aggressive posture, and so on.

(h) Orientation

This refers to the position of one person in relation to another and signals certain interpersonal attitudes — for instance, people in a co-operative situation will tend to sit side by side, in conversation or discussion at 90°, in confrontation or negotiation they will face each other.

The height at which a person is sitting in relation to another will also impart meaning to the relationship — the person at the higher level tending to be dominant.

Case example 5.2   BHS cafeteria seating

The following report appeared in *Catering and Hotel Management* (May 1981).

At Doncaster and Maidstone British Home Stores have passed through a three stage phase in reducing the seating in their restaurants by 15 per cent but at the same time increasing total seat usage at peak hours by 30 per cent. This has been mainly accomplished through installing a higher proportion of two-seater, rather than four-seater units.

Originally the restaurants at Doncaster had 214 seats with about 60 per cent four-seater tables and 40 per cent two-seaters.

What with the habit of shoppers using a further seat as a stand for their parcels and the natural reluctance of anyone newly arriving to share a table, it was found that the majority of four-seater tables were occupied by two or even only one person.

So when the premises were being renovated the proportions were reversed with now 60 per cent two-seat tables and 40 per cent four-seaters. Almost immediately the seat usage at peak hours rose from 50 to between 60 and 70 per cent.

At the Maidstone store now the proportion has been divided into almost three equal parts; a third for two-seaters, a third four-seaters and a third banquettes.

Of course, a number of these tables for two are, in fact, set a mere six inches apart, which seems perfectly sufficient for one pair of customers to feel that they are sitting completely separated from the next. But this is only effective when access to both sides of the tables is equally easy.

So instead of the traditional attitude of squeezing into the space as many people as possible, considerable attention has been given to the most suitable width of the aisle. The minimum is now set at 3 ft and this graduates up, according to usage, until in the centre and the main aisles the width is 5 ft.

(i) Bodily contact

In the UK bodily contact is less common than almost anywhere else in the world, being restricted to hand-shaking upon greeting and saying farewell, and contact within the family. In other cultures, bodily contact occurs freely, such as kissing and hugging amongst adults of the same sex in Eastern Europe and the Middle East, rubbing noses amongst Eskimos and so on.

(j) Non-verbal aspects of speech

The verbal meaning of a communication is affected by the numerous different ways of expressing the information, such as voice quality, intonation, pitch and flow; stress on particular words or syllables; the timing of the communication, including the speed and the incidence of pauses; as well as non-linguistic sounds such as 'ers' and 'ums', grunts, whistles, clicks of the tongue, and so on.

In discussing gestures, we have identified three main functions which are relevant not only to actions, but to all forms of non-verbal communication (NVC). They can support verbal messages by providing *feedback* on how the message is being received, especially looking at a person's face and eyebrows; *synchronisation* of conversation by such things as nods, shifts of gaze, posture; and evidence of *attentiveness* to the communication, signalled by orientation, gaze and posture. Second, NVC is important in *managing social relationships* by showing interpersonal attitudes, such as friendliness, contempt and sexual attraction; emotions especially through facial expression and tone of voice; and self-image, how people would like to be seen and treated, through their appearance, voice quality and manner. Third, NVC can be used in a limited way to completely *replace verbal messages*. For example, customers may ask for the bill by catching the waiter's eye and pretending to write on the palm of their hand.

Symbolic and graphical representation

In addition to those forms of communication that are clearly language – either verbal, and body language, which is non-verbal, we are subject to and use a great number of symbols, sounds and illustrations to convey messages. These methods can be divided into those that are designed to impart information and those which also attempt to affect a person's attitude or emotional state.

Task 5.3

Look at the following and identify what each of them signifies:

The advantage of using such representations are:
1. Overcome linguistic or reading difficulties. It is possible for signs and pictures to communicate effectively with people of different nationalities and cultures and of different age groups. For instance, the graphical representation of male and female on toilet doors, pictures of individual dishes on children's menus, maps and so on.
2. Convey information that cannot be put easily into words. Examples of this are the use of maps, diagrams, plans and pictures.
3. Communicate effectively in a very short space of time. In certain situations where people may be unable to read or hear instructions (such as in a moving car), or reluctant to take in information due to lack of interest, a symbol can convey meaning extremely quickly, as in the case of road signs, company logos and poster advertising.
4. Influence behaviour unconsciously. Some significant information can be imparted through the use of colour, design, sounds and smells. People, for instance, are made to walk faster through Waterloo Station during the rush hour by the playing of marches, bread shops attract custom by expelling their attractive baking smells onto the street, whilst as we have already seen in Chapter 3 colour schemes affect the atmosphere of a room and human behaviour.
5. The message is transmitted to the world at large and response is elicited only from those people for whom it is relevant.

Task 5.4

To illustrate the difficulties and complexities of graphic design, you might like to create a symbol to represent the following words or concepts: exit, down, through, danger, public house, friendly, warm.

5.4 HOW TO BE AN EFFECTIVE COMMUNICATOR

Research has shown that only a proportion of the total information imparted is absorbed by the people for whom it is intended. Therefore, it is important to consider all aspects of the communication if it is to be effective. The following considerations may help you to become an effective communicator.

(1) Credibility

The receiver of a message is influenced not only by the content but also by the person who is sending the message. Therefore, they are more likely to respond favourably if the sender is seen to be an authority or in authority, reliable and consistent as a source of information, warm and friendly, trustworthy and dynamic. If any *one* of these factors is not present, then the sender will lack credibility and the communication will suffer.

(2) Personalised

Research[3] has shown that making people aware of your personal involvement or viewpoint improves the acceptability of the message. Where appropriate therefore we should use a personal pronoun, so taking responsibility for the ideas and feelings we represent, rather than vaguely ascribe them to 'most people' or 'the management'.

(3) Construction

This is obviously of prime importance. Messages should be short, sharp and simple. They should use common and familiar words. They must make good use of active verbs to give life to the communication. A message should include clear, concise statements of all necessary information. When dealing with complex topics it is important to group items of information logically and progessively to make it readily understood and to space out new information with items that are familiar (see case example 5.1 on the readability of union agreements).

(4) Appropriateness

When constructing the message, consideration must be given to the target audience so that the style of presentation and the language used are appropriate. Compare, for instance, the language used in *The Times* with the *Sun*.

Task 5.5

Identify the usual style of greeting adopted by people in the following situations:

1. Restaurant manager with guests.
2. CB radio enthusiasts.
3. Answering the telephone at work.
4. Making a formal speech.

This may involve the use of quite technical language or jargon that would not be understood by a non-expert or lay person. An example of this in the catering industry is the use of menu French (which in fact is not readily understood by the public, hence the growing usage of menus with English explanations or dish names).

(5) Relevance

Before you can listen to a radio broadcast, you might first switch on the radio. In the same way before you can effectively communicate you must switch on the 'receiver'. This process involves attracting and gaining attention and quickly making them aware of the importance and relevance to them personally of what you are saying. Therefore in a complex statement the best sequence of presentation will be to refer to (1) the impact that the message is likely to have on the receiver, (2) other people, (3) then things in general and finally (4) dry ideas of concepts involved.

(6) Style

We shall examine in more detail leadership style in Chapter 8. In this context, style refers not only to the manner of the communicator, but also to the style of the presentation. For instance, at an informal meeting both parties are likely to be seated, at a formal presentation the speaker is likely to stand whilst the audience is seated, and in the case of a subordinate receiving a reprimand, the subordinate is likely to stand whilst the superior remains seated.

(7) Congruence

We have already seen that NVC has a powerful influence. Argyle et al.[4] discovered that non-verbal style has more effect than verbal contents and that when verbal and non-verbal messages are in conflict the verbal contents are virtually disregarded. The communicator must therefore consider the non-verbal cues people are signalling as well as what they are saying.

(8) Environment

There must be as little distraction as possible from the external environment, such as noises from the street or machinery, activity and passers-by, to allow the receiver of the communication the best opportunity to comprehend the message. For example, it is essential during an interview to ensure no interruptions by telephone calls or visitors. The pressure of time can also be inhibiting to effective communication and you must therefore allow plenty of time for getting the message across.

(9) Repetition

We have already pointed out that two or more channels may be needed for communicating the same message. There is no harm in repeating yourself if it gets the message across so long as alternative modes of expression are adopted and as soon as the message is understood, repetition ceases.

(10) Feedback

It is not sufficient to assume that you are communicating well — you must make sure that your audience has understood the message you are trying to convey.

This can be done through monitoring the person's non-verbal cues such as facial expression, direction of gaze and posture and also by eliciting a response through questioning or testing. Longer-term retention of the message will be achieved if praise is given when it is clear that the receiver has understood the message completely.

Receiving messages effectively

In the same way that we can establish guidelines for good communication, we can also identify factors that will help you to be a responsive recipient of messages. Good listening is composed of two basic elements — first, being open to receive messages and ensuring that this openness is obvious to the communicator. It is important to concentrate on what is being transmitted and to listen actively, to question any misunderstandings immediately, to ask for clarification and repetition, to show through non-verbal signals such as gaze and posture, that the message is being received and understood. Second, good listening involves ensuring the understanding of the message and the accuracy of your interpretation of its content. This can be achieved by paraphrasing the original message and repeating it to the sender, trying to reflect to the sender the feelings that have been transmitted, and negotiating over the interpretation of these contents and feelings. At all stages, one must be aware of the non-verbal signals you are receiving and attempt to be as objective as possible, so that no emotive barriers to understanding are created.

5.5 BARRIERS TO COMMUNICATION

If you refer back to our model of the communication process (see Fig. 5.1) you will see that at all stages in the process 'interference' can occur. This interference presents barriers to good communication and we will aim to identify some of the problem areas.

Task 5.5   feedback to the authors

In order to complete the communication process and provide feedback on the book, please photocopy this exercise, complete the questionnaire and return it to the authors, c/o College Division, Holt-Saunders Ltd, 1 St Anne's Road, Eastbourne, East Sussex BN21 3UN. Please ring your response to the following:

Position

student	1
lecturer	2
manager in the industry	3
other (please specify)	4

Course
(if you are studying)

BTEC National Diploma	1
BTEC Higher National Dip.	2
HCIMA	3
Degree	4
Other (please specify)	5

Readability

Easy to   Difficult
read   to read
1   2   3   4   5

Ease of understanding

Easy to   Difficult
understand   to understand
1   2   3   4   5

Relevance

Very   Not
relevant   relevant
1   2   3   4   5

Enjoyment

Very   Not
enjoyable   enjoyable
1   2   3   4   5

Appropriateness of tasks

Very   Not
appropriate   appropriate
1   2   3   4   5

Appropriateness of case examples

Very   Not
appropriate   appropriate
1   2   3   4   5

Value for money

Good   Poor
value   value
1   2   3   4   5

Overall rating

Excellent   Poor
1   2   3   4   5

Any other comments

Please give any other comments on any aspects of the book you would like us to know. Thank you very much.

(1) At the source

It is all very well, as we have done earlier, to identify those features essential to effective communication but real life does not always make the implementation of such features possible. For instance, people tend to adopt a particular leadership style which they feel is appropriate to the situation and with which they are comfortable. This may, however, conflict with the need to be warm and friendly as a communicator. Likewise, someone of status in an organisation, who wishes to encourage discussion, comment and feedback may deliberately avoid personalising their statements so that subordinates are not influenced by their boss's own opinions. Another problem may be physical impediments such as stuttering, a nervous tic or other mannerisms which prevent the sender from effectively presenting the information clearly and concisely, without distractions. Lastly, through lack of knowledge or information the sender may inadvertently or deliberately omit facts or distort the situation. The sender's emotional state can obviously have some distorting effect, since it is difficult for someone in a state of aggressive arousal or nervousness to communicate.

(2) The message itself

If one does not adopt the techniques outlined previously regarding the construction of messages, it is very easy for them to lack clarity and logical sequence, to be phrased incorrectly using the wrong type of language and for the important points to be lost. Similarly, the presentation of the message can be at fault simply through illegible handwriting, not speaking audibly, or not using audiovisual aids where appropriate. Finally, there can be misunderstandings about the purpose of the message — what is meant as a suggestion by the boss can be seen as a directive by subordinates.

(3) The channel used

We have pointed out that distractions are undesirable in the communication process and these are allied to physical problems such as open-plan offices, lack of privacy, lack of ventilation and so on, over which the communicator may actually have little control. Whilst it may not be feasible to modify the physical environment, it may be possible to carry out the exchange at a more favourable time, for instance to talk to the chef in the kitchen, wait until after the service when things have quietened down, so that you may approach him in his own surroundings where he may feel more at ease. As well as considering the physical environment one must also consider the psychological. An atmosphere of conflict or competitiveness will affect the willingness of individuals to communicate properly and messages received could be consciously misinterpreted.

Communicating to large numbers of people has particular problems such as their physical location, the wide range of personalities involved, the resource and cost implications and the difficulty in receiving feedback from them all. The Industrial Society suggests one way of overcoming this problem is to use 'briefing groups' whereby the communicator passes the message to a small number of immediate subordinates, who in turn pass it on, and so on. This does, however, lead to possible distortion of the message as it passes from person to person, since the message will tend to be short-ened, by stressing selected key points, and modified by individual bias. There is also the danger that the message will lose its immediacy and as people tend to remember best what has happened most recently, feedback will be poor.

(4) The receiver

The final barrier to communication may be at the receiver's end of the process. The receiver may have feelings of insecurity ensuing from a lack of understanding about the reasons for the communication, the sender has failed to 'switch the receiver on'. The receiver may have a lack of trust in the sender which may lead to them being scared or too embarrassed to seek clarification. Cultural reasons may make people reluctant to ask or answer questions, as in the case of Far Eastern people who do not wish to lose face by showing a lack of understanding.

Attempting to transmit too much information at one time may overload the receiver. This may be evident from the receiver's failing to recall the information, dis-tinguish fact from opinion, or to categorise incorrectly the information in stereotypes. In extreme cases, the receiver may switch off completely.

Finally, we must recognise that individual differences in perception may lead the receiver to interpret the message in a way quite different to the intended outcome.

5.6 CONCLUSION

For most people, communication is something we all take for granted. Whilst we give some thought, although probably not much, to what we are saying, we give very little thought to how we should say it. However, in certain fields of endeavour the approach is very different, for instance in acting, advertising and teaching. In these instances, the method is in many respects more important than the message. It is therefore some-what surprising in an industry such as the hotel and catering industry, where communi-cation is both vitally important and very widespread, that not more thought goes into the communication process. What has tended to happen is that depending on their role within the organisation, management and staff have become specialists in certain types of communication. The receptionist should be extremely good at face-to-face, personal interaction with people; the chef communicates symbolically with the customer through the appetising presentation of food; the advance reservations clerk is extremely well-versed in the use of the telephone; the waiter is an expert in inter-preting and communicating non-verbal signals; and so on. For managers it is import-ant to develop the widest range of communicating skills, so that they are able to use the most appropriate method for the circumstances. Managers have to be flexible enough to explain to an employee who cannot read English or understand it very well what is meant by statutory sick pay, and to discuss with a customer the finer points of fly fishing. It is sad to relate that the present management style of many people work-ing in the industry is very much prescribed by the demands upon their time of paper-work of all kinds. The result of this is that foreign employees receive a memo about sick pay which is meaningless to them and the customer never gets to meet the man-ager.

1. *This poster demonstrates the importance of communication.*

2. *First contact is made by telephoning to reserve a table.*

3. *The customers are greeted at the door by the manager.*

4. *The menu is a very effective way of communicating with the customer...*

5. *Personal contact is also of prime importance.*

6. *This restaurant sends the order through to the kitchen by computer.*

Case example 5.3

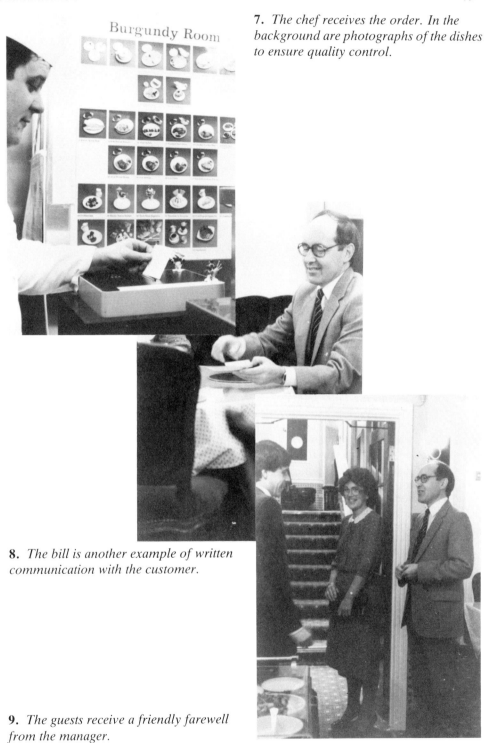

7. *The chef receives the order. In the background are photographs of the dishes to ensure quality control.*

8. *The bill is another example of written communication with the customer.*

9. *The guests receive a friendly farewell from the manager.*

Case example 5.4   Customer contact skills — a comparative study of native and non-native English speaking staff (with kind permission of the HCITB)

Introduction
As a result of contacts between the Hotel and Catering Industry Training Board and the Industrial Language Training Service (ILT), a language and communications survey was carried out at a 4 star hotel employing about 90% of foreign staff in its restaurant section. To acquire comparative data, observations were also carried out at a similar hotel, in a nearby city, which employed all English staff in its restaurant.

Findings
Customers contact
The English spoken by the ethnic minority staff often appeared at first glance to be adequate for the performance of their jobs. However the examples given below — which are of language used by English staff and ethnic minority staff in identical situations — reveal ethnic minority staff's inability to produce language needed for satisfactory customer contact.

English   a) Your table is ready when you are ready.
E.M.   b) Your table is ready now.
English   a) Would you like to follow me, please?
E.M.   b) This way please.
English   a) Here is the menu/for you/madame.
E.M.   b) Menu, please.
English   a) Would you care for some bread — Vienna roll or Melba toast?
E.M.   b) Bread, sir.
English   a) Have you decided what you would like (to eat), madame?
E.M.   b) Are you ready to order?
English   a) Would you like your roast beef well done, medium or rare?
E.M.   b) Which way do you like your steak?
English   a) Gentlemen, are you taking coffee?
E.M.   b) Do you want coffee?

Notice how English staff are able to create an atmosphere of politeness and individual care for each customer through the use of more language in longer sentences — whereas the e.m. staff, with limited language, use forms which (especially if produced with "un-English" stress and intonation) can often be interpreted as abrupt or off-hand — it is not easy to convey politeness by using short clipped sentences.

   The English staff agreed that choosing appropriate language was an essential part of their job — whereas the e.m. staff were more concerned with communicating with the customer in terms of basic comprehension. Another example illustrates this lack of appropriate language.

   A guest, having finished his meal and waited some time for the bill, had left his table to stand by the exit for the waiter. As the waiter approached showing two other people to a table the guest said "I've been looking for you. Can I have my bill?" with obvious signs of impatience. An appropriate response would include an acknowledgement, an apology and an assurance of attention — "Yes sir, I'm sorry. I'll be with you in a moment." In fact the response was "Yes, alright" in a flat intonation that to an English person signals offhandedness.

Staff need to be able to respond to a wide variety of customer initiative from casual friendly remarks to stormy complaints, for example:

	A guest arrives late for a reservation
Guest:	I'm sorry I'm late.
Response:	'Oh, that's quite alright, Madame' or more informally 'Oh, don't worry about it, Madame.'

	A guest remarks while being served:
Guest:	We've been out all day in the rain looking around.'
Response:	'Have you? What did you see?'

	A guest is looking at the menu and mutters something inaudibly, to no one in particular.
Response:	'What's that, sir?'
Guest:	'Oh, I'm looking at "Fresh gateau".'
Response:	'Oh yes, that's very good.'

The survey revealed that many e.m. staff were unable to respond to such a degree.

Language for non-routine or difficult situations
The survey also showed that similar but more serious problems occurred as soon as either the language or situation departed from the predictable and/or became more complicated — since the ethnic minority staff lacked the necessary command of English to cope with non-routine events. Where misunderstandings did occur, total breakdown was often avoided more by goodwill on the customer's part than by the linguistic ability of the overseas staff.

The English staff were asked how they reacted and what language they used in certain difficult situations, some of which had been observed at the hotel, for example, the practice of group members of coming into the restaurant one by one — rather than all together. The English waiters said they had a series of language strategies for minimising the problem.

For example:
"Are you part of a group sir, or by yourself?"
"Are there some others coming?"
"Would you like to wait for the others or start now?"

Ethnic minority staff did not possess such strategies.
The ability to initiate/respond to this degree of flexibility requires:
a) considerable command of the language
b) awareness of what is appropriate to the individual customer
c) confidence to initiate/respond as and when appropriate

Conclusion
Ethnic minority staff, while well equipped in many of the main areas of professional exertise are frequently prevented — through inadequate language skills — from achieving satisfactory customer contact.

REFERENCES

1. Laver, J. & Paterson, D.G. (1951) Readability of union contracts. *Personnel*, **28**.
2. Dahle, T.L. (1954) Transmitting information to employees. *Personnel*.
3. Johnson, D.W. (1974) Communication and the inducement of co-operative behaviour in conflict. *Speech Monographs*, **41**.
4. Argyle, M. (1970) Communication of inferior and superior attitudes by verbal and non-verbal signals. *British Journal of Social and Clinical Psychology*, **9**.

6 Interpersonal Behaviour

Man is not born human. It is only slowly and laboriously in fruitful contact, co-operation and conflict with his fellows, that he attains the distinctive qualities of human nature.

Robert E. Park

OBJECTIVES: to explain the terms 'interpersonal behavour' . . . to outline the factors affecting interpersonal relationships . . . to understand the concept of self-image . . . to describe the roles that people adopt . . . to identify problems associated with role behaviour . . . to describe alternative approaches to the development of social skills

6.1 INTRODUCTION

WHEN interviewing new recruits or prospective students for the hotel and catering industry the most common response to the question of why that person wants to come into the industry is because they enjoy 'meeting people'. Although this seems a rather shallow explanation it is true to say that success in hotel and catering operations depends to a large extent on the ability of the staff to 'meet people' and deal with them efficiently, be they the guests of the establishment or other members of staff. It is very important to understand the underlying principles of interpersonal behaviour to be able to cope effectively with this interaction and to develop the individual's social competence or social skills.

The diagram in Fig. 6.1 illustrates the complexity of interpersonal behaviour, showing that the interaction which occurs between two or more people is a continuing process affected not only by the personal characteristics, perception and social skills of those taking part but also by the situation in which the interaction takes place.

6.2 THE INTERACTIVE PROCESS

The process of social interaction has been related to that of a motor skill[1] such as driving a car or playing tennis. The interaction process involves the reception and

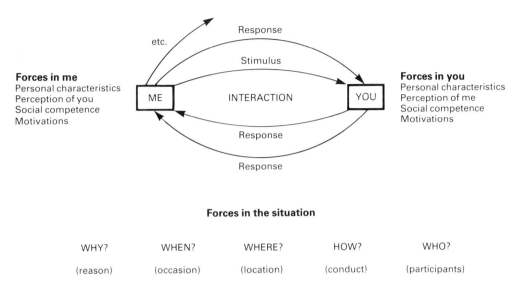

Figure 6.1 *The complexity of interpersonal behaviour.*

interpretation of perceptual cues, making appropriate responses both verbally and non-verbally and the opportunity to receive feedback and take corrective action. In the diagram this process assumes the form of a spiral with the initial remark from *me* eliciting a response of some sort from *you*. This response will in turn generate a response from *me* and so on until the interaction reaches its conclusion. Similarly, when playing tennis one player serves the ball, the other player tracks the service, monitors the first player at the same time and makes an appropriate return; the rally continues until one player wins the point or the ball goes out of court. This analogy perhaps stresses the competitive nature of social interaction which is not present in all situations, but it also emphasises the special features of social skills in that the performance of one player, although linked, is independent of the other player and there is therefore a need to have ways of co-ordinating the interaction if it is to be as effective as possible.

Forces in the individual

Fig. 6.1 illustrates that this central process is likely to be affected by forces in the individuals involved in the interaction.

Personal characteristics

All the individual differences discussed in the earlier chapters are of importance here. Although it would appear that personality or level of intelligence would be good predictors of a person's social behaviour, it has been found[2] that people can behave socially in quite different ways depending on the situation they find themselves in; in one situation a person may be dominant and outgoing, but in another may be shy and retiring. However, there are certain fundamental attributes which do seem to persist from one interaction to another; these include a person's need for dominance or dependence, their need for aggression or warmth in relationships, their extraversion or introversion, stability or neuroticism, their perceptual style (i.e. the predominant way in which they perceive or categorise the world around them), their social and cultural background and their self-image or self-esteem. The conclusion to be drawn here is that although a person's behaviour may not be as consistent as we would expect from one situation to another, there will be an identifiable range of behaviours from which any particular response may be drawn.

Perception of people

The selection of the appropriate response from individuals' ranges of behaviour will be affected by the way they perceive the other person in terms of their personality, age, status and so on. The factors involved in the perception of other people have already been discussed in Chapter 3.

Social competence

Just as some people are more skilled in manipulative motor skills (such as chopping vegetables or using a spoon and fork) so different levels of social skills can be identified, and similarly social skills can be improved by training and experience. The interaction between two socially skilled people will be very different from that between two socially less competent people. The question of social skills and social skills training will be looked at in more detail in this chapter.

Motivations

In any interaction each individual will have their own personal objectives or needs to be satisfied, and these needs are likely to vary from situation to situation. First, a person may be looking for support, protection or guidance as in the case of a new employee during induction or a tired guest arriving at reception; any new situation will tend to stimulate this dependent approach. Second, a person may be looking for warmth or friendship in the relationship and may behave in such a way as to encourage a friendly response. Another motivating force in social situations may be a need for power to control other people's behaviour; supervisors and managers would be expected to have high needs in this respect. A fourth need is for approval, confirming what people think about themselves in a favourable way, bolstering their self-image and self-esteem. The sex drive has been found to affect social behaviour and encourage interaction with others, but is inhibited in Western society by social taboos and codes of conduct. Similar codes of conduct will restrict the behaviour of people who feel a high need for aggressive behaviour and unacceptable physical aggression may become channelled into direct and indirect verbal aggression.

Perhaps the most common reason for people coming together and engaging in inter-personal behaviour is simply that they have to complete some appointed task. A guest who wishes to order a meal will find it very difficult to do so without interacting in some way with waiting staff. People working on the same service line will need to converse to get their work done. These examples illustrate that a great amount of social interaction takes place not because people particularly want it to, but because it has to; once social interaction does occur then the other motivations will be brought into play.

Interaction between people cannot, however, occur in a vacuum; it must be affected by the situation in which it takes place.

Forces in the situation

Reasons for interaction — why? One influence on the interaction will be the goal or purpose of the meeting. It is possible to identify a number of situations all of which will have a slightly different influence on the interaction process. First, the main purpose may be to obtain information as is the case with a receptionist taking a booking over the telephone or conducting an interview. In this case each person has an accepted part to play; it is acceptable for instance for the interviewer to ask personal questions and the interviewee will be expected to respond truthfully. In the case of a waiter taking an order for a meal it is acceptable for the guests to take a long time to make their selection, to change their minds and so on.

A second purpose for social interaction is to attempt to change another person's beliefs or attitudes and good examples here include sales reps attempting to convince customers about the superiority of their products or political candidates canvassing for votes at an election. Again, each party to the interaction is aware of the role the other is playing and their behaviour will be affected accordingly. Problems may arise when the waiter who is taking the order attempts to take the part of the sales rep and influence the customer's choice, unless the guest is prepared to accept this change of emphasis. It is essential that all staff who come into contact with the guest receive training in sales techniques so that they can recognise and take advantage of this type of situation effectively.

A third situation is when one person is giving information to another as is the case in training or giving instructions. It is important to distinguish here between imparting information to one other person and to one hundred people.

Fourth, one person may be attempting to change another person's emotional state such as trying to cheer somebody up or trying to calm down an irate guest who is complaining about your standard of service. Again, especially in the case of dealing with complaints, it is imperative that the staff concerned receive training in how to handle this kind of situation. There can be nothing more frustrating than for a guest to complain vehemently that a steak was cooked badly in a microwave oven when you know for a fact that you do not have a microwave oven.

A fifth purpose for social interaction arises from working together with colleagues. Nearly all jobs in the hotel and catering industry involve some co-operation between individuals or between groups. For example, it is essential for the kitchen staff and the counter staff on a self-service counter to co-operate to ensure that there is a continual supply of food available but that holding time is kept to a minimum; without that co-operation customers will either have to wait for their chosen meal or receive an inferior product. It is unfortunate that co-operation between certain departments in the hotel and catering industry seems so poor, particularly between the critical areas of kitchen to restaurant and reception to housekeeping.

The final purpose relevant to our discussion is that of supervision, either looking after one individual or supervising the work of a group. Included here, for example, would be the chairing of a committee or a head waiter organising the staff ready for service.

Occasion of interaction — when? The influence of time on interaction would not seem to be particularly great, but one only has to think of a guest coming down to breakfast early in the morning after over-indulging the previous night to be greeted by clattering plates and loud voices to realise that there is an appropriate time for all behaviour. It is this 'appropriateness' that is of prime concern here. Whereas in the evening guests may have a long time to spend over their dinner, at lunchtime they will most likely have more limited time and staff dealing with them should realise these implications. Similarly a receptionist checking in guests late at night should be aware that they are likely to be tired and hungry and want to get to their room as quickly as possible. At the other end of the day, some London hotels have set aside special facilities for guests who have arrived on the early morning flights from America and arrive travel weary. The important thing here is to recognise the influence that the time of day can have on an individual's behaviour and compensate accordingly.

Location of interaction — where? The location in which the interaction takes place has two major effects. The physical characteristics of the setting are obviously important; it is very difficult to conduct a meaningful discussion on cost control with the head chef in the middle of a busy and noisy kitchen, much better to find a quiet corner in an office somewhere. The second aspect of location concerns whose office the discussion takes place in. Every person likes to establish an area of territory which they feel belongs to them and which others enter at their peril. A good example of territory is where a family spend a morning on the beach and having set up their deckchairs they build a small wall in a circle round their encampment. The family go home at lunchtime, but the now empty circle of sand stays empty for the whole of the afternoon, despite the beach being crowded. It is easy to see that there will be a different atmosphere to the discussion whether it takes place in the manager's office or in the chef's office. Managers may generally find staff much more amenable and open to communication if they approach them on their territory rather than summoning them into managerial space, but they must also realise that they are entering the staff's territory and act accordingly. Another aspect of territory relates to the individual's personal space, as we have identified in Chapter 5: that space which keeps people slightly apart in queues or makes them sit at opposite ends of a park bench.

A person whose space is violated will either back away or in extreme cases become aggressively defensive, but a person who likes close contact will feel rejected if their partner constantly backs away.

Conduct of the interaction — how? The conduct of the interaction must be influenced by the method of communication being used. A good example here is the effect of the

telephone which limits the amount of non-verbal feedback so making it more difficult
to interpret the communication and to synchronise the conversation.

Participants in the interaction — who? The interaction will be affected by the roles the
people are occupying at that particular time and also by their relative status. The
interaction between the headwaiter and the head chef will be very different to that
between Tim and Roger after work across the road in the pub. The effect of the 'role'
of the person will be discussed in more detail later in the chapter.

Task 6.1   the predictions exercise (Fig. 6.2)

Your own rating	Your prediction	Statement	Partner's rating	Partner's prediction	Difference you	Difference partner
		1. Capital punishment should be introduced				
		2. Sports are character building				
		3. Children should obey their parents				
		4. I am careful in handling money				
		5. I like to be the centre of attention				
		6. I usually hold my anger inside				
		7. I am easily embarrassed in front of groups				
		8. I consider myself to be quite intelligent				
		9. Blood sports should be banned				
		10. I like my physical appearance				

Figure 6.2 *Predictions.*

This task must be completed with the help of a partner.
In the column headed 'your own rating', indicate the degree of your agreement or disagreement with the following statements on a scale as below.

Total disagreement   0 1 2 3 4 5 6 7 8 9 10   Total agreement

Now in the column marked 'your prediction' write down your prediction of your partner's response of agreement or disagreement with the statements. With your response now covered your partner should complete the columns marked 'partner's rating' for his or her own response and 'partner's predic- tion' for his or her prediction of your response. In the 'difference you' cloumn enter the difference between your prediction and your partner's actual response and similarly in the 'difference partner' column enter the difference between your partner's predictions and your actual scores.

An analysis of the previous task will show considerable discrepancies be- tween the individuals' rating and their partners' prediction of their response, even between close friends. There are three main explanations of these dif- ferences. First, when individuals write down their response they may give the response for how they would *like* to be rather than how they *actually* are in order to protect their self-image and self-esteem. Second, the individual may deliberately display a false front to the world and it is this image the partner is reflecting, and finally the individual may be displaying an image to the world of which he is unaware. These problems have an obvious influence on the way people interact.

6.3 OTHER FACTORS AFFECTING RELATIONSHIPS

Self-image

The term 'self-image' is how you see yourself and consists of a core of such things as name, sex, body image, occupation and additional items such as social class, personal- ity, religious or political beliefs and so on. In addition to this self-image, people have an 'ideal' image of how they would like to be, probably built up from admired models of behaviour, just as fans of a particular group will adopt their style of dress and mannerisms. This ideal is the goal that the individual tries to achieve and in interaction with other people will tend to present this image for approval or rejection. Approval from other people will reinforce the particular image adopted and will contribute to the individual's self-esteem, that is the degree to which people approve of and accept themselves. The way in which the self-image develops is not wholly understood but is likely to be affected by the reaction of others, comparison with others, the roles a per- son plays and identifying with models. The reactions of other people do have a pro- found effect on the development of self-image and we tend to come to see ourselves in the way that other people see us, especially those we are in close contact with such as parents and friends. The response of our friends also provides a comparison be- tween their image and our own and especially during adolescence there is pressure to conform to the behaviour and image of the peer group. Individuals play many dif- ferent roles in the course of their life and these will have an effect on self-image. For instance, a person who works for a time as a waiter will adopt some of the waiter's characteristics into their self-image and these will persist outside the work environ- ment and even if the person changes jobs. The modelling process also shows up here: when commis chefs are promoted to chefs de partie they will tend to adopt the behaviour of their most admired colleagues as they look to find ways of handling the situation. In this way the individual takes various models at various stages and parts of each will go to form the overall self-concept.

Self-projection

Effective interaction depends to a large extent on the growth of understanding between the individuals concerned and breakdowns or problems in interaction can derive from a lack of this basic information and understanding. This process can be illustrated by the Johari window shown in Fig. 6.3.

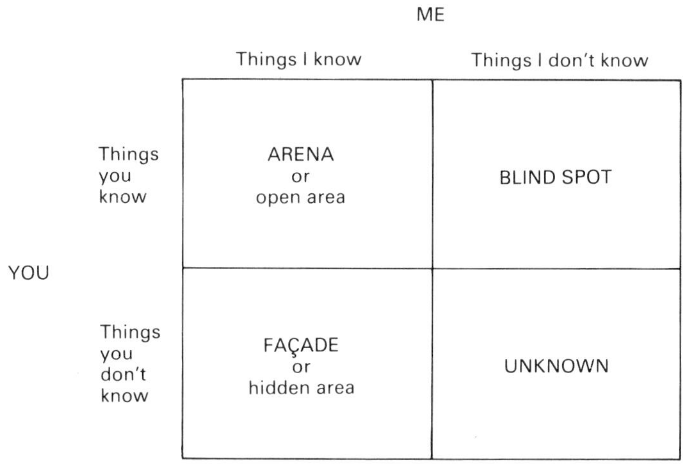

ME

	Things I know	Things I don't know
Things you know	ARENA or open area	BLIND SPOT
Things you don't know	FAÇADE or hidden area	UNKNOWN

YOU

Figure 6.3   *The Johari window.*

The arena or open area contains the things I know about myself and about which others are also fully aware; there is a free and open exchange of information and feelings in this area. For interaction to be its most effective this open area should be as large as possible. The blind spot contains information that I do not know about myself, but which others do know. This information may be in the form of verbal cues, mannerisms, the way I say things or the style in which I relate to others. I may not be aware of the signs of anxiety which I am transmitting when I meet someone, but they may perceive it quite easily. In the hidden area are the things about me which I do not want other people to know; so although I may be very nervous, I put on a façade of being very confident so that people do not see the 'real' me. The unknown area contains things which neither I nor others know about me, but may be there even so. For instance, I may have some latent ability which has not yet developed or it may be simply childhood memories which have faded over time.

In order to improve the interaction between people it is necessary to expand the open area and this can only be done by a conscious effort and in an atmosphere of trust. For instance to move from the hidden to the open area requires sufficient trust and confidence for one person to disclose information about themselves to others which they would normally prefer to hide. To move from the blind spot to the open area requires feedback about how people are perceived by others which the individual must be prepared to accept. Venison[3] suggests that it is the prime responsibility of hotel managers to improve customer relations by engaging in as much direct customer contact as they can to elicit feedback from guests about the services being provided, so as to defuse potential complaints, and by being sincere and open in their communications both with guests and staff develop good interpersonal relations throughout the establishment.

6.4 ROLES

As well as developing a self-image, projecting themselves in particular, people also adopt roles. A role can be defined as the pattern of behaviour typical of people occupying a particular position. This consists of the work they do, the traditional ways of behaving, the attitudes and beliefs they hold and the clothes or uniform they wear. For example, a man who is a top-class hotel manager is expected to dress smartly in black jacket and pinstripe trousers, to glide regally round the establishment, greeting every customer and employee alike by name and title, to never lose his temper and to dine elegantly every evening in the restaurant. The individual does not occupy just one role, but a wide variety of roles at different times of the day or week. Thus the same hotel manager may be a father, football referee, and a tenor in the local operatic society. Individuals quickly identify the role they are expected to play and adapt their behaviour accordingly when placed in a new situation. This is illustrated by Lieberman's research[4] into workers' attitudes towards management. Initially, he collected information from 2000 employees regarding their opinions and feelings towards management. After two or three years he discovered that those promoted to foremen had developed distinctly pro-management attitudes, whereas those elected as union officials had strong anti-management attitudes. The attitudes of the remaining workers remained constant.

Task 6.2

Consider a typical week and prepare a list of all the roles you have played. Show where you act out these roles as in Fig. 6.4.

The behaviour of the person playing a role is determined largely by the expectations of the people with whom they interact. This group of people is known as the 'role set'. Fig. 6.5 illustrates a typical role set for a person employed as a waitress. All the differing expectations of these people will basically define how she behaves when working at her job.

However, the concept of role behaviour is not as straightforward as it first seems, since it assumes that people are prepared to readily adopt patterns of behaviour imposed from outside and suppress their own individuality. This causes serious role problems.

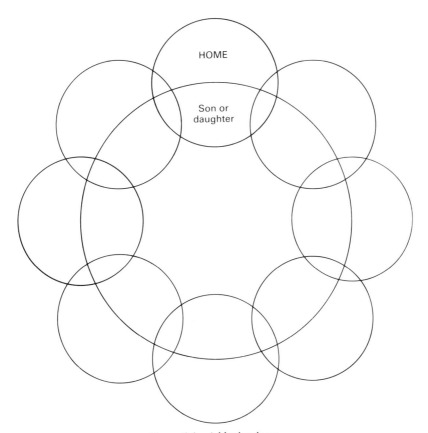

Figure 6.4 *A blank role set.*

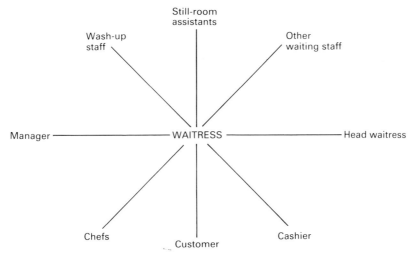

Figure 6.5 *A typical role set for a waitress.*

Problems with roles

Role ambiguity

This arises where either the occupier of the role or the members of the role set are uncertain about precisely what that role is and the expected behaviour pattern. The management trainee is often a classic example of someone in an ambiguous role. It is usual for the trainee to be placed at an operative level during the early stages of training. Their own expectation is to act as a normal member of staff in that job, but fellow workers are likely to perceive them as a member of the management team and act accordingly. Even when the management trainee is given supervisory or managerial responsibility they are unlikely to be given corresponding authority; this places considerable strain on their interaction with staff, especially those they may well have worked with previously at an operative level.

Role incompatibility

There are situations in which the person occupying a role is unsuited to the particular demands placed upon them. This may be due to their personality, level of intelligence, attitude, beliefs or their own self-concept. Thus a person who is relatively introverted may find it difficult to occupy a role that involves meeting lots of people, or an employee may eventually be promoted past the position which they are intellectually capable of handling (this is referred to as the 'Peter Principle');[5] or a worker in a team who due to a religious upbringing has a strong work ethic and may not find the accepted productivity level of their co-workers complies with their own ability; or lastly entrants to the hotel and catering industry who are attracted by the glamour or the impression that they will be helping and serving people are often disillusioned when they discover that the industry is primarily concerned with making a profit.

Role overload

When an individual is confronted by so many differing role expectations that they are unable to cope, they are said to be suffering from role overload and will display symptoms of dissatisfaction, fatigue and tension. This often is due to additional tasks or responsibilities being added on to a position. An example might be the assistant manager in a hotel who is already responsible for personnel and training, being asked to act as duty manager and becoming in addition health and safety officer, the chair of the staff social committee and security officer.

Multiple-role conflict

We have already identified that one person will inevitably occupy several roles, and it is when these roles are expected to be carried out at the same time that conflict can arise. A person will be behaving in a way that is acceptable to one role, which may be totally unacceptable to another. When a member of the family telephones someone at work, they will be treated not as a relative but as co-worker or client, so that the style of communication may be a lot more formal than at home. One reason for not allowing members of staff to drink in the bars of the hotels in which they work is that bar staff in their work role are expected to require payment for drinks, but friends and co-workers might expect to be dispensed drinks for nothing.

Role-set conflict

In Fig. 6.5 we identified a possible role set for a waitress and it can be seen from the large number of people with whom contact is made that it is unlikely they will all have identical expectations of the waitress's behaviour.

The customers expect the waitress to serve them in the time they have available whereas the chef expects them to wait until the food has been correctly prepared and the manager may wish all customers to be served within a certain time scale. This shows that each member of the role set has very definite expectations of the person's behaviour, but that these can be incompatible.

A group of workers that are particularly susceptible to this type of conflict are 'front-line supervisors'. This is due to the fact that they are at the interface between workers and management both of whom have very different expectations. Six particular problems have been identified.[6]

1. The supervisor is not involved in management policy decisions, but is expected to carry them out.
2. Although no longer part of the shop-floor work force the supervisor relies completely on their co-operation.
3. The supervisor has no real authority.
4. One of the supervisor's prime concerns is to maintain group morale while at the same time being expected to monitor, control and correct staff performance.
5. It is unlikely that the supervisor will be promoted to a management position but must maintain and uphold the management viewpoint.
6. The supervisor's background is often more like that of the subordinates than that of the superiors, it is therefore easier to identify with the subordinates when the opposite may be being asked for.

Reducing role problems

Since all of us adopt roles unconsciously in most interpersonal relationships, should a problem arise it is often difficult to resolve. Having identified that the problem arises from role behaviour there are four possible ways of resolving the situation. First, the detailed definition of the expected behaviour for a job can be laid down. This will be based on a job description, but should also include behavioural, as well as task details. It is not sufficient to say that a waitress should serve customers, but to specify the timescale over which service takes place. Second, in some instances it may be necessary to change the job so that the present incumbent is able to function more effectively. A third solution may be to train the individual to cope more effectively with the job as it stands. For example, a commis chef may be sent on day release to college to gain further qualifications before being promoted to chef de partie. Lastly, careful selection of new employees may reduce the likelihood of role problems occurring in the first place.

Task 6.3

Recommend the most appropriate of the four methods for reducing role problems in dealing with each of those identified.

6.5 SOCIAL SKILLS TRAINING

It should be evident from the previous discussions that the interaction process is so
complicated that to function effectively most people would benefit from some help
and guidance. This is particularly true of the hotel and catering industry where there
is a great deal of interaction. It has been suggested[7] that such 'social skills' are
unteachable. Pell bases this view on his experiences which suggest that if attempts are
made to change attitudes, this 'is a slow process and it is unrealistic to expect any real
change after a course which lasts two or three days', whilst other techniques such as
transactional analysis break down under stress and the staff resort to their instinctive
response which 'might be the right one or the wrong one'. Pell's solution is that in the
long run it is essential to select the right people, and that good employee selection procedures will achieve much more than social skills training.

Whilst we acknowledge that selection is very important, we take the view expressed
by Boella[8] that we can make positive contributions that facilitate staff learning social
skills. He cites four factors that management should consider:

1. Job design 'so that staff want to, and can, deal courteously with customers'.
2. Physical aspects of the job, so that social problems are not created by poor layout,
    lighting, noise level, heating, ventilation, etc.
3. Conditions of employment, in particular poor remuneration or over-reliance on
    tips.
4. Courtesy training, i.e. training in very simple courtesies, greetings and routines to
    avoid 'conflict situations'.

Furthermore, we would suggest that social skills training techniques should not be dismissed lightly. As long ago as 1969 the HCITB expressed the opinion that 'training in
social skills is vital'.[9]

Since then they have invested a great deal of time and effort into this area of training.[10] There are broadly three approaches to social skills training (see Fig. 6.6).

Cognitive approach

This method of social skills training relies on traditional teaching methods through
lectures, discussions, case studies, and reading. The underlying principle is that if the
individual understands the way people interact and the reasons for their behaviour
they are in a better position to cope with interpersonal relations. In many respects this
chapter is reliant on this method. The most significant technique to apply this cognitive approach is transactional analysis as developed by Eric Berne[11] and applied extensively in this country by Traveller's Fare, the catering operation of British Rail (see case
study 6.1).

Figure 6.6 *Approaches to social skills training.*

The essence of transactional analysis is that you can adopt one of three main roles during interaction which will influence the way you behave. These are the role of 'parent' who controls, criticises, sets standards and makes rules, but also protects, cares for and looks after; the 'child' role is typified by screaming, stubbornness, rebellion but also compliance, adaptability and servility; third there is the 'adult' role which is rational and level-headed persons who arbitrate between the other two. These are called 'ego states' and are evident in every individual, normally with the adult in control but the parent or child being displayed when the need arises. TA attempts to analyse any communication process according to the ego state of the participants. For the interaction to be effective the ego states must be complementary. That is to say, the initial stimulus and the response must fit together, in this way adult stimulus and adult response will be complementary, as will a parent stimulus to a child response.

Problems in interaction arise when the stimulus and response cross, so that if you adopt a parental role but the response you receive is also of a parental nature then conflict will ensue. As well as complementary and crossed transactions, a third possibility is the ulterior interaction where on the surface there seems to be a complementary transaction, but underlying this one of the participants is adopting a superficial role. These situations are best illustrated by an example of each type of transaction.

Complementary transaction

Waiter: Are you ready to order now, sir?
Customer: I certainly am

In this example both participants are adopting an adult role.

Crossed transaction

Waiter: How did you find your steak, sir?
Customer: I looked under the chips

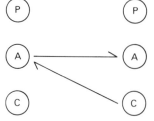

This shows an adult stimulus being answered by a childish response. This could result in either annoyance or humour. The exact reaction will depend on the social skill of the waiter. Thus the annoyance response might be:

Waiter: That's not quite what I meant, sir!

which would be a parent to child transaction and could result in a further breakdown of interaction, whereas the humorous approach might be:

Waiter: And was it there, sir?

This is a child response to the customer's stimulus and therefore complementary so that the transaction can now proceed smoothly.

Ulterior transaction

Wine waiter: Well, the Bordeaux '64 would go
                rather well but is expensive. Perhaps
                you'd prefer the '71?
Customer: No, no, a bottle of the '64 please.
                It's such a good vintage.

This shows on the surface an adult to adult rational exchange, but underlying it is the implication that the waiter thinks in a childish way the customer is not able to afford the best, while the child in the customer must now have it irrespective of the cost. Thus the TA approach teaches staff to identify the three ego states and encourages them to adopt a complementary ego state, thereby avoiding crossed or ulterior transactions.

Behavioural approach

This is achieved through traditional training methods and approaches social skills as any other technical skill based on the views of Argyle outlined earlier in the chapter. This approach relies heavily on role playing where the trainee tries out a variety of

9 Complaints

ALWAYS LISTEN

"NO TOILET ROLL AGAIN"

BRING IN YOUR BOSS . . . . .

"THIS FISH SMELLS BAD"

"THERE'S A HOLE IN THIS TOWEL"

THANK AND APOLOGISE

TRAINER

Objective: To deal effectively with complaints.

1. Ask Questions
Ask your trainees for the answers to these
questions, which relate to their Card:

Q Why do complaints tend to come to you?
Q To whom can you go for help?
Q Why is it important to listen?

2. Exercise
Pose as a complaining customer and ask the trainee
to deal with you. Give guidance as necessary,
stressing your company's specific complaints
procedure.

Some examples could be:
    Customer complains of slow service in restaurant.
    Customer complains that tap drips in wash basin.
    Customer complains that wrong room key was
    handed over.
    Customer complains of being overcharged in the bar.

It's even more useful if you can think of examples
which relate to the individuals and their jobs.

Figure 6.7 *A trainer card (HCITB).*

techniques in a simulated situation. With role playing the trainee receives instruction in the particular techniques to be used and is then allowed to practise these techniques and receive feedback on how well he or she has performed. An example of this type of training is the development of interviewing skills, where trainees, following initial instruction, are often videotaped conducting interviews on applicants so that they may then actually see themselves performing, allowing for a thorough critical review of their achievement. In this way, the correct behaviours are reinforced and poor performance can be rectified. This particular approach has been adopted by the HCITB in their 'customer relations training packages' which consist of a series of training sessions on different aspects of social skills ranging from posture and hygiene to diplomacy and selling. An example of a 'trainer card' for one session is shown in Fig. 6.7 showing the style adopted.

Another behavioural method is profile training. This approach is based on a series of group exercises where the individuals are encouraged to categorise people's behaviour. By appreciating how other people are behaving, they can then adapt their own behaviour to give the most appropriate response. Another of the major features of profile training is that trainees are given accurate feedback on the way they are behaving at all stages so developing their self-awareness.

No one 'profile' is appropriate since the first part of the technique is to identify those behaviour patterns that are adequate in a particular situation and those that should be avoided. Once established, individuals are observed and their performance in the various categories measured. They are then set specific targets to increase the desirable behaviour by specific amounts thereby reducing undesirable behaviours. For instance, behaviours that would be deemed appropriate in the work situation might be to innovate, give clarification to subordinates and identify problems, and undesirable behaviour might be shutting out suggestions, defending one's actions and jumping the gun. Once people have begun to adapt, they can progress to identifying different profiles for different situations so that, for instance, the chef would begin to adopt different approaches towards commis, supervising colleagues and customers.

Affective approach

The third approach does not try to prescribe specific behaviour but attempts to change a person's attitudes and feelings, thereby increasing their sensitivity to other people and themselves. Through this, it is hoped they will become more socially skilled. The basic format of this method is the T-group which consists of a group of 8 to 12 people who meet to discuss and analyse their own interpersonal behaviours. Two organisations in the hotel and catering industry that have been known to use the technique are the Carlton Tower hotel in the late 1960s and the then 'Popular Division' of Trusthouse Forte in the early 1970s.

T-group training would normally follow the following pattern over a period of five or six days. In the first instance, the group meets with the skilled trainer present but no direction is given as to what the group is expected to do. Members react in a variety of ways, displaying annoyance, humour or by retiring into themselves according to their individual personality and self-image. As the sessions progress the trainer begins to provide inputs relating to the group's interaction and individuals' behaviour, mainly by asking questions; this also encourages group members to give and receive feedback in the best possible way. By this process, trainees develop critical self-awareness and become more willing to share their experiences, feelings and attitudes with other members of the group. At times this can be a painful process, but the group members by now provide a sympathetic environment for self-disclosure and personal development. At the end of this highly intense period of self-evaluation, trainees emerge more sensitive to others' feelings and needs, more self-assured and display more acceptable social characteristics such as humour, helpfulness, generosity and so on.

It is apparent from our discussion that some of these techniques have only been applied rarely in the industry. By far the most common approach has been that developed by the HCITB, primarily because it fits in with the normal style of on-the-job training, it does not require specialist expertise and it can be seen to work. Both TA and T-groups have indirect effects upon staff. The latter tool is particularly time-consuming and generally thought to be only suitable for management personnel. In fact, where 'ordinary' employees have attended T-groups results have been favourable. For instance, Peter Venison states of the Carlton Tower experience that 'the team spirit and co-operation which ensued the return of the final group was greater than I have witnessed in any other hotel environment'.[12] Likewise, T-group training with THF produced results such as a reduction in staff turnover, improved customer response and increased self-awareness.[13] The research concludes that such training is undoubtedly suitable for all grades of staff and that 'operative' staff enjoy and respond well to this type of training.

6.6 CONCLUSION

It is no accident that this chapter occurs at the mid-point of this book. The understanding and application of interpersonal skills is the linchpin of our approach to human relations. In the previous chapters we have identified the areas of knowledge that an individual must be aware of to be an effective manager of people. This chapter shows how to integrate this knowledge and apply it skilfully in any situation where interpersonal interaction takes place. In the succeeding chapters we consider groups and organisations, leadership and decision-making, and the consumer. The successful management of all these areas relies completely on applying the principles outlined here.

Many of the case exercises in other chapters fulfil the role of examining interpersonal behaviour and we recommend that you also look at these to identify the forces in each situation and attempt to establish the roles adopted by the various participants (see case exercises 3.1, 7.1, 8.1 and 8.2).

Case example 6.1   Customer relations training in British Transport Hotels

This case example describes how one company — British Transport Hotels Ltd — used the techniques of transactional analysis as part of a programme to improve staff effectiveness. In the mid-1970s BTH was one of the largest companies in the hotel and catering industry, employing about 11 000 people. Its activities were all associated with rail travel: operating 29 railway hotels, catering and retailing at 185 stations and catering on 900 train services daily.

The BTH management team recognised one of their key result areas was improving staff effectiveness — particularly customer relations skills. All hotel and catering employees need customer relations skills, but this was especially important when dealing with BTH customers. When people travel they are often under considerable stress. Struggling with luggage, rushing for trains, unexplained delays and missed appointments all heighten a customer's anxiety and cause frustration. Like most hotel and catering workers, BTH employees experienced the pressure of extreme peaks of business (for example during rush hours). Put these two together — a frustrated, anxious traveller and a harassed catering employee — and the situation can be explosive. Often a trigger, such as a product complaint, would result in a customer 'unloading' a morning's frustration onto the catering staff — and sometimes vice versa. And, of course, these incidents would make the employees feel even more harassed and frustrated, making them even less ready to deal with the next customer.

The problem was complex — the pattern of business, the environment, the systems of work and equipment, the style of supervision and the selection of staff were all contributory factors. The BTH management team started on a programme of activities to deal with these factors. Staff training was just one aspect of this programme — and clearly something more than the existing training in technical skills was necessary. Staff needed to develop the ability to deal with difficult customer situations, including an understanding of how their own behaviour could contribute to the problem.

At this time TA had already been used for customer relations training in other industries — for example, airlines and banking. TA is particularly useful for this form of training because its concepts can be learned easily by people with no previous knowledge of human relations. The BTH Training Department reviewed existing TA training packages in use in other organisations and after discussion with managers in BTH drew up a set of training objectives. In simple TA terms these objectives were:

1. Identify ego states.
2. Analyse transactions.
3. Demonstrate how to deal with difficult situations.

The training programmes had to be designed to reach large numbers of staff quickly. It was also decided that a maximum of one training day per employee could be devoted to this activity. In order to meet these requirements it was considered advantageous to design the package around a series of short, filmed incidents. These were made using professional actors, portraying BTH employees and customers, in a range of typical situations. The first part of the film was designed to help trainees learn to identify ego states. The second part dealt with the analysis of transactions. Both parts of the film involved participative exercises. There was also a filmed introduction to the training course featuring the company's chief executive.

The complete Training Course lasted for six hours and consisted of nine sessions:

1. Introduction (using film)
2. Understanding ego states
3. Identification of ego states (using film)
4. Strokes and stamps

5. Understanding transactions
6. Analysis of transactions (using film)
7. Dealing with difficult situations
8. Role play exercises
9. Programme review

A typical course consisted of 10 trainees led by a member of the BTH training department. After the course, most trainees felt that they were more competent to recognise and avoid potentially difficult situations and to deal with customer complaints when they arose. There were other trainees who felt that the training programme was interesting — but that it added little to their customer relations skills. At a departmental level, the training appeared to be most effective when an entire work group and their supervisor attended. The supervisor's attitude and example was crucial to the success of the programme. TA gave the work group a common language for discussing customer relations and it is interesting to note that some TA jargon has persisted for many years.

At a corporate level it was difficult to evaluate the effect of the training — measures like complaints and commendations showed no demonstrable improvement. As already stated training was only one part of the solution — and as often happens in training, it was difficult to establish that TA had been particularly effective in solving BTH's customer relations problems. In the following years the emphasis of customer relations training changed from developing individual interpersonal skills (using TA) to teaching specific procedures (for example, say 'Good Morning, how can I help you... would you like anything else?'). TA, however, was developed as one of the main vehicles for management training and career counselling; but that's another case study.

REFERENCES

1. Argyle, M. (1978) *The Psychology of Interpersonal Behaviour*. Harmondsworth: Penguin.
2. Gergen, K.J. & Marlowe, D. (1970) *Personality and Social Behaviour*. London: Addison-Wesley.
3. Vension, P. (1983) *Managing Hotels*. London: Heinemann.
4. Lieberman, J. (1956) The effects of changes in roles in the attitudes of role occupants. *Human Relations*, **9**.
5. Peter, L.J. & Hull, R. (1969) *The Peter Principle*. New York: William Morrow.
6. Sasser, W.E. (1980) Let first-level supervisors do their job. *Harvard Business Review*, March–April.
7. Pell, R. (1980) Are social skills unteachable? *Hospitality*, **5**.
8. Boella, M. (1981) Are social skills unteachable? *Hospitality*, **17**.
9. HCITB (1969) Food Service. Wembley: HCITB.
10. Cooper, C.L. & Oddie, H. (1972) An evaluation of two approaches to social skill training in the catering industry. Southampton: University of Southampton.
11. Berne E. (1961) *Transactional Analysis in Psychotherapy*. New York: Grove Press.
12. Venison, P. (1983) op. cit.
13. Cooper, C.L. & Oddie, H. (1972) op. cit.

7 Groups at Work

We are essentially cultural animals with the capacity to formulate many kinds of social structures, but a deep-seated biological urge to co-operation, towards working as a group, provides a basic framework for those structures

R.E. Leakey, *Origins*

OBJECTIVES: to define 'group' . . . to differentiate between formal and informal groups . . . to identify the functions of group . . . to discuss those factors affecting group performance . . . to identify the characteristic features of a developed group

7.1 INTRODUCTION

JUST as individuals cannot fail to communicate in the course of their work, it is also extremely unlikely that they will not be part of a 'group', particularly in the hotel and catering industry which relies heavily on team effort and co-operation. In fact, everybody in their working and social life is a member of a wide variety of different groups.

Task 7.1

Before reading how we define a 'group', attempt to identify the groups that you might belong to.

This task should have resulted in an extensive, and apparently dissimilar list of collections of people ranging from the family to a darts team or class of students at college. We therefore need a definition of what does and what does not constitute a group for the purposes of our analysis, that is to say we shall concentrate on the grouping of individuals at work.

7.2 DEFINITION

There is no problem in finding a definition of what constitutes a group because it is a term in common use and as a concept not too difficult to understand. However,

102

behavioural scientists do not seem to be able to agree over one single, comprehensive definition, but have tended to isolate individual factors in group make-up. These include the following.

Perceptions of membership

A group has been defined as 'any collection of people who perceive themselves to be a group'.[1] This is possibly the criteria you have used in order to answer Task 7.1

Interpersonal interaction

A second definition is 'a number of persons who communicate with one another often over a span of time, and who are few enough so that each person is able to communicate with all the others, not at second-hand, through other people, but face to face'.[2]

Purpose

Another definition suggests that a group is 'composed of two or more persons who come into contact for a purpose . . .'[3]

Motivation

A group is '. . . necessary to the satisfaction of certain individual needs in each' member of the group.[4] This definition stresses that members belong to a group to satisfy their personal needs — primarily for security, sociability and status.

Interdependency

A fifth definition of a group is 'a set of individuals who share a common fate, that is, who are interdependent, in the sense that an event that affects one member is likely to affect all'.[5]

Mutual influence

A group may be defined as 'two or more persons who are interacting with one another in such a manner that each person influences and is influenced by each other person'.[6]

Structural relationships

According to this definition a group is 'a number of individuals who stand in definite status and role relationships to one another and which possesses a set of values or norms of its own regulating the behaviour of individual members . . .'[7]

We take the view that all of these definitions help to contribute to an understanding of the nature and function of a group. However, for our purposes we suggest the following definition 'a group is comprised of two or more people who have frequent interpersonal interaction, with common objectives, achievable only through group membership, and whose behaviour is affected by being part of that group'.

Task 7.2

Review the list of groups you belong to — add to it any further that you have now identified and remove those which do not conform with our definition.

7.3 FORMAL AND INFORMAL GROUPS

The distinction between formal and informal groups within an organisation is fundamental. Formal groups are those created by an organisation to carry out some specific task and their structure, membership and procedures will be largely dictated from outside the group. Because of these features they tend to have well-established patterns of communication, and are resistant to change. They can be either set up for a limited period of time, although generally they are relatively permanent. Examples of such groups include committees, a management team, the crew of a fast food store, and trade union branches.

Informal groups, on the other hand, are not set up by management, but arise naturally out of the social interaction at the workplace. They tend to grow up through friendship and common interest, their behaviour is self-determined and the membership is likely to be small and change constantly as do therefore the patterns of communication. Due to their nature, it is more difficult to identify examples of such informal groups categorically, but any group of friends in the workplace may constitute an informal group. One specific example that one of the authors encountered whilst managing a hotel was of four women who lived in the same neighbourhood and travelled to work together. Although they were employed in different capacities, in the kitchen, bars and reception, this informal group was effective in approaching the manager in order to improve the female staff changing area.

Research at another hotel, however, showed that 'personal associations amongst hotelworkers were only moderately strong at work and weak out of work'.[8] The exception to this was in the Housekeeping Department of the hotel being studied, due to the strong cultural links between the maids who were all of West Indian background. Thus nearly three-fifths of the hotel workers would not be bothered if they were moved from their usual work group to work with another, whilst over half were happy never to see the people they worked with outside the hotel. No doubt these results would have been more pronounced if it were not for the strong socio-cultural links of the hotel's chambermaids.

It is more common for such groups to be influenced by the formal group structure of the organisation, and both formal and informal groups are apparent in most working situations.

Task 7.3

Review your list of groups that you belong to and decide whether each one is formal or an informal group primarily.

7.4 PURPOSES OF GROUPS

These can be divided into major areas. First, those purposes or functions related to the task and the organisation's aims, and, second, those related to the individual member's social needs. With regard to the organisation's goals, Handy[9] identifies ten major purposes:

1. The distribution of work.
2. The management and control of work.
3. Problem-solving or decision-making.
4. Information processing.
5. Information, and ideas, collection.
6. Testing and ratifying decisions.
7. Co-ordination and liaison.
8. Increasing commitment and involvement.
9. Negotiation or resolving conflict.
10. Inquest or inquiry into the past.

Task 7.4

Look at the following list of groups that might be found in the hotel and catering industry and attempt to identify which of the above purposes apply to each one:

1. Bi-annual meeting between management and shop stewards.
2. Weekly management and supervisors' meetings.
3. A five-minute meeting for briefing banqueting staff before a function.
4. Monthly meetings between contract caterers and representation of the client's staff.
5. A company's board meeting

This task illustrates that many groups have more than one function and are involved in a multitude of tasks and roles. But it is important to realise that the structure and organisation of a group set up for one purpose may not be appropriate for the same group to carry out a different purpose. For instance, a board meeting which sets out to allocate priorities for company expansion may find it difficult to then move on to discussing staff training and development.

The second main area to consider is that of the individual's objectives in group membership. Groups provide an opportunity to satisfy a number of individual needs — notably the needs as identified by Maslow for security, affiliation and status. They give members a sense of protection and can be actively involved in the defence of members' interests. By the very nature of groups, individual members achieve a sense of 'belonging', whilst certain roles or positions in groups enhance the individual's status and influence. Thus groups are also providing an opportunity for individuals to compare themselves with other group members and to confirm their own self-image.

Groups can also enable individuals to complete a task or carry out a role that they could not easily achieve on their own of which a prime example is the teamwork involved in preparing and serving a meal in a restaurant. Likewise, the individual can use the group to achieve their own personal objectives which may or may not coincide with the work they are employed to do or the objectives of the company employing them. For example, supervisors may use their group to press for an increase in their own salary. Finally, groups have the function for individuals of stimulating and encouraging mutual help and co-operation, which may have the benefit of creating a happy working environment.

7.5 GROUP EFFECTIVENESS

We have seen why organisations and individuals may need groups, but as yet we have not identified what it is about a group that makes it an effective and appropriate way of dealing with the situation.

Psychological base

All individuals require a social framework in which to exist, and work in groups, both formal and informal, provides this framework. Research evidence[10] has also shown that the presence of other people, both as an audience and as colleagues, affects a person's state of arousal and therefore their performance. The degree to which such arousal is

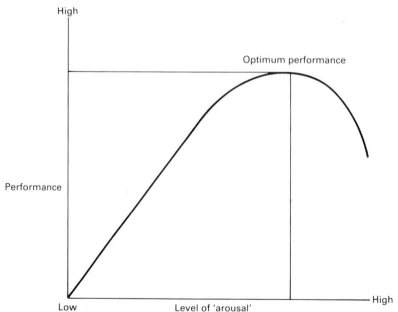

Figure 7.1 *Idealised representation of the Yerkes–Dodson law.*

beneficial appears to be linked to the concept identified by Yerkes and Dodson, who found that where the level of arousal was low, performance was weak due to a lack of interest, and that when a person was highly aroused their performance was also not at their best due to stress and anxiety. Thus the optimum performance was achieved when the person is neither under- or over-aroused (See Fig. 7.1). The implications for group performance suggest that groups are particularly good at dealing with relatively simple tasks.

Production of ideas

Although there is a lack of consensus about how good groups are at producing ideas we would suggest the following. First, a group is unlikely to produce a greater number of ideas than an individual given the same amount of time and similar thinking strategies, such as brain-storming. Second, groups will tend to produce better quality ideas in that they will be better evaluated and thought out, since they will be subject to criticism from the group members. Third, groups select riskier options in solving a problem than individuals might be prepared to select on their own, because groups provide shared responsibility and security, and for reasons of self-image individuals act more 'courageously' in public than they might do in private. Finally, due to the procedural nature of groups, they tend to take longer to react to decisions as everyone feels obliged to have their say.

Commitment

People are more likely to carry out a decision that they have had a hand in making than one that has been imposed upon them. It is therefore critical if effective implementation is important to involve groups in the decision-making process.

Job satisfaction

Since humans are social animals who have a need for interpersonal interaction, groups at work are likely to improve the job context and hence job satisfaction, and this in turn will reduce absenteeism and labour turnover.

Productivity

There are obviously certain tasks or jobs that cannot be done by a single person, but must be tackled by a team, and often jobs that one person could do are done more productively by a team. Making beds is a good example.

Case example 7.1   The Kalmar plant

Volvo's Kalmar car-assembly plant is the most visionary experiment in job redesign yet.

The shape of the building is designed to provide a lot of sides and corners. Each corner provides a home for teams of 15–20 workers with their own workshops. There are more than 20 of these small shops, each with its own entrance and facilities such as change room, sauna bath, coffee and conference room, coffee machines and even a view. Duplicate facilities are built in to provide for a possible second shift with its own territory. Employees are allowed free use of phones for local calls to keep in touch with the outside world. A true little village.

Around these villages glide wagons, silently controlled by electronic impulses from under the floor. A wagon, a low platform carrying the chassis or body, can be called in by one of the workshops when the workers are ready for it. The wagon can be tilted to any angle, stops instantly if it bumps into any person or thing, and is constantly checked by computer for work faults which are fed directly back to the workshop for rectification.

Teams are required to produce a daily quota, breaks and idle time are not monitored or controlled. The quota was fixed by union negotiation, not imposed by management.

'It all sounds too good to be true,' comments John O'Meara of Witwatersrand University Business School in South Africa after visiting Kalmar, 'but is it really working?' The answer was that the new plant had so far exceeded expectations.

7.6 FACTORS AFFECTING GROUP PERFORMANCE

The promotion and development of groups are affected by three major variables, namely those relating to group membership, those associated with the group's task and the environment in which it exists.

Membership variables

Size

There is obvious conflict involved in arriving at the optimum size for any group. On the one hand, the more group members there are, the more skills and expertise are available to carry out the group task. On the other hand, increasing size can result in difficulties in organisation, a reluctance by some members to participate, an increase in conflicting viewpoints, a greater likelihood that members will form sub-groups, and absenteeism and low turnover will increase. A group should therefore be as small as possible yet contain all the skills required to accomplish its task.

Members' characteristics

In the first place, the group members collectively must have all the requisite skills and abilities needed for the task, but in terms of social interaction there must also be a high degree of compatibility. This does not necessarily mean that all group members must be identical, in fact a degree of contrast is essential for the dynamism of the group.

Members' status

A wide variety of different studies have shown that group members who are perceived by their fellows as having a higher status will have a greater influence over the performance of the group than lower status members.

Individual objectives

We have already seen that an individual's objectives in group membership may not be entirely compatible with the group objectives. Individuals tend to have what is known as a 'hidden agenda' including such things as impressing the boss, or doing as little as possible, or maintaining the status quo. As long as these objectives remain hidden, they will adversely affect the group's development and effectiveness.

Task variables

Nature of the task

This will obviously affect the type of group. A group which is required to be creative must have a different structure from one that is concerned with information distribution.

Time scale

One must also consider the pressure of time upon the group, as this will allow less freedom for the group to develop in its own way and less time to consider individual needs. This must therefore have an impact on the quality of work produced.

Importance

The greater the perceived importance of the group task to the individual the more committed they will be to the group's objectives and similarly the more important the task is to the organisation as a whole the more attention the group is likely to receive.

Precision

Some tasks allow for an exact and detailed identification of a group's objectives and procedures which can assist in the early stage of group formation as it reduces ambiguity about the group's purpose.

Environmental variables

Organisation

All organisations have an established way of doing things or 'in-house style' and this is bound to affect the ways in which the group can develop its own rules, procedures and structure.

Physical

Not only is the group affected by the organisational environment, but also by the physical circumstances in which it meets, such as the amount of noise, shape and size of the meeting place, ventilation and the seating arrangements.

Generally, the closer people are together the more likely interaction is to take place and therefore be an effective group.

Relationship with other people

This factor relates not only to the perceived status of the group within the organisation and therefore the amount of status and influence it has, but also to the degree of inter-group dependence and competition. A group may not be able to perform its function without the co-operation and effective running of one or more other groups, as for instance the relationship between chefs and waiting staff.

7.7 THE FORMATION AND DEVELOPMENT OF GROUPS

Before a group is formed, the person or persons forming the group must be aware of the variables above and their likely impact upon the chances of the group being successful. Tackman[11] suggests groups are likely to follow four distinct developmental stages which he calls forming, storming, norming, and performing. What happens at each stage will have implications for task performance and social interaction.

Stage 1 — forming

With regard to the task, members will try to establish exactly what the task is, what the best way of accomplishing it should be and what resources and information they will require. Socially, this will be a time of establishing personal identity in the group, at the same time looking for acceptable leadership and behaviour.

Stage 2 — storming

Most groups go through a period of conflict, when the original consensus is challenged and redefined; this usually arises due to discrepancy between the individual's expectations and actual experience of what the group is doing. Socially, this may be expressed by the individuals attempting to assert themselves and resisting group pressures to conform. Assuming that the group goes through this stage, a secure foundation for trust between members is likely to be established.

Stage 3 — norming

It is at this stage that the group develops cohesion. Members begin to look on each other as part of the group. This leads to an open exchange of opinions and ideas, a willingness to listen and accept others' views about the task in hand, and a general increase in the social harmony of the group, through the establishment of new standards and individual roles for each group member.

Stage 4 — performing

Only when the three previous stages have developed successfully will the group achieve the highest levels of performance. Constructive attempts will be made to complete the task and solutions to any problems should begin to emerge. Interpersonal relations will be settled and co-operative.

7.8 CHARACTERISTICS OF DEVELOPED GROUPS

The importance of the working group was first shown clearly by Elton Mayo and his colleagues in a detailed study of workers' behaviour at the Western Electric Company factory in Hawthorne, near Chicago, between 1924 and 1932. Mayo had been called in by the management because production at the factory was thought to be too low. While experimenting with different lighting levels Mayo found that all changes seemed to increase output and to test this reaction further he set up the Relay Assembly Test Room. Here five young women were segregated from the rest of the factory and various changes were made in their working conditions and rest pauses. Throughout the period of the experiment, even during the times when conditions were made worse, the women's output steadily increased. When interviewed they said:

1. They enjoyed working in the test room and worked harder there because they felt special.
2. They did not regard the observer as a normal supervisor because he explained things to them and reassured them.
3. The experiment seemed to show that management was interested in them.
4. They helped each other at work and had developed close friendships with each other away from work.
5. They felt united and had a common purpose.

In an attempt to prove his theories, Mayo took a group of men and simply observed their behaviour in their normal conditons — the Bank Wiring Observation Room. The following points were noticed:

1. The men worked to an unofficial level of output; if anyone worked harder than this he was abused by the others.
2. Reported figures for output were false; they showed a constant, instead of a variable output.
3. The men often exchanged jobs contrary to management instructions; they often helped each other.
4. The supervisor knew that this was going on, but did nothing to stop it. He was not regarded by the group as their leader. One member of the group who told the supervisor of these practices was made an outcast and nicknamed 'squealer'.
5. Unofficial leaders in the group were more influential than the official leader, the supervisor.

Mayo's work helped to establish certain characteristics of developed groups, primarily concerning group norms, cohesiveness and structure.

Group norms

These consist of shared patterns of perceiving and thinking, shared methods and styles of communication, interaction and appearance, common attitudes and beliefs and shared ways of doing things.

Task 7.5 the Hawthorne experiments

Attempt to identify what the group norms were for the Assembly Test Room and the Bank Wiring Observation Room.

It is possible to identify two main areas — those relating to the task and those concerned with social behaviour. Task norms include how fast people should work, how hard or long, and what standard of work should be achieved. Ideally the organisation would like the supervisor to set those norms within a framework of the organisation's objectives. However, as can be seen from the Hawthorne experiments, unofficial leaders within the group itself may emerge to establish and control what the task norms will be. Social norms include attitudes towards trade unions or management, modes of dress and hair style, and common codes of communication, both verbal and non-verbal. In this area too, leaders can emerge to set these norms and are often not the same persons who are task leaders[12] because within the group the task leader is likely to be the most respected or experienced member, whereas the social leader is the most liked (the socio-metric choice).

There is considerable pressure applied to individuals who do not conform to group norms. This pressure may be physical as was the case in the Bank Wiring Observation Room, where hard-working members of the group were 'knuckled' to make them slow down to the group norm, or it may be psychological sanction, where the member is verbally abused or ostracised. In extreme cases, non-conformity will result in expulsion from the group. This pressure to conform can have considerable effect as was demonstrated by studies conducted by Asch.[13] In this experiment subjects were asked which of three lines on a card was the same length as a fourth presented with them.

The task was so simple that on their own, people were almost 100 per cent correct. However, in group situation where individuals were placed unknowingly amongst the researcher's colleagues, the results were rather different. When these colleagues unanimously made a patently wrong choice, a surprisingly high proportion of the subjects agreed with them.

Group cohesiveness

This is the degree to which group members view the group to be attractive and rewarding, and therefore the extent to which they would be prepared to make sacrifices to protect the continued existence of the group. Some of the characteristics of a cohesive group are a very close adherence to group norms by all group members, a strong identification with the group's purpose, a willingness to accept responsibility for the completion of the task and also the capacity to endure frustration even to the extent of defending the group from outside threat. The advantages of such groups are:

1.   Assuming group norms are appropriate high standards of work are achieved.
2.   Increased co-operation amongst group members.
3.   Greater job satisfaction.
4.   Development of pride, loyalty and prestige.

There can, however, be certain disadvantages such as:

1.   The lack of congruence between the group's production norms and the expectations of the organisation.
2.   Increased hostility to other groups.
3.   New group members will find it difficult to be accepted.
4.   Cohesive groups are resistant to change and therefore find it difficult to adapt to new situations.

Group structures and roles

One of the most interesting areas of study in group dynamics is the structure of the group composed as it is, of a series of interlocking roles. By structure we mean the established pattern of group interaction. This will have been affected by:

1.   Age of the group — as the group develops through the stages we have identified the pattern of interactions will change until an accepted structure is reached during the performing stage. The longer the group is together, the more rigid this is likely to become.
2.   Previous interactions — if any of the members of a group have had previous friendly contact they will tend to form a nucleus for everybody else.
3.   Task needs — the way in which the task is organised will affect the structure, for instance a group teamed together on a production line will tend to concentrate around those people in the centre of the line with those at the ends being isolated, whilst the kitchen partie system tends to encourage the formation of several small subgroups within the brigade.

4. Communication needs — we shall be looking at the effects of differing communication patterns, but in its simplest form those people who need to communicate with each other for the completion of the group task will tend to form a structural link, for example as in a fast-food store as shown in Fig. 7.2.

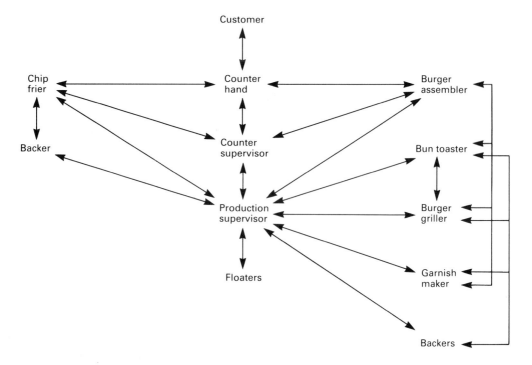

Figure 7.2 *Communication in a fast-food store.*

5. Status of members — as we have seen one of the dangers associated with groups is that members who are perceived as having high status, either informally through the force of personality or formally through their position in the organisation, may influence the group and therefore create a structure centred around themselves.
6. Intra-group feelings — any strong attractions between members, or conversely, strong antagonisms, for purely personal reasons will be bound to affect group development.

One way of determining the structure of the group is to use the techniques known as sociometry. One technique involves each individual being asked to select the two people they would most like to work with and those they would most like to socialise with. These choices which must be made in private are then plotted onto a sociogram (see Fig. 7.3). It is possible to identify from sociograms the following patterns:

SOCIOGRAM – GROUP STRUCTURE

TASK ORIENTATION

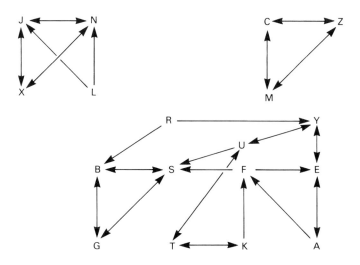

SOCIAL ORIENTATION

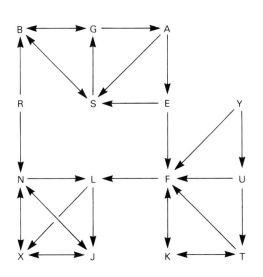 

Figure 7.3 *Two sociograms of one group of people.*

1. Isolate — not wanted by anybody.
2. Pair — select each other but are not chosen by anyone else.
3. Clique — mutual selection between three or more people.
4. Star — the most popular person being selected most often.
5. Chain — choices show a linear linkage between members and hence mutual inter-dependence without mutual attraction.
6. Sub-group — a number of members of the group connected to each other, but not to the main body.

Task 7.6

Look at Fig. 7.3 which shows two real-life sociograms of one group of people, one based around work, the other on social relationships.
  Identify the examples of each of the patterns listed above. Compare your findings of the task-oriented sociogram with the social-oriented sociogram.

As well as having a 'position' in group, each member may also have a distinct 'role' to play. These roles can be divided into three main types — task, maintenance and self-oriented.[14] It is apparent that for a group to function effectively all of the task and maintenance roles must be performed by some person or persons in the group at some stage. Some members will perform more than one role and it is the leader's responsibility to ensure that task and maintenance roles are completed, but individual roles are avoided. Examples of such roles are shown in Table 7.1.

Table 7.1   *Example of roles within a group.*

Task	Maintenance	Self
Initiator	Encourager	Blocker
Information-giver	Compromiser	Aggressor
Information-seeker	Harmoniser	Playboy
Co-ordinator	Peacekeeper	Sympathy-seeker
Evaluator	Gatekeeper	Comedian
Opinion-seeker	Observer	
Decision manager	Commentator	
	Standard setter	

Case exercise 7.1   Outside caterers' management meeting

Huelin's Caterers had recently won the contract to operate all the catering facilities on a race course in the north of England. The following is a short extract from the meeting held two weeks before the first race meeting to discuss final arrangements.
  Alan Huelin is the managing director and has been running his own firm for twelve years. Terry Reader is the executive head chef of the firm who has been with them for nearly a year after working in a large hotel in Manchester. Graham Brace is the company's deputy accountant responsible for all control aspects of the operation and is based at the firm's head office in Birming-

ham. Paul Saxon is an assistant manager who has been with the firm since leaving college three years ago and will be responsible for all the executive boxes during the meeting. Ann Townsend is the company sales manager responsible for promoting special functions and public relations on the race course. They are now discussing supply and deliveries to the site.

TERRY: There is no way you can do that. You've got to have the meat delivered at least a day in advance.

PAUL: I think bar stocks should be on site in good time too. We don't know what sort of problems we are going to run up against.

GRAHAM: That's all very well but I have got a lot to do. If I'm expected to keep good control of stocks levels, I don't really want to have to go all the way up there and back on the day before the meeting as well as all the other days.

ANN: You could always stay up there, Graham. We probably won't need to, once things are organised, but I think it would be a good idea for Graham and myself to be up there for the five days at least for this first meeting.

TERRY: That's all very well, but it costs money.

ALAN: How do you feel, Graham, about staying up?

GRAHAM: Well, I've got lots of things on my plate . . .

ANN: Haven't we all, but this is quite an important contract.

ALAN: We're getting off the track here, but I think we should have both Ann and Graham staying over at least for Wednesday and Thursday evenings. Now what about getting the deliveries in?

TERRY: Well, I've got to have them in plenty of time, but I've got no storage space. Much of the prep. will have to be done the evening before and God knows where I'm going to store it.

ANN: Could we hire a refrigerated lorry at such short notice?

GRAHAM: Why didn't we know about this before? These things cost a lot of money you know.

TERRY: Well I was under the impression the walk-in fridge was going to be repaired before we took over the contract.

PAUL: It's all right chef. I've looked into that; it will definitely be done before the next meeting, I promise.

ALAN: Right then, we hire a refrigerated lorry. Paul you're in charge of that and we get meat and veg. suppliers to deliver the day before. All right, Terry?

The meeting continues . . .

From our lists of basic task, maintenance and self roles try to identify from the discussion above what role or roles the participants are displaying.

7.9 GROUP COMMUNICATION

Sociometric techniques can help us to identify the established patterns of communication in the group. Considerable research has been carried out on such patterns, notably by Leavitt[15] which has identified desirable and undesirable patterns of communication. [16] Looking at these simple patterns — the wheel, all channel and circle (see Fig. 7.4) — the conclusions are that the wheel is always the quickest to reach a solution, the circle the slowest.

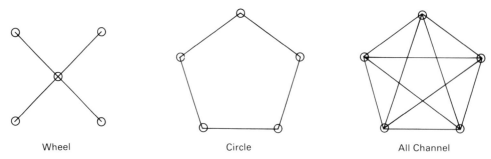

| Wheel | Circle | All Channel |

Figure 7.4   *Some patterns of communication within a group.*

With regard to the quality of decisions, the best solution is likely to be reached by the all-channel system, whereas the quality of the wheel's decision will depend largely on the ability of the person in the middle. Concerning satisfaction of members in general, the greater the interaction the higher the satisfaction so that the all-channel system will have the highest satisfaction, the circle the lowest, whilst in the wheel the person in the middle will be high, those at the extremes low.

Task 7.7

Go back to case example 7.1 and identify the type of communication pattern before and after reorganisation.

To summarise, wheels are ideal for fast results where quality is not vital although morale may be low for all but the leader. Circles are always bad, being slow, inflexible and providing little satisfaction. All-channel systems have obvious advantages with regard to speed, quality and morale, but they take time and do not stand up under pressure.

7.10 CONCLUSION

There are very few operations in the hotel and catering industry that are entirely performed by individuals, most activity is carried out by groups of workers working as a team. The grouped nature of the work is reinforced in this industry by staff wearing distinctive uniforms, which clearly differentiate between one type of employee and another. As well as helping to create a 'team spirit', however, such uniforms also establish a status for each group that detracts from the effective operation of the organisation as a whole. Whatever the problems, an understanding of how groups work together is fundamental to any manager, for it is usually by being put in charge of a group that identifies an individual as a manager. At the same time as leading a group, the manager will also be part of a group, that is the management team of the unit.

REFERENCES

1. Handy, C.B. (1976) *Understanding Organisations*. Harmondsworth: Penguin.
2. Homans, G. (1950) *The Human Group*. London: Routledge & Kegan Paul.
3. Mills, T. (1967) *The Sociology of Small Groups*. Englewood Cliffs, NJ: Prentice Hall.
4. Cattell, R. (1951) New concepts for measuring leadership in terms of group syntality. *Human Relations*, **4**.
5. Fielder, F.E. (1967) *A Theory of Leadership Effectiveness*. London: McGraw-Hill.
6. Shaw, M. (1981) (3rd edn) *Group Dynamics*. London: McGraw-Hill.
7. Sherif, M. & Sherif, C. (1956) *An Outline of Social Psychology*. London: Harper & Row.
8. Lowe, A. (1979) *New Methods of Decision-making*. Birmingham: University of Aston.
9. Handy, C.B. (1976) op. cit.
10. Zajonc, R.B. (1960) *Social Psychology*. London: Wadsworth.
11. Tackman, B.W. (1965) Development sequence in small groups. *Psychological Bulletin*.
12. Bales, R.F. (1955) *Role Differentiation in Small Groups*. Englewood Cliffs, NJ: Prentice Hall.
13. Asch, J. (1952) *Social Psychology*. Englewood Cliffs, NJ: Prentice Hall.
14. Benne, K.D. & Steats, P. (1948) Functional roles of group members. *Journal of Social Issues*, **4**.
15. Leavitt, H.J. (1951) Some effects of certain communication patterns on group performance. *Journal of Abnormal and Social Psychology*, **46**.
16. Shaw, M. (1981) op. cit.

8 Leadership

And if the blind lead the blind, both shall fall into the ditch

St Matthew, Chapter 15, verse 14

OBJECTIVES: to define 'leadership' . . . identify different styles of leadership . . . to describe the probable effects of leadership styles on individuals and group members . . . to select an appropriate style of leadership for a given situation . . . to identify the role of decision-making and problem-solving in management and relate it to the leadership situation

8.1 INTRODUCTION

OVER the years a large number of people have attempted to define 'leadership' but none of these has proved to be totally satisfactory. From these definitions, however, one is able to identify certain common strands:

1. Generally speaking, within the work situation a leader is someone who occupies a particular position in that organisation, for example, the head waiter in a restaurant, the floor housekeeper, or the kitchen superintendent in a hospital.
2. A leader is recognised by those concerned as being the focus of a group, for example the member of staff selected by their peer group to represent the interests of that group on a staff social committee may be such a 'leader'.
3. A leader can be seen to be a person within an organisation who can exert influence upon individuals, groups or the organisation as a whole. One could argue that consumers in the hotel and catering industry fulfil the role of leaders in as much as they exert an influence over the service that they receive.
4. Another strand of leadership is the ability to help a group to function effectively as a group. This will involve not only enabling the group to complete its set task more effectively but also to maintain good personal relationships between the group members.
5. Finally, the overall responsibility of a leader is to get other people to do what the leader wants them to do as willingly as possible. It must be realised, however, that

there may be conflict between what the leader would like the group to carry out and what the organisation requires the leader and his group to achieve.

Therefore the most effective leader should be able to identify these interrelated strands and weave them into a leadership style which combines his positional, focal, charismatic, social and functional roles.

Task 8.1

Consider the different groups to which you may belong, such as family, college class, sports club, orchestra, or at work. In each of the groups identify the person whom you regard as the leader and attempt to explain your selection on the basis of the five points listed above.

8.2 LEADERSHIP STYLES

Of the many attempts to classify styles of leadership, we have selected four major contributions of relevance to the hospitality industry.

McGregor

McGregor's contribution to management thought[1] was largely in the field of staff motivation as discussed in Chapter 2. However, one can also apply his theory X and theory Y to leadership style. If we look at Fig. 8.1 we can see a diagrammatical representation of these two theories. On the one hand leaders who believe in theory X will adopt a leadership style which involves them in coercing, controlling, and instructing staff in the exact way of carrying out their tasks. Such leaders can be described as 'boss-centred' and their leadership style as 'telling'. On the other hand, the leader who believes in theory Y will allow their staff to decide their own way of approaching their tasks, with help and guidance from the leader. This type of leader can be described as 'employee-centred' and their style as 'consulting'.

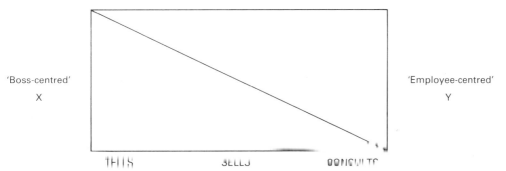

Figure 8.1 *Leadership style based on McGregor's theory X and theory Y.*

Fig. 8.1 also shows that leadership style exists between the two extremes dependent on the extent to which the leader inclines towards the X or Y theory. In this way, a third major leadership style can emerge which can be described as 'selling'. That is to say the leader would still make all the decisions, but would then attempt to convince the staff that they are the correct ones rather than impose them.

Blake and Mouton

We have already identified that the socio-emotional leader, the person who looks after the welfare of the group, must co-exist with the task leader, the person who takes decisions about how the work is to be done. In fact, to be an effective leader these two roles must be combined. Two behavioural scientists, Blake and Mouton,[2] have translated this concept into leadership terms, using their managerial grid, shown in Fig. 8.2.

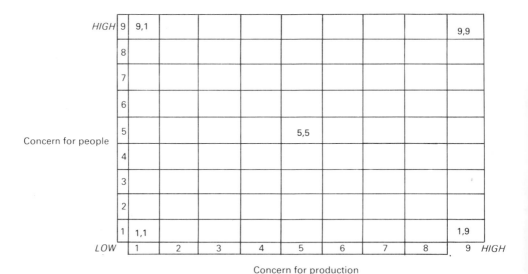

Figure 8.2   *Blake and Mouton's managerial grid. Reproduced with permission.*

Essentially, Blake and Mouton's concept of leadership is concerned with the symbiosis between concern for people and a concern for production. Within these two extreme dimensions, a variety of leadership styles have been identified five of which are shown on the diagram above. A style which shows little concern for people or for production, shown as position 1,1 on the grid, can be termed 'impoverished management'; it achieves very little apart from keeping the manager in a job. Second, there is a style which displays a high consideration for people, but favours a happy working environment more than production, position 1,9 on the grid. This is referred to as 'country club management' and achieves very little apart from keeping the staff happy. A third style, 9,1 above, concentrates on getting the job done and ignores the feelings of the staff, and is consequenctly called 'task management'. Fourth, a leader who attempts to produce as much as possible, whilst maintaining staff morale, will probably arrive at a style of leadership that can be thought of as 'middle of the road', position 5,5 on the grid. Finally, a leader who, by gaining the commitment of the staff, maximises output and reaches 9,9 on the grid could be said to reach 'Utopia'.

Blake and Mouton are concerned that leadership theories have tended to be based on an analysis of the effects of different leaders, which in turn has led to assumptions about leadership style. These studies, such as the Ohio State University study, have started from statements about leadership behaviour and have gone on to reduce leadership down to a smaller number of specific elements. For instance, in Fleishman's study the result is just two dimensions which he termed 'initiating structure' and 'consideration'. These elements are seen as two discrete and independent variables. Blake and Mouton, however, argue that leadership should be studied from the point of view of the interactive process rather than traits or attributes ascribed to leaders. They therefore stress that their two variables are interdependent and it is not possible to measure them separately. They take the view that every leader should attempt to achieve a 9,9 orientation in dealing with any situation which requires leadership. This orientation they see as being participative and conflict-resolving, with clearly established goals.

Fiedler

Fiedler's contingency theory of leadership is based on research that also establishes a task-oriented leadership and a style oriented towards achieving good interpersonal relations, but is very different from that of Blake and Mouton. His studies to measure leadership style examined how workers rated their co-workers and how leaders perceived group members to be like themselves. People who rated co-workers favourably tended also to assume their colleagues to be like themselves and would therefore be those leaders who are mainly concerned with successful interpersonal relations. People with little regard for their co-workers and who perceived little similarity to themselves tended to be task-oriented leaders. From this Fiedler developed his contingency model of leadership which suggests that a group's performance will depend on, or be 'contingent' upon, the appropriate matching of leadership style with the group and the extent to which the situation provides the leader with influence over the group. Thus there are three 'critical dimensions' which affect the leader's most effective style: first, the positional power that a leader holds by virtue of his or her authority; second, the extent to which the task to be performed is clear-cut or vague; and third, the extent of the group's respect and trust for the leader. It is important to note that the first two of these dimensions are outside the leader's direct control and are dependent upon the organisational context (see Chapter 10). Fiedler suggests that no one style of leadership is always effective. Task-oriented leaders are most effective when situations are either very favourable, i.e. when position power is high, task structure clear and leader–group relationships good, or very unfavourable, i.e. unclear position and task, poor relationships; whereas human relationship leaders are most effective when the situation is only moderately favourable or unfavourable.

Task 8.2

Consider the following example and decide if the manager should adopt a task-oriented style or be human relations oriented.

John Sims is the owner-manager of a small country hotel which has been owned and operated by his family for nearly twenty years. When his uncle retired five years ago, John took over the management after having worked abroad for several years. Most of the staff have worked at the hotel for several years and staff turnover is very low. The hotel has always ben fairly successful and John has recently re-invested the previous year's profits into the refurbishment of the restaurant and bars. He would like to follow this up with a new marketing campaign, a revitalisation of the hotel's reputation and an upgrading of the restaurant in the various good food guides. This will obviously necessitate some retraining of staff, devising new menus, improving existing skills, and so on. How should he go about this?

Likert

Likert's analysis of leadership style[3] is probably the most widely read and understood. He classifies leadership styles under four main headings.

(a) Autocratic

Autocratic leaders make all the decisions for their group and then instruct them how to undertake their tasks. Within this classification, we can identify a 'hard' autocrat, who would show little or no concern for the feelings of the workforce. On the other hand, a 'soft' autocrat, whilst still giving the orders, does so with apparent concern.

(b) Persuasive

Persuasive leaders still make all the decisions, but rather than impose them prefer to sell their ideas to the group. However, if the group rejects their ideas they would still impose their decisions without the group's acceptance where necessary.

(c) Consultative

This type of leader, before making a decision, would consult with their staff as to what they considered to be the best course of action. They would then make their own decision, which may or may not be influenced by the opinions expressed by staff. In this way they hope to gain acceptance of their ideas by ostensibly involving those whom they are leading.

(d) Democratic

With this style, leaders would present to their staff the opportunity to participate freely in the decision-making process and they would accept any decision that was reached in this way. They would be extremely reluctant to make any decisions on their own.

Task 8.3

Speculate which style of leadership, based on Likert, the following personality types might choose to adopt.

1. Stable/introvert.
2. Stable/extravert.
3. Neurotic/introvert.
4. Neurotic/extravert.

8.3 SELECTING AN APPROPRIATE LEADERSHIP STYLE

By analysing leadership styles as we have done above, it may appear that one must adopt one particular style, boss-centred, country-club or whatever, or following on from Task 8.3 that certain personality types will automatically become certain types of leader. However, it is possible to adopt more than one style of leadership and it may in fact be advantageous for someone to select the appropriate style for a given situation. For instance, let us consider the following six leadership situations:

(a) You are the catering manager of a unit which is being refurbished and a new kitchen is to be installed.
(b) As Chair of the staff social committee, you must decide how to redecorate the staff recreation room.
(c) Imagine the head waiter of a restaurant, who must determine next week's duty rotas.
(d) In two weeks' time, you are holding a large residential conference, the eating, seating and sleeping arrangements have to be finalised.
(e) An advertisement for the local newspaper has to be designed for the opening of your new wine bar.
(f) The owners of the hotel you manage wish to reinvest some of their profits into the business and a decision has to be made how best to extend the premises.

Before reading on, consider which leadership style would be most appropriate for these situations and give reasons to support your choice.

We would suggest that the appropriate leadership style for these six situations are as follows.

(a) Consultative

There is a need to involve the staff as they are more closely involved with the working environment and may therefore be able to make a valuable contribution to the kitchen design. Furthermore, it is the staff who will have to operate within the redesigned layout and they would therefore have some commitment to that design.

(b) Democratic

There is a tendency for leaders who are elected democratically to apply a democratic leadership style. Furthermore, this situation provides the ideal opportunity for allowing staff to determine their own working environment.

(c) Consultative

This style enables leaders to gather information about the needs of the staff and then relate these to the needs of the organisation. They should, in effect, adopt a 'middle-of-the-road' position. However, this assumes that staff are aware and tolerant of the constraints placed upon leaders by the organisation. It may be that if they were intolerant and uncooperative, leaders may have to adopt a persuasive, if not autocratic, style.

(d) Autocratic

In this situation, the leader is so constrained by the needs of the customer, she or he is in effect not making a decision, but communicating the decisions made for her or him by the client. Tasks need to be completed in a particular way to meet with customers' requests and staff need not be consulted.

(e) Persuasive

The design of advertisements and public relations effort of the operation are outside the expertise and concern of most staff. In this situation therefore decisions will be made by the leader with or without external advice from experts, and then the decision reached will be communicated persuasively.

(f) Consultative

Once again, although the leader will be capable of making a decision alone, benefits would almost certainly derive from consulting the staff who are directly involved in the day-to-day operation of the business. The ideas they put forward may not always be adopted, but may form the basis of an overall assessment of the possibilities.

The suggestion of the exercise above is that leadership behaviour should be adapted to the needs of the particular situation. This approach is based loosely on the idea of a 'contingency' theory of leadership. As we have seen, Fiedler suggests that leadership style should depend upon the relationship between leaders and the people under them, and upon the structure of the task to be undertaken. His conclusions following research in a wide variety of organisations indicated that a 'structuring' style should be adopted when conditions were either very favourable or very unfavourable to the leader and that when conditions were modestly favourable, a 'supportive' style was best. He went on to suggest that apart from these two possible approaches, managers are unlikely to want to or be able to change their style, and that rather than expect managers to adapt rapidly and often to different circumstances and people, it may be better to organise the work groups, formal power of managers and their tasks, to suit the managers.

Whatever the style of leadership adopted, managers must be aware that their subordinates may not perceive it in the same way that they do. In Lowe's study three types of decision areas were identified: (a) task decisions, e.g. working methods on individual jobs, payment systems and overtime levels; (b) operational decisions, e.g. departmental organisation, equipment purchase, discipline methods, budgeting; (c) strategic decisions, e.g. broad policies, recruitment, redundancy. The three main groups in the hotel — managers, supervisors and workers — all agreed that *all* forms of decision-making should be approached in a more participative way, with task type decisions being more delegated than either operational or strategic decisions. When asked about the actual management style, as opposed to the most desirable, a different picture emerged from each group. The workers felt that management made all the decisions without reference to them; supervisors believed that management were participative when making decisions closely relevant to the work group; and managers thought themselves to be more participative than they were perceived to be by both of the other two groups.

8.4 LEADERSHIP AND DECISION-MAKING

An alternative way of approaching the selection of an appropriate leadership style is to consider the nature of the decision to be reached under two headings. First the quality of the decision, i.e. the extent to which the solution must be accurate and correct. For instance, surgeons must have a high degree of quality in all the decisions they make, since an error could prove fatal, whereas on the other hand, someone selecting a meal from a menu is only making a low-quality decision. Second, the acceptability of the solution to the people who will be affected by it. An example of this could be the selection of a uniform for members of staff: this must have a high degree of acceptability to those people who will wear it. Once these two dimensions to any decision or problem have been identified, it is possible to suggest an appropriate leadership style (see Fig. 8.3).

Dimension		Leadership style
Quality	Acceptability	
LOW	LOW	AUTOCRATIC
HIGH	LOW	PERSUASIVE
HIGH	HIGH	CONSULTATIVE
LOW	HIGH	DEMOCRATIC

Figure 8.3 *Leadership style and decision-making.*

Fig. 8.3 suggests certain leadership styles since it is impossible to be dogmatic about the style to be adopted.

We would therefore argue that the autocratic style is suited to decisions requiring low quality and low acceptability, since it is the style that is the least time consuming and these are decisions about which no one cares greatly in any case. With decisions of high quality and low acceptability the persuasive style could be adopted as this enables the people most qualified to make the decision to carry out this role, whilst still

recognising the importance of maintaining employee relationships. Third, for important decisions of great concern to staff, the use of the consultative style ensures that a
decision of high quality is reached with the additional benefit of commitment and
involvement of the staff. Lastly, although time-consuming the democratic style is ideal
for situations which necessitate staff acceptability but do not require any particular
quality, although this is not to say that high quality decisions will not be made using
the democratic process.

Task 8.4

Refer back to the six leadership situations outlined in section 8.3 and classify
them according to the two dimensions of quality and acceptability. To what extent does your classification accord with our recommendations on appropriate leadership styles?

8.5 DECISION-MAKING AND PROBLEM-SOLVING

One could argue that the principal role of the leader is that of decision-maker, and
therefore in discussion of leadership the question of how decisions are made must be
included. It is generally accepted that effective decision-making involves a systematic
approach which can broadly be outlined as:

1. Defining the problem.
2. Collecting information.
3. Developing solutions.
4. Selecting the optimum solution.
5. Implementing the solution.

An example of this systematic approach could be reaching a decision about where to
go on holiday. The first stage is to establish what sort of holiday will meet the needs
of the people concerned and this is usually followed by a visit to a travel agent to
obtain brochures and other relevant information. The prospective holiday-makers
now look through the brochures and identify those holidays that meet with all their
requirements, arriving at a short list of possible alternatives. The next stage is to select
from the short list the holiday that best suits all the parties concerned, before going to
the travel agent to book it.

(1) Defining the problem

The first stage in the problem-solving process must be to identify accurately the exact
nature of the problem by distinguishing between the cause of the problem and the
effects that are evident. For instance, an inadequate induction programme for new
members of staff working in the catering industry may well lead to a variety of apparent problems such as high staff turnover, poor customer relations, unsatisfactory
working relationships and so on. Thus a rigorous examination of the problem areas

must be undertaken to identify the root cause. It is also important at this stage to establish what the objectives of solving the problem are; that is to say that it should be laid down in detail what it is hoped to achieve, so that it can be assessed at a later date the extent to which the solution has been effective. For instance, in the case of high staff turnover, since it is impossible to eliminate it completely, a realistic solution might be to set the objective of reducing it by 50 per cent of present unsatisfactory levels. A technique to aid the definition of the problem is to prepare a written statement outlining not only the major causes identified, and the desired objectives of the solution, but also those people who are party to that problem and its solution. For, at all stages in the problem-solving process it is important to be aware of the human relations implications of implementing such a process.

(2) Collecting information

Once the problem has been clearly identified, it is necessary to collect all relevant information which will contribute to its solution. The first task must be to decide what information is required and the best ways of obtaining it. For example, continuing with the problem of staff turnover, such information would include statistics of numbers of employees, number of separations over a given time, analysis by department, data relating to reasons for leaving and so on. Such information may be obtained from personnel records, departmental heads, interviews with leavers, or even questionnaires circulated to present staff. The second task is then to examine this information to establish its accuracy, validity and reliability, as no decision can be made based on unreliable data. It may then be necessary to collect additional information from new or different sources, if the original data are not adequate. Finally, it may be necessary to arrange the information into a form which facilitates comprehension and assimilation, such as by using tables, graphs, diagrams and so on.

(3) Developing solutions

The great danger in attempting to solve a problem is to latch on to a single solution which appears to be correct. The systematic approach demands that a number of alternative solutions are generated so that the optimum answer, which closely meets the objectives set, is arrived at. There are two ways of developing these alternative solutions.

Conservative

The conservative approach is to apply logical, deductive reasoning to the problem. In the case of staff turnover, this approach would lead to an examination of selection procedures, induction, rates of pay, motivational skills of supervisory staff, and so on. The aspects that are developed would depend upon the information collected, which in our example might include statistics showing a large percentage of staff leaving within two weeks of their start date, interviews at which staff stated that they were leaving because they had been offered higher rates of pay elsewhere and other such data.

Lateral

The lateral approach to developing solutions to problems is much less inhibited than the conservative approach and is sometimes called 'brain-storming'. This technique involves noting down as many solutions as possible to the problem, without regard to their viability or logical basis; no suggestions should be rejected immediately. The best method of achieving this, advocated by the guru of lateral thinking, Edward de Bono,[4] is to collect a small group of people conversant with the problem and to allow them to throw up ideas which cannot be challenged. One member of the group acts as secretary to note down all such suggestions. It is only at a later date that these are subjected to more rigorous examination, but at no time should they be rejected out of hand. This method encourages the development of creative and original solutions which may not otherwise have arisen. For example, one way of eliminating staff turnover is to cease employing any staff, possibly by replacing them by machines. Both the conservative and lateral approaches have advantages and disadvantages, which are outlined in Fig. 8.4.

CONSERVATIVE

This approach can be carried out by the individual leader involving other people if necessary.

One person may reflect on the problem and develop solutions at any time of the day or night, whatever he or she may be doing.

Due to the above, the actual time taken to develop solutions may be very short, as they are largely thought out during other activities.

Solutions developed logically are completely thought through.

Logical thought is a skill which is largely developed during the normal educational process of the individual.

Due to the conservative nature of the deductive approach, all solutions will tend to be acceptable to all parties concerned as they will be within their range of experience.

This approach allows the leader to select whichever style of leadership he or she considers to be appropriate e.g. autocratic or consultative.

LATERAL

This approach should involve at least four or five persons to be its most effective.

Solutions are only developed within the time allocated to the brain-storming session.

Time must be given up by several individuals for a lateral thinking session and further time is needed to develop the ideas generated into workable solutions.

Solutions developed are merely the seeds for further consideration.

Brain-storming is an additional skill which must be learnt by the participating decision-makers if it is to be truly effective.

Solutions developed, whilst being creative and original may well represent unacceptable changes to some of the parties concerned.

This approach which by definition involves other people commits the leader to a democratic participative style.

Figure 8.4 *A comparison of the conservative and lateral approaches to solution development*

(4) Selecting the optimum solution

This stage in the problem-solving process is crucial; there is little point in developing several excellent alternatives if the best of these is ignored and at the same time it will be difficult to implement a solution that is sub-optimum. For these reasons, it is imperative to adopt an objective and systematic appraisal. This takes the form of identifying constraints, predicting likely effects and relating solutions to the predetermined objectives. Constraints are usually related to the resources of the operation and typically include finance, staffing, working environment, consumer reaction and so on. As well as such apparent physical constraints, the decision-maker will also have to work within the formalised restrictions of the company's overall policy objectives, for instance, although it may be physically possible to increase occupancy rates at a luxury hotel by taking coach parties, this is likely to be contrary to the established policy of the business. The prediction of likely effects is the most speculative aspect of decision-making, particularly where human relations are concerned, because as we have already seen human beings are unpredictable and traditionally resistant to change. This necessitates a weighing up of the pros and cons of each alternative solution as rigorously as possible and recognising the direct and indirect implications in both human and physical terms. There have been numerous examples in the catering industry where attempts to solve one problem have led to problems in other areas of the operation, such as the hotel that purchased housekeeping trolleys to allow their chambermaids to work more effectively only to find that they would not fit in the service lifts; the restaurateur that accepts an outside catering function, only to leave the restaurant depleted of staff and equipment at a busy time; and the hospital that has replaced counter service with vending machines for night workers, only to find the machines are little used due to lack of personal contact. Finally, in many cases decision-makers may often find the optimum solution easy to identify, if they have accurately defined the problem and set realistic objectives (as outlined above). In the final analysis, it is the meeting of these predetermined objectives that determines the optimum solution.

Leaders have the option of drawing upon a range of techniques that may assist them to select the optimum solution, developed from a variety of disciplines, economics, sociology, management science and the behavioural sciences. These include such techniques as work study, critical path analysis, programme evaluation and review technique, cost benefit analysis, game theory approach and many others. The decision to use these techniques will depend upon the complexity and scale of the problem and the expertise and resources available to the decision-maker.

(5) Implementing the solution

Theoretically, if decision-makers have successfully selected the optimum solution they should find it relatively easy to implement. This implementation will draw on their expertise from a wide range of skills not only in terms of human relations, such as motivational skills, leadership style and communications, but also in terms of finance, marketing, technical aspects and other related managerial skills. One of the major problems to be overcome, as we have already seen, is resistance to change. This topic will be further investigated when we consider the management of human relations in

Chapters 9 and 12. Whatever the problems involved, leaders may benefit from a formalisation of their proposals into a written implementation plan, which identifies the action to be taken at various stages. The final element of the process is to institute a procedure that reviews the effectiveness of the solution implemented in human, financial and physical terms in order to evaluate the overall success or failure of the decision.

Task 8.5

For each stage of the decision-making process outlined above select appropriate methods of communication (refer to Chapter 5 which discusses these methods).

8.6 CONCLUSION

In this chapter, we have been discussing the concept of leadership. We have attempted to arrive at a definition of leadership and we have identified a variety of leadership styles. We have gone on to suggest that the type of decisions that leaders have to make will affect their choice of leadership style and that they should adapt their style to meet the needs of the situation. This raises three important points. First, in selecting an appropriate leadership style managers must at all times be aware of the likely effect this will have upon the individuals and groups with which they come into contact. Consider for a moment, how you would feel as an employee and decide what sort of manager you would like to work for — would you like yours to be autocratic or consultative? Do you prefer to be told what to do or make your own decisions? Once you have considered the type of boss you would prefer, look back to the questionnaire you did as Task 8.2. Would you behave in the way you would like your boss to behave? Furthermore, it should be obvious to you that other people may prefer to be treated in a different way to that which you would prefer. It is too easy to believe that because people are in a subordinate position that they like to be given orders, for as we have pointed out in Chapter 1, all individuals whether they are chambermaids, waiters, or kitchen porters, will have their own views and preferences. This brings us to the conclusion that when selecting a leadership style, leaders must not only consider the type of decision to be made, as we have advocated, but also the people whom this decision is likely to affect. For instance, a low-level decision concerning the wash-up facility may need to be made, but the staff involved would neither expect nor like to be consulted. The second point we would like to make is that although we advocate an adaptive approach to leadership, there are disadvantages as well as advantages. Briefly, the advantages are:

1. Better decisions should be made as the type of decision has been considered before tackling the problem.
2. The feelings and motivations of the staff concerned have also been taken into account.
3. The managers themselves are continually assessing their own performance.
4. The managers should be freed from having to make unnecessary decisions.

However, we can also identify disadvantages:

1. Leaders may be ill at ease using a style which is not ideally suited to their personality.
2. Inept managers, who appear to change their style continually, may well confuse and disenchant their subordinates.
3. The adoption of a single style may well lead to familiarity and security amongst staff, they would know exactly where they stood and the organisation would operate like a well-oiled machine.

Task 8.6

Consider prominent figures who have obviously adopted a single leadership style, such as Margaret Thatcher, Brian Clough, Arthur Scargill. To what extent has their 'success' been due to this fact?

Finally, we would like to make it quite clear that although advocating the adaptive approach and suggesting appropriate styles to adopt in given situations these are our own subjective views. We have attempted to give reasons for the choices we have made, but we are aware that other individuals, with other experiences, could equally well support an alternative view.

We hope that we can be seen to have been descriptive and not prescriptive, not offering a recipe for success but a basis on which individuals can make their own choices.

Case exercise 8.1   A question of standards

This study is based in a general hospital with 600 beds somewhere in the Midlands. The catering section employs nearly 60 full-time and 70 part-time members of staff, most of whom are members of a trade union. The management structure comprises a catering manager, two assistant catering managers, a kitchen superintendent, who reports directly to the manager, and two head chefs. The trade union members of staff are represented by a shop steward who is employed as one of the three storekeepers.

The catering manager's name is *Graham Leadom*. He is aged 45 and has worked in the National Health Service since leaving catering college with his craft qualification. He was appointed as assistant catering manager of this hospital seven years ago, and was promoted to his present position just over six months ago. *Mick Williams* is the kitchen superintendent. He is 26 years old and joined the hospital as a head cook two years ago. His promotion occurred at about the same time as Graham Leadom's. He has City and Guilds 706/1 and 706/2 qualifications and is at present studying for a NEBSS certificate on a day release basis. Before getting married, his previous experience was in four-star hotels. The shop steward is *Martin Carey*, who has held this position for the last five years. He is 52 years old, and joined the hospital six years ago when the engineering firm that he worked for made him redundant. Although his union branch has participated in national actions, there have never been any local disputes between union and management whilst he has been shop steward.

The following conversation took place in the manager's office at 3.00 p.m. one Tuesday:

CAREY: Excuse me Graham, have you got a minute?

LEADOM: Of course, Martin, but I have got an appointment with the chief nursing officer in five minutes. What can I do for you?

CAREY: Well it's a bit difficult really, Graham. But it's about that Mick Williams. Some of my members have been getting a bit upset, very upset really.

LEADOM: Oh, I'm sorry to hear that . That's not good enough. What's Mick done to upset them this time?

CAREY: Well, you know the new menu cycle that we started yesterday? It seems that Mick has been telling the cooks not to follow the standard recipe, but to do it his way. When they did this yesterday, not only did it not turn out as nice as it generally does, but they damn near held up the conveyor 'cause it took so much longer to do. In fact, a couple of the lads missed their tea-break trying to follow his instructions. Then he had the cheek to have a go at them because they took so long over it. It's all very well him coming up here with his fancy qualifications, but my lads are only cooks, not chefs in some posh hotel. He'll have them doing crêpes suzette next.

LEADOM: Oh dear! I don't think he will. This does sound rather serious. Which particular menu items were altered?

CAREY: I don't know exactly, but does that really matter? You can't go mucking around with standard recipes just like that, otherwise why do we have them? Besides which you have a meeting with the cooks every six weeks to discuss the menu and the dishes on them. What's the point of having meetings to decide things, if someone comes along and changes it all?

LEADOM: Yes, I agree, Martin. I'll certainly have to have a word with him. As it happens, I'm seeing him tomorrow morning anyway, and I can discuss it with him then. I'm sure we can get things sorted out, but I must go and see the CNO now. I'll come and see you tomorrrow to let you know what's going on.

The next conversation took place at 10.00 a.m. the following day:

LEADOM: Before you go, Mick, there is something I'd like to discuss with you. Martin came to see me yesterday with a complaint that you've changed some of the standard recipes.

WILLIAMS: What's it got to do with him? He wouldn't know a standard recipe if he saw one. I don't know why you put up with these union people, Graham. He's only the ruddy storekeeper, how would he know if a recipe is different or not?

LEADOM: Well, some of the cooks went to see him. You can't keep putting their backs up.

WILLIAMS: Look, we've been through this before. If you want me to run this kitchen properly, I've got to do it my way. If some of the cooks don't like the way I do things then they can always leave. But most of them know I'm good at my job and they respect me for it. Those that want to learn have learnt a hell of a lot from me about how to do things right since I've been here. And I've made sure we've kept within the budget, which is more than my predecessor could.

LEADOM: I know you're a good chef, Mick, but there's more than that needed to be a good supervisor. You've got to take the feelings of the staff into account before you do anything. They've got to know what's going on.

WILLIAMS: They know what's going on all right, because I tell them. Look, are you telling me I can't change a standard recipe without checking with you first?

LEADOM: No, I'm not saying that, although I would like to be consulted. But it's the way you go about things. Some of those cooks yesterday didn't even get a break, and it's over that sort of thing that the union could get very funny.

WILLIAMS: All right, Mr Leadom, I'll make sure they get their breaks, if they put the work in, and we can discuss the question of standard recipes at the next catering meeting on Friday, if that's all right with you?

LEADOM: Very good, Mick. But I hope you'll remember what I've said.

Read through the case exercise and attempt to identify the leadership style of both Graham Leadom, the catering manager, and Mick Williams, the kitchen superintendent. Outline the reasons for your choice. If you were the catering manager in the case exercise, which style of leadership would you adopt to deal with:

(a) The shop steward.
(b) The kitchen superintendent.
(c) The aggrieved members of staff.

What problems might arise if a manager and her or his assistant tend to have different leadership styles?

Case exercise 8.2 Drinks all round

This study takes place in a marquee in the grounds of a large country house after a coming-of-age party. A firm of contract caterers was employed to provide and serve the buffet supper. The party was a great success and the customer so pleased that as there are twelve bottles of chilled champagne left over, he insists that the staff should share them amongst themselves. As five members of staff are involved, this is causing problems.

The manager is thinking

It's a very kind gesture but it's causing a lot of problems and bad feeling. In the end I expect I shall have to sort it out myself but I don't really want to do that. Much better if we can all agree. Of course, I spend a lot of my time sorting things out. I did a lot of work before the party; I had to discuss the menu with the customer and then with the chef; I had to make sure all the equipment had been ordered and that it had arrived; I arranged for the staff and during the evening I not only had to make sure everything was running smoothly, but had to lend a hand where it was needed. In fact, I take full responsibility.

The chef is thinking

Without me there wouldn't have been a party. I planned the menu, and made sure that everything was cooked and ready for the evening. I had to carve the joints during the evening for the guests and some of them wanted me to serve them with the salad. I seemed to be making coffee for hours too. What's more a few bottles of champagne would do nicely for my parents' silver wedding next week.

The wine waiter's thoughts are

Serving wine is difficult at the best of times, you must keep it at the correct temperature, but that's very difficult if you've got buckets of ice everywhere for the white wines and ice keeps melting. The red wines very nearly got too warm inside this hot marquee. There's not much room to work either, not to mention having to wash up the glasses, which isn't my job really. But I expect I'll be lucky to get more than one bottle of champagne out of this lot.

One of the waitresses is thinking

I was in charge of the waitress service. We had to lay up the tables beforehand and that wine waiter didn't overdo himself — he did just manage to arrange his glasses. As for the clearing up, we did all that. Packing away all the china into boxes takes a long time.

The other waitress thinks

This is the first party of this kind that I've done and I think it'll be the last. They can keep their champagne, I don't like the stuff anyway. I've never worked so hard. I thought I was a waitress not a pack horse. I've been run off my feet. That manager didn't do much, but I expect he'll end up with half the champagne. He's welcome to it.

Suggest what the likely outcome would be if the manager adopts the following leadership styles:

1. Autocratic.
2. Consultative.
3. Democratic.

Outline a possible solution to the problem identified in the case exercise using a logical/deductive approach.

Apply lateral thinking to the problem of allocating the bottles and try to come up with a number of alternative solutions. For instance save the bottles to launch ships with!

REFERENCES

1. McGregor, D. (1960) *The Human Side of the Enterprise.* New York: McGraw-Hill.
2. Blake, R.R. & Mouton, J.S. (1964) *The Managerial Grid.* Houston, TX: Gulf.
3. Likert, R. (1967) *The Human Organization.* New York: McGraw-Hill.
4. De Bono, E. (1970) *Lateral Thinking: A Textbook of Creativity.* London: Ward Lock.

9 Supervisory Management

OBJECTIVES: to identify the functions of management . . . to outline the conflicting demands and expectations of first line supervisors . . . to describe particular techniques used by supervisory management

9.1 INTRODUCTION

IN most industries there is a clear demarcation between blue-collar and white-collar workers. In such industries the lowest level of management is the line supervisor who is still regarded as a blue-collar employee; it is not until middle management that a person is regarded as being a white-collar employee. In the hotel and catering industry the demarcation between these two categories of employee is not so clearly defined. The position is further complicated by the nomenclature used by different organisations within the industry, in particular some people in supervisory positions are likely to have the job title 'manager' — for instance, many restaurant managers in hotels, assistant managers in large industrial catering units and so on. Likewise there are employees whose background would suggest they are supervisors, who are clearly managers, for instance executive chef and chef managers of small industrial catering units. By implication this suggests that there is a distinction between supervision and management. In fact our view is that both have very similar functions, which we shall examine in some depth shortly. The distinction between the two rests upon at what level those functions are carried out or delegated. A supervisor is in direct contact with the workforce, a manager has supervisors reporting to him or her. Our emphasis throughout this book is to look at those aspects of human relations that need to be understood by lower level and middle management and therefore our analysis and discussion of management is very much concerned with the activities and responsibilities of people employed on this borderline.

9.2 PROBLEMS CONFRONTING THE FIRST-LEVEL SUPERVISOR

We shall immediately look at some particular problems that have been identified as confronting the first-level supervisor.[1]

1. Supervisors' age and training are often more similar to the workforce they supervise than the group with whom they are supposed to identify, namely management.
2. Supervisors are separate from the workforce, but depend heavily on its co-operation.
3. Supervisors are the first level of management, but have little real authority.
4. Supervisors are expected to maintain high morale, but spend most of their time checking their subordinates' standards of performance or being involved in administrative detail.
5. Supervisors are not involved in management policy-making but are expected to meet its demands and defend it against criticism.

In this chapter we shall be examining both the theoretical and practical aspects of the manager's job, but we would emphasise that all the preceding chapters and those following are implicitly concerned with this too.

9.3 THE FUNCTIONS OF MANAGEMENT

The first and frequently quoted analysis of the process of management was by Henri Foyal, who stated 'to manage is to forecast and plan, to organise, to command, to co-ordinate and to control'.[2] Modern views are quite clearly based on Fayol's analysis, but their emphasis has changed, since his five functions are clearly identifiable with the classical theory of organisation (see Chapter 10).

A recent guru of management thought outside the classical school is Peter Drucker. He also identified five basic 'operations' in the work of managers.[3]

In the first place they set objectives, they decide what has to be done to achieve those objectives and communicate them to the people whose performance is needed to achieve them. Second, managers organise by dividing work activity into manageable jobs. Next managers motivate and communicate, making a team out of the people responsible for various jobs. The fourth element is the job of measurement analysing, appraising and interpreting performance. Finally, managers develop people; direct people or misdirect them. They bring out what is in them or they stifle them. They strengthen their integrity or corrupt them.

A more modern update of Fayol's six elements is the analysis by E.F.L. Brech who emphasises management as a social process, thus preferring to replace 'command' by 'motivation'. He also includes organising as part of the planning process, believing that Fayol's emphasis on organising was due to his familiarity with large-scale enterprises where problems of hierarchy, delegation and communication were evident.[4] Brech's view is therefore a process of planning, motivation, co-ordination and control with feedback to future planning and a repeat of the cycle.

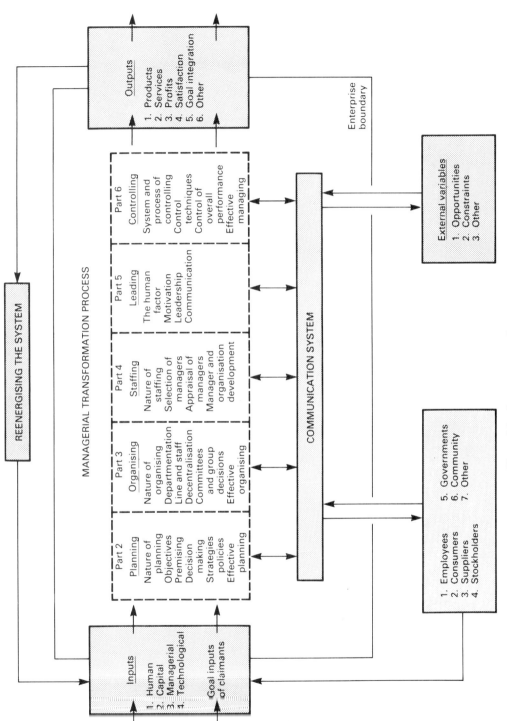

Figure 9.1 *Systems approach to management.*

Levels of management	Typical job titles in the hotel and catering industry	1. Planning, organising	2. Motivating	3. Communication	4. Leading	5. Controlling
Top management	Managing director, Chief executive	Overall policy — long term establishes organisation structure	Policies on promotion, remuneration and reward	Policy statements, annual accounts, in house journals	Position	Corporate aims and policies
Senior management	General manager, Regional manager	Policy interpretation medium-term goals. Determines unit structure	Decisions on promotion etc. Providing an effective working environment	Memoranda and meetings. Letters	Modelling and Directing	Budgeting, targeting. Design systems
Middle manager	Assistant manager, Catering manager	Policy, implementation — short-term plans	Job design and personal effort	Memoranda and meetings. Verbal face to face	Modelling and Participating	Periodic monitoring and data collection
Supervisor	Head waiter, Head chef	Operating and day-to-day problem solving	Personal approach	Verbal, face to face	Participating	Day-to-day monitoring and implementing systems

WORKFORCE

Figure 9.2 *Management function and management level*

Lastly, there is the systems approach to management which Koontz et al. have proposed[5] (see Fig. 9.1). They see management as the conversion of inputs through planning, organising, staffing, leading and controlling into system outputs. For them, co-ordination is not a separate function of management, it is 'the essence of managership . . . each of the managerial functions is an exercise in co-ordination'.

It is outside the scope of this book to support or propose a theory of management, but we have selected those functions which we see as being of particular importance and relevance in managing people. These functions are as follows — planning, motivating, communicating, leading and controlling. Within each of these functions different levels of management will undertake different activities. See Fig. 9.2.

In previous chapters we have already considered the concepts of motivation, communication and leadership. We regard these as intrinsic to the role of lower and middle management. Without the necessary knowledge and associated skills of these areas the manager would be unable to function (particularly in the catering industry which is so dependent upon people) for you cannot motivate, lead or communicate with plant and machinery. However, before the manager can undertake these three functions the planning process must take place and control must be exercised. For lower and middle level management the planning and control elements tend to be laid down by more senior managers for implementation. This view is reflected in Fig. 9.2. It should also be noted that we have tended to analyse the five functions in terms of lower and middle managers and hence will not discuss concepts such as policy-making, budgeting and corporate aims.

9.4 PLANNING AND CONTROLLING

The major focus of planning and controlling is on organisational effectiveness and not the individual's effectiveness.

'It is the heart of the organisation. It clarifies the individual perspective, expectations about what should be done, but whilst it obviously influences individual behaviour it is concerned with the whole and not individual parts. In simple terms these two functions answer two basic questions — what are we doing? And how well are we doing?' (see Fig. 9.3).[6]

Process involved	PLANNING		CONTROL	
Basic question	What are we doing?		How well are we doing?	
Secondary question	Where are we going?	How do we get there?	How do we know?	How can we improve?
Operation	Set goals and objectives	Allocate resources and draw up plans	Measure the criteria of quality, quantity, cost and time	Utilise feedback response time and change

Figure 9.3 *A description of planning and control.*

Brech summarises the relationship between the two as follows: 'planning lays down the programme to be followed and the standards or budgets to be attained. Control watches to see that the programme and the standards or targets are adhered to or brings to light the reasons why not'.

In many respects control is inherent in planning. First, policies are laid down and rules established in order to achieve corporate aims and specific goals. In planning and deciding these goals control is being automatically imposed.

Second, the structure of the business is organised and again control is built in by specifying authority, responsibility, communication channels and the interrelationship of different parts of the organisation. Third, decisions are made concerning recruitment, selection and training policies which also controls the activity of employees. Fourth, systems of performance appraisal and scales of remuneration are estabished, also inhibiting freedom of action. Fifth, budgets are established linking the financial resources available to specific organisational goals and providing the financial parameters of the operation. Lastly, the appropriate technology is selected in terms of machines, automation and computers. The operation of such technology also controls the organisation's activity by prescribing how and when certain tasks must be achieved. Computers and information technology have had a significant impact on the extent to which employees in organisations are controlled.

Whilst planning and control are essential to the organisational health of the enterprise, from the human relations approach there is evidence that control creates pressure on employees and increases anxiety in them. T.R. Mitchell (op. cit.) expresses it well: 'by definition control systems are designed to regulate behaviour and the regulation of behaviour implies loss of freedom. People react negatively to this loss of freedom, and the resultant behaviour can be damaging for the organisation'.

In order to avoid such a response, research indicates that five principles should be adhered to:

1. Understanding. Employees will appreciate some degree of explanation as to why control factors such as rules, budgets and so on are necessary and an outline of the reasoning behind their implementation.
2. Fairness. All controls should be perceived as fair to everyone concerned. Evaluation of procedures should be open to discussion.
3. Participation. If it is possible to involve people in setting up of control procedures they will be more likely to implement and adhere to them.
4. Flexibility. Control systems should always be flexible enough to take account of marginal differences in performance particularly where individuals are concerned.
5. Feedback. A control system is useless unless it provides those in authority with the information they require in order to manage the business effectively. Making such feedback available to all levels in the organisation may help to develop and indeed motivate the staff.

9.5 PUTTING MANAGEMENT FUNCTIONS INTO PRACTICE

The trouble with management functions is that first-line managers do not think, act or behave in these terms. They do not say to themselves 'at 10 o'clock today I am going to motivate my staff' or 'this afternon I am going to communicate with colleagues'. In reality they say to themselves 'at 10 o'clock this morning I have an appraisal interview with Phil Pearson' and 'this afternoon I am explaining the new statutory sick pay regulations to my staff'. Therefore we propose to look at four common activities undertaken by management particularly at lower levels namely interviewing, training, conducting and attending meetings and implementing change. There are two reasons for this approach. First, we hope to show the integrated nature of management functions that necessitates the selection and implementation of some or many of the interpersonal skills we have identified. Second, by dealing with the reality of what a manager actually does we will introduce the reader to new interpersonal skills.

Interviewing

The supervisor is involved in a wide variety of interview situations ranging from the formal selection interview to an informal chat over a coffee. All these situations have similarities in that they are attempting to achieve specific goals through the gathering and imparting of knowledge, where the interviewer has the major influence on the conduct of the interaction, for instance the interviewer decides when and where the discussion will take place. The most common forms of interview are, one, the selection interview where the manager is involved in the recruitment of new staff; two, the appraisal interview when the manager is involved in assessing subordinates' performance and agreeing future targets; three, the disciplinary interview where she or he attempts to exercise control over an employee's unacceptable behaviour; four, grievance interviews where subordinates feel they are being badly treated and require remedial action; the counselling interview where the manager is concerned with the personal problems of the staff which may only indirectly affect the work situation; and lastly the exit interview where the manager tries to find out the underlying reasons for the termination of an employment contract, either when an employee is dismissed or resigns.

In all these interview situations there are four fundamental problems to the effective conduct of the interaction.

Anxiety

Interviews induce considerable anxiety not only on the part of the interviewee, who may feel threatened or whose self-image and esteem are open to criticism, but also for the interviewer, whose expertise as a manager is in question and who may feel uncomfortable to the personal nature of what is to be discussed. A further complication is introduced by the status difference between the individuals concerned. This is especially true in situations where the individuals' roles are not so clear or important; for instance, in a counselling situation where the employee may be worried about talking to the 'boss' about problems at home.

Reluctance to talk

The most effective interviews are those where the interviewer says very little and allows the interviewee the largest share of the conversation. Some interviewees are very reluctant to talk and embarrassing silences can ensue. It is the interviewer's responsibility to encourage the interviewee to talk as freely as possible.

Underlying feelings

One of the major purposes of any interview is to discover the underlying causes of people's behaviour or their underlying attitudes. In this situation, however, interviewees will present their most favourable image and attempt to hide any unfavourable characteristics. The interviewer's responsibility is to make the interaction as open as possible and to bring these feelings to the surface. The openness of the interview can also be restricted by the roles that people play. People have stereotypical expectations of the way interviews are conducted.

Bias

As we have seen any interpersonal perception is open to the bias introduced by the interviewer's own value systems and personal characteristics. Interviewers must attempt to remain as objective as possible and avoid their inbuilt biases.

In Fig. 9.4 we have attempted to outline effective techniques for interview situations and identify the ways in which these help to overcome the problems outlined above.

Task 9.1

Attempt to categorise each of the techniques shown in Fig. 9.4 under the five functions of management. For instance, the first technique — 'clarify aims and objectives' — is the planning function.

Training

In looking at the tasks in which a supervisor is directly involved, training is perhaps the one that stands out. Training is normally described as being either off-the-job, conducted away from the workforce and usually involving the imparting of knowledge, or on-the-job, conducted actually in the place of work and usually concerned with developing skills. However, we see any situation where supervisors perceive their subordinates' behaviour as less than acceptable as indicating a need for training, which the supervisor should carry out on an immediate, ad hoc basis. Rather than seeing poor performance as requiring criticism or disciplinary action, on most occasions simple training and guidance will be more effective. Thus in many respects for us the titles supervisor and trainer are almost synonymous. Ad hoc training will involve all of the five functions of management we have identified, as well as an application of the basic learning theories we identified in Chapter 3. There is no right or wrong way of going about this training since unstructured training of this sort will depend upon the task the employee is undertaking, where it is taking place, whether or not there are other staff or customers present, the relationship between the supervisor and the trainee, the immediacy of the problem and the extent to which the observed behaviour deviates from the required standard of performance. Let us take a simple example of a public house which usually has a rather large number of part-time staff. It is important

Interview techniques	Interviewing problems to be overcome				
	Reduce anxiety		Reluctance to talk	Identifying underlying feelings	Bias
	Inter-viewer	Inter-viewee			
Clarify aims and objectives	✓				✓
Collect and study necessary information	✓			✓	
Invite interviewee to attend in appropriate manner		✓			
Plan sequence of interviews	✓				✓
Prepare layout of room		✓	✓		
Ensure no interruptions	✓	✓	✓		
Choose surroundings free of noise and distraction			✓		
Open interview in friendly but controlled manner		✓	✓		
Ask open questions			✓	✓	
Do not express personal judgements			✓		✓
Maintain continuity in discussion		✓	✓		
Encourage interviewees to extend useful statements				✓	
Listen with interest			✓	✓	
Observe non-verbal behaviour				✓	
Beware of halo effect					✓
Make notes openly		✓			✓
Show normal politeness and courtesy		✓	✓		
Sum up during interview and at the end	✓	✓		✓	✓
Allow time for completing notes after interview					✓
Use standard rating scales					✓
Reinforcement techniques			✓	✓	

to the licensee that the staff serve full pints of draught beer. Upon observing a member of staff not doing this the approach could vary quite widely. To a fairly experienced bar- man he might just say in passing 'Come on, you know better than that', to a recent employee he may take them to one side, show them how to pour the beer correctly and emphasise the importance of filling the glass. If a customer was complaining that the glass was not full enough he might only deal with the customer and not speak to the member of staff until later and for a trustworthy, well-experienced barman he might merely ask after the transaction was completed 'Why didn't you fill the glass, Jack?' The only test of whether an ad hoc approach to training has been effective is whether or not the employee performs the task correctly in the future and feels happy about doing it that way.

Our discussion above contrasts vividly with the general approach adopted to on-the- job training in the hotel and catering industry which tends to be very formal, rigid and structured. This is primarily due to the all pervading influence of the HCITB, which has had nearly 20 years to investigate, develop and 'impose' training methods on the industry. It is interesting to note that the most recent publications of the training board are noticeably less pedantic about how to train staff, for instance 'Training your staff' HCITB 1982. It is clear from their literature that it is the supervisor who is almost inevitably the on-the-job trainer. In this respect the supervisor's role is typical of those problems that beset the supervisor that we identified earlier, see p.138, for it will be management who will have determined the training plan, but the supervisor who will implement it; the supervisor is in an organisational role that demands great individual flair; upon completing the training, management holds the supervisor responsible for the trainees' performance; and intrinisic in the training is the concept that the supervisors will be motivating staff to learn things, although they may be unwilling to do so. We can identify the role of the supervisor in the training process from Table 9.1.

Table 9.1   *The training process.*

Stages	Person responsible	Documentation
Identification of knowledge and skills required	Personnel manager	Job description
Assess staff's present level of knowledge and skill	Personnel manager/ Training officer	Interview records Application form Curriculum vitae Staff records
Identification of training needs	Training officer	Training records Staff appraisal forms
Prepare training plan	Training officer	Company manuals HCITB publications
Implement training	On-the-job instructor i.e. supervisor	Lesson plan
Evaluation of instruction	On-the-job instruction and unit management	Training records
Evaluation of training programme	Training officer	Training plans Performance appraisal

Most on-the-job training has a standard approach, which can be broken down into five stages.

Planning

This includes identifying the people for whom the training is appropriate, what the objectives of the training are, and where and when the session is to take place. The next step is to break the task to be taught down into its component parts and identify the perceptual cues which highlight the correct performance of each stage of the task, so that trainees will know what to look or listen for during the completion of the task. For instance, when chopping an onion the trainee is taught to *look* for blemishes on the skin, *feel* the correct way of holding the onion, and so on. The final step is to put together the total lesson plan which will also list the necessary resources, tools and equipment and identify an appropriate environment for conducting the session.

Starting

At the start of any training session it is necessary to get the trainees in the right frame of mind i.e. feeling at ease but raring to go! This is best achieved by arousing the trainees' interest in the task through displaying a finished product, performing the skill, humour, question and sometimes shock (particularly those areas concerned with health and safety at work). Second, it is important to make trainees aware of the need for being able to complete the task, especially in relation to the trainees themselves. Third, the overall content of the session must be established and trainees should be made aware of the objectives which they will have achieved at the end.

Carrying out the instruction

The foundation of a good piece of instruction is a well-planned and well-presented demonstration of the skill to be learnt. The trainer should first demonstrate the complete task at normal speed, so that the trainee sees the eventual expected level of performance. Then the trainer should break the demonstration into small, discrete steps, stressing the perceptual cues. At all times the trainer should keep the trainees involved by asking questions which will also check their level of understanding.

Allowing the trainee to practise

The only way that a trainee is going to develop skilled performance is by supervised practice. Following the demonstration of each step of the task trainees should be allowed to practise until they are proficient. Once all the steps have been covered the complete task should be demonstrated again at half-speed with questioning throughout and then the trainees can practise the complete task with the supervisor monitoring their performance by correcting, guiding and praising where appropriate.

Evaluation

On completion of the training session trainees are for a few days given frequent opportunities wherever practicable to practise the new skill they have acquired. During this time they will receive further guidance from the supervisor and experienced colleagues; once trainees have achieved the required standard, their performance of the task will become routine and evaluation by the supervisor will take place on an ad hoc basis.

Meetings

There is a general tendency throughout industry to increase the number and frequency of committee meetings and all supervisors are likely to find themselves participating in meetings and calling and chairing meetings of their own. The general purpose of committees is to solve problems and make decisions which are acceptable to those present and require their commitment for implementation. In some cases the emphasis of a meeting is on generating creative solutions to problems. In others simply at achieving consensus and disseminating information. Committees should be able to generate more and better solutions than individuals by combining their members' skills, abilities and knowledge and by providing interaction to stimulate new ideas.

It is more likely perhaps for low-level managers to be committee members than chairpersons. To be an effective committee member one must consider the following factors.

Preparation

It is essential to be prepared adequately for the meeting by studying the agenda and associated documents, discussing any relevant points with your subordinates and ensuring that any information is ready for you to take to the meeting.

Communication

At committee meetings all communication should be kept as concise and as relevant to the points under discussion as possible.

Problem-solving

It is important to remember that the purpose of committees is to make decisions and solve problems for the organisation as a whole, and that departmental factors, although important, should not be stressed at the expense of an effective overall solution.

Objectivity

It is necessary at all times to be as objective as possible to prevent departmental or personal bias misdirecting the committee process.

The skills of chairing a committee are difficult to tie down, as they involve all the skills of communicating, interpersonal interaction, group dynamics and leadership we have already looked at. It is also true to say that experience of committee membership is essential to chairing a committee. There are, however, certain specific areas which deserve attention.

Preparation

Just as the committee member must prepare for the meeting so must the chair consider his or her agenda, anticipate any particular problem issues and if neccesary discuss these with individuals beforehand.

Creating the right atmosphere

It is the chair's responsibility to ensure that the meeting progresses smoothly and he or she should encourage members to contribute their views as necessary. It has been found[7] that those who encourage the expression of minority views lead to more effective and more widely acceptable solutions to problems.

Guiding the discussion

The basic procedure for any item should be to outline the problem, summarise the background and outline the benefits and disadvantages of various courses of action.

Following this introduction the meeting should be opened for discussion where the chair plays an active role, not in discussion content, but in controlling discussion flow by such techniques as summarising, focusing on issues and problems, evaluating proposed solutions and consideration of sub-problems.

Concluding the discussion

Once the discussion has reached its optimum point the chair should call for consensus. It is important that all members of the committee should be able to agree to the proposed course of action as any dissent will weaken its implementation and potential effectiveness. At this stage also the chair should identify what action is to be taken by which members of the meeting and ensure that they understand what they are required to do and when.

Task 9.2

As in Task 9.1 try to identify aspects of the five functions of management we proposed in chairing and attending meetings.

Case example 9.1   Meetings in a typical hotel

The following is a list of the type of meetings and their frequency held at the Brentwood Post House, a three-star 120 bedroom hotel operated by Trust-house Forte.

Type of meeting	*Frequency*
Heads of department	weekly
Management	weekly
Staff consultative committee	every 6 weeks
Departmental training meetings	weekly
Staff social committee	twice per year
Finance	weekly
Interviews	most days
Sales think-tank	every 6 to 8 weeks

As well as these formal situations, impromptu meetings are held after close of business quite often, with such meetings being as effective as the formal ones.

Coping with change

The hotel and catering industry, due to its close relationship with the customer and the need to adapt to these customers' changing demands, constantly tries to introduce a variety of changes to its product, service and administrative systems which it is hoped will be better for both staff and guests. These changes will be largely decided by higher level management but it will be the job of the supervisor to ensure that they are implemented smoothly and with minimum staff resistance. Changes could be of an apparently minor nature, such as requesting all guest-contact staff to wear name badges or changing the brand of coffee served to customers, or of more major significance such as the refurbishment of the unit or the restructuring of work schedules. Whether or not the change appears on the surface to be a major or minor alteration, the important factor is not the scale but the degree to which the staff perceive the change will have an effect on them. In our four examples, staff are likely to either be unconcerned about change, as in the case of coffee used, or in favour of change, as in the case of smartening up their work environment. But they may well resist change which they regard as threatening as in the other two examples given.

People do not resist change because of the change itself. There is resistance because change means having to readjust behaviour and because of some or all of the fears identified below.

Unemployment

Any change which seems to carry risk of creating unemployment or redundancy, especially at a time of high national unemployment, will be bound to meet resistance.

In the refurbishment of a restaurant, for instance, it would be important to stress that no staff changes were being considered or that any necessary changes would be accomplished with staff co-operation.

Earnings

All employees are concerned about the size of their pay packet and changes likely to affect bonuses, commission and overtime will meet considerable resistance. In the catering industry some employees' income is also derived from tipping, which will equally be jealously guarded.

Loss of skill

Whenever a person has spent time developing a skill they will resent any attempt to reduce the importance of their skills.

Loss of self-esteem

We have seen that a person's self-esteem is fundamental to their behaviour and that a person's employment, their status and job satisfaction are important parts of that image. Management are particularly prone to resist change which threatens their self-esteem.

Failure

When new skills or techniques are introduced to the job, people will be fearful about their ability to master these new skills. The greater the difference between old and new methods and the longer the employee has been working that way, then the greater will be the likelihood of resistance.

Social integration

The Hawthorne experiments (see p.111) demonstrate the effect that social groupings have upon the work environment. Any change affects the social group both in a formal way by readjusting staffing structures and informally when previous interactions are reduced. For example, people may worry about reorganisation of the people they work with every day, but may be equally worried when a restructuring of other departments means that they do not meet their usual dining companions in the staff cafeteria.

Uncertainty

When any change is planned it is important to make sure that people are made fully aware of the true nature of the change. If people hear about proposed changes through gossip or by overhearing other people discuss it, the uncertainty this causes will be intense and once rumours are established they are difficult to put down.

It is therefore important to realise that staff resistance to change is based on very understandable and real fears about their future and also that the fears staff do express may not be the true reasons but simply the ones they feel able to express. When introducing change, in order to reduce these fears the following stages should be adopted.

1. Forecast the likely effects of the change. As part of the considerations for implementing the change all the people who will be affected should be identified and the likely effect upon them predicted.
2. Consult those affected. The people identified above should be consulted to discover their feelings about the proposed change and to attempt to discover ways of reducing potential anxiety. Such consultation may be informal when staff individually or collectively are approached by their supervisor or formal when often through their shop steward employees are asked to express their opinions.
3. Analyse feedback. Having consulted with staff and identified potential problems the plans for the implementation of change can be analysed to find ways of reducing anxiety.
4. Introduce the change. The way should now be clear for the change to be introduced, but at all times staff must be kept informed of what is happening.
5. Follow-up. Once the change is introduced staff should again be consulted to discover any problems they may be having with the new procedures and to put things right.

Case example 9.2   Resistance to change

In 1975 a survey (Shamir, B. 'A Study of Managers and Staff Attitudes' [1975] Cornwell, Greene, Bertram, Smith & Co.) was conducted into the attitudes of management and staff to a number of proposed innovations, such as the replacement of room service by vending machines, the introduction of convenience foods, and developing multi-skilled personnel. With regard to 'automating' room service, managers were generally in favour of kettles in each bedroom but against vending machines, which were seen as unprofitable, reducing the service element and not effective sales agents for the hotel.

Sixty-five per cent of employees, on the other hand, were in favour of self-service devices in rooms, but their opinion was affected by whether or not it would bring them personally more work.

Concerning the introduction of convenience foods, chefs were worried about their loss of skill and loss of status, believing that by not personally preparing a dish for a customer a lot of self-respect and pride in their work would be lost. Management recognised these misgivings, but still regarded convenience foods as essential due to the shortage of good chefs and their high wages, believing that the customer would be unable to differentiate between fresh and convenience products.

The proposal to introduce multi-purpose employees was probably the most far reaching of the study. The idea of employees crossing traditional departmental boundaries seems ideally suited to the special demands of the catering and hotel industry. Employees were divided on the issue. Half of them (the professionals such as chefs, waiters, receptionists) were against the idea as it would reduce their prestige and job satisfaction, whereas the

other half (porters, chambermaids and so on) were in favour as it would provide more interesting work, more co-operation and higher status.

Managers were generally in favour of the idea, but they said it would only
work if a completely new workforce, who had no previous experience of the
industry, was recruited and trained, and paid higher rates of pay.

REFERENCES

1. Sasser, W.E. (1980) Let first-level supervisors do their job. *Havard Business Review*, March–April.
2. Fayol, H. (1916) Administration industrielle et générale. *Bulletin de la Société de l'Industrie Minérale*, **3**.
3. Drucker, P. (1954) *The Practice of Management.* New York: Harper.
4. Brech, E.F.L. (1975) (3rd edn) *The Principle and Practice of Management.* London: Longman.
5. Koontz, H., O'Donnell, C. & Weinrich, H. *Principles of Management.* New York: McGraw-Hill.
6. Mitchell, T.R. (1982) *People in Organizations.* New York: McGraw-Hill.
7. Maier, N.R.F. & Solem, A.R. (1952) The contribution of a discussion leader to the quality of group thinking: the effective use of minority opinion. *Human Relations*, **5**.

10 Organisations

In the world of mules
There are no rules

Ogden Nash

OBJECTIVES: to define the term 'organisation' . . . to outline the traditional role of organisations . . . to compare alternative organisation structures . . . to outline four approaches to organisation theory . . . to establish the extent to which organisation theories apply to the hotel and catering industry

10.1 INTRODUCTION

SO far, we have emphasised individuals and we have seen how they may function more effectively if they work together in groups. However, even in an industry such as hotel and catering with its high proportion of very small units, the majority of workers do not work for themselves, nor as a separate group, but as part of a larger organisation. Such organisations may be entrepreneurial in nature where the business is owned, operated and managed by a single person or a small number of partners in the business. Larger businesses will tend to be organised as private or public companies where ownership is in the hands of shareholders and management is undertaken by a board of directors who employ a management team. Apart from the private sector, catering is operated by both public corporations such as British Rail and government bodies such as the National Health Service, education service and armed forces. Whilst all of these bodies are organisations, it is obvious that they are very different from each other. This chapter will look at why organisations exist, how they are structured and the relevance of organisation theory to the hotel and catering industry.

10.2 WHAT IS AN ORGANISATION?

Organisations exist for many of the reasons that we have identified as benefits arising from putting individuals to work as groups. These include the fact that some tasks cannot be achieved by one person alone; several people working together can complete a task more quickly than individuals; most individuals need social contact and have more job satisfaction when working as part of a group; and theoretically, groups increase efficiency by allowing individual members to specialise and become superproficient in one aspect of the joint venture. However, organisations differ from groups in several ways.

Size

Generally speaking, an organisation would consist of several or indeed many groups with some individuals within the organisation never coming into contact with other employees.

Legality

Most if not all organisations have a clearly identifiable legal status through compliance with various Companies Acts or by being government bodies.

Existence

Most organisations have a definite starting point, during their lifetime accumulate both documentary and material evidence of their existence in the form of share certificates, plant, machinery, annual reports and so on; and cease to exist at an equally well defined time.

Structure

Organisations are social structures, but whereas a group will determine its form internally the structure of an organisation is prescribed theoretically from above by management although as we shall see in practice they are in turn affected by a large number of external factors.

Aims

All organisations exist for a purpose. Ostensibly in the private sector the main aim has been to maximise profit although alternative possibilities exist such as increased market share, maximising return on capital employed, achieving a target percentage in terms of mean growth, sales maximisation, and so on. In addition to these business aims, organisations may also have implicit social aims such as safeguarding the environment, maintaining employment, creating a good public image and achieving status. The aims of organisations in the public sector are not so different since they too are concerned with achieving the maximum provision with the minimum resources. In order to achieve these overall aims, organisations will tend to set targets for individual groups which collectively will fulfil the organisational purpose.

These characteristics lead us to the traditional view of work organisations, as outlined by Capey and Carr.[1]

1. Organisations consist of people in groups performing specific tasks at prescribed times.
2. The organisation attempts to match the dominant skills and abilities of each individual employee with the specific tasks it has set.
3. The individual tasks are essential and indissoluble from each other to achieve the corporate aims of the organisation.
4. To ensure that individual effort meets corporate aims there is a formal system of control and co-ordination.
5. The controlling and co-ordinating function is undertaken by management and confers upon managers' status rights and obligations.

It is easy to believe that organisations are designed consciously but as C. Handy states 'most organisations are not designed, they grow'[2]. This lack of conscious planning is derived from the fact that businesses are dynamic entities that change their market position, lose and gain employees, are subject to external social, legal and economic pressures and so on. At each stage in their development there are a great number of choices to be considered about the most desirable and effective structure to adopt at that time.

In large organisations decisions about these choices are not made by supervisors or lower level managers, but an understanding of the principles involved is essential for two reasons. First, by understanding the rationale or organisational design the supervisor/manager will be able to understand the structure of the organisation for which he works and should therefore contribute more effectively to its operation. Second, most of these principles can be applied to individual units as well as large firms. This is particularly relevant to the hotel and catering industry which is composed of many small units and in terms of other industries has very few large-scale firms.

Some of the questions to be considered are to what extent should the workforce be specialised? How many subordinates can a manager control? To what extent and on what basis should there be departmentalisation? To what extent should formal rules and regulations be laid down? How adaptable is the structure to the changes imposed from outside and evolving from within?

10.3 ORGANISATION STRUCTURE

Basically, the structure of any organisation is determined by the extent to which those at the top of the organisation wish to control the activities of their subordinate workforce. There are some notable examples of bosses who wanted to run their own show such as Freddie Laker of Laker Airways or Colin Chapman of Lotus Cars. In the main, however, those at the top recognise that they cannot physically cope with managing the entire operation and they must delegate their authority to a chain of command below them. Thus there are two underlying concepts essential to the understanding of an organisation. These are the span of management and the delegation of authority.

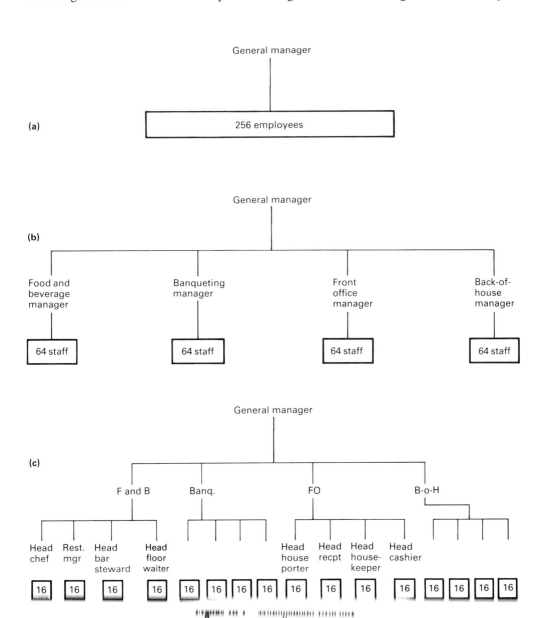

The span of management refers to the fact that a manager cannot supervise an unlimited number of subordinates. Imagine, for instance, a hotel with 256 staff all of whom report directly to the general manager (Fig. 10.1a). Every problem that arises, every query to be answered, every decision to be made would come to him or her. The demands upon time would be too great, on memory and abilities overpowering, and mental processes would be susceptible to breakdown. To overcome this a second level of management is introduced; typically in a hotel these might be a banqueting manager, food and beverage manager, front-office manager, and back-of-house manager. This has solved some of the problems for our general manager, who now only has to deal with four people each of whom is a specialist in their own field (Fig. 10.1b). These assistant managers, however, in our highly theoretical model still have 64 employees reporting to them whom they must manage effectively. In a hotel, of course, in terms only of time the business operates 24 hours a day, 7 days a week all year round, thus making effective supervision even more difficult. For these reasons, a third level of management is introduced and the managers each have four department heads reporting to them (Fig. 10.1c).

In our example our effective span of management has been four, that is managers have four subordinates reporting to each of them. Particularly at upper levels of management and certainly within large organisations rather than individual units it is generally accepted that the span of management should be between three and six subordinates reporting to their boss, but this does depend on several factors. First, it will depend upon the extent to which the policies of the organisation are clearly stated and how comprehensive they are. If everything is well defined each manager will need less time for decision-making, problem-solving and so on and can therefore have a larger number of subordinates than an organisation whose policies may be confused, contradictory or non-existent. Second, the span of management can be greater where subordinates are competent, experienced and have a high degree of expertise. Third, the nature of the business activity will influence the span, in particular the extent to which it is routine and uncomplicated or rapidly changing and complex. Fourth, the physically closer subordinates are to their boss, the greater the span of control since effective interaction is made easier. Lastly, there is the extent to which the organisation can effectively use experts or specialised management staff to assist those managers directly responsible for the manufacture of the product or provision of the service.

Joan Woodward has identified[3] that most firms have two kinds of management function based on a study of a number of firms in Essex in the 1960s. The 'task' functions are vital to the achievement of the organisation's primary objectives. These are usually four: production, sales, accounts and research and development. Managers responsible for task functions are known as 'line' managers. The 'element' functions help and support the task functions, the most notable example being the personnel department. Managers of the element functions are known as 'staff' managers. In addition to the different roles of line and staff managers there are differences in the authority that each manager holds.

Generally, staff managers act in an advisory capacity to line managers who always make the ultimate decisions about the operation. At the same time staff managers within their own particular spheres of influence can exercise direct authority outside their own departments. For instance, a personnel manager in a hotel responsible for health and safety at work could take direct action to rectify malpractice in a kitchen although the operation of the kitchen would normally be the responsibility of the food and beverage manager.

Task 10.1

Look at Fig. 10.2 showing the organisation structure of a large hotel and identify the line and staff organisation.

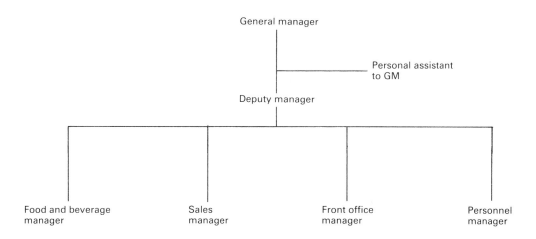

Figure 10.2 *Organisation structure of a large hotel.*

Whilst Woodward's analysis is useful it does present problems when applied to the hotel and catering industry as opposed to manufacturing industry. In large hotel and catering organisations line management tends to be regarded as the management structure within each unit, and staff management is regarded as the management structure at head office. In hotels this is partly because all assistant managers whether they have a 'task' or 'element' function are expected to take a turn at duty management. Also in order to be appointed a general manager it is quite common for assistant managers to work in various line functions and staff functions, which is not the case in the manufacturing sector.

An inevitable consequence of reducing the span of control is an increase in the number of levels of management (see Fig. 10.1) and an increase in the total number of management personnel employed. In our hotel example, three levels of management with a span of control of four has resulted in 21 managerial positions. The choice then is between extending the number of management levels or the average span of control. Both have their drawbacks. By extending the span we encounter those problems we previously identified resulting from having too many people reporting to and being supervised by one person. There are, however, disadvantages in having several levels of management. These include the cost of management salaries, difficulties in communication between top management and the workforce and a lowering of staff morale due to the distancing of those people who ultimately make the real decisions

10.4 AUTHORITY AND DELEGATION

However an organisation is structured it will not be effective unless all the participants have a clear idea of their authority. One of the earliest principles of management is that there should be 'unity of command', that is to say that everyone from the lowest employee up knows exactly who their boss is. The reasons for this are to avoid conflict, and to ensure that everyone is working towards the corporate aims of the organisation, for implicit with authority goes responsibility, that is to say that authority is invested in a person when they are made responsible for achieving certain objectives. A potential supervisor or manager must realise that in accepting a position of authority and the formal right to command another person to perform a certain act, he or she must be prepared to accept the responsibility that goes with it.

It is fairly self-evident that the person with the ultimate authority and responsibility for achieving the organisation's aims is the person at the top, the managing director, company chairman or president of the corporation. However, by introducing different levels of management this ultimate authority must be delegated to subordinates; thus the finance director would be responsible for all financial aspects, and the personnel manager for staff recruitment, training and so on. As you move down the hierarchy, managers are set more and more specific objectives to achieve and planning and decisions tend to be short term rather than long term. To be effective, delegation necessitates that subordinate managers are first given all the information they require to meet the objectives laid down for them and second they are allowed to make all the decisions incumbent in their job, within the broad policy framework laid down by the organisation. Effective delegation has two major benefits for the organisation — decision-making is immediate and where the action is, and there is increased job satisfaction for management personnel. The great danger of delegation is that by giving authority and responsibility to managers, they may be incapable of meeting objectives through incompetence or lack of experience or they may pursue their own personal objectives rather than corporate ones which could lead to financial loss.

Bases of authority

So far we have implied that organisations give managers authority by giving them a formal position, but, as we shall see, to have effective authority a manager must have far more than just a title and a desk. The traditional formal view of authority is that subordinates comply with a manager's command because it comes from a legitimate source. A more recent alternative view is acceptance theory which suggests that employees only accept orders and instructions given to them within well-defined limits, usually defined both implicitly and explicitly by the terms of their contract of employment. Unless subordinates are prepared to accept the manager's requests they can have no authority. Whichever view of authority is preferred research has indicated[4] that managers are reluctant to use their position as a means of achieving subordinate compliance. What other ways are there then of influencing the actions of others?

As well as the legitimate authority resting in the position the manager holds we can identify four other sources of authority.

Reward and punishment

A manager often has the power to give promotion or pay increases to his subordinates or on the other hand to reprimand and ultimately dismiss the employee.

Make the job easier

Managers are often in a position to control the flow of information to subordinates which may help or hinder their work; to control the way in which work is organised and the physical and social environment in which it is carried out and also to influence subordinates' status in the organisation, by placing them on committees, or introducing them to higher level managers for instance.

Expertise

People are generally willing to comply with those they regard as the expert in that particular field. This does not necessarily mean academic qualifications, but someone who obviously knows their job inside out and who does it well. Due to the nature of this influence and its high degree of acceptability to subordinates expertise may give rise to someone having greater authority than their position intends. For instance, in a large kitchen the sous chef who shows more expertise than the head chef may command more respect and hence authority than the legitimate head.

Personal power

There are without doubt individuals who by their personal characteristics alone command respect and hence authority. This is very often called 'charisma'. In our view, however, personal power is not just something you are born with, but it can be learnt. Indeed we would argue that a major purpose of this book is to show potential managers how through effective communication, motivation and interpersonal behaviour they may become respected managers in their own right and not simply for the position they hold.

10.5 DESIGNING THE ORGANISATION

So far we have seen that out of growth and necessity organisations increase the number of their management personnel. Apart from the span of management and the role of authority there is yet a third drive towards allocating managers specific responsibilities and departmentalising the organisation, that is 'specialisation'. The concept of specialisation is that individuals become more expert in carrying out tasks the more practice they have and the fewer skills they have to master.

The prime example of specialisation is in manufacturing industry where durable goods such as televisions or motor cars are mass produced with each worker playing a very small and usually repetitive part in the whole process. In the hotel and catering industry the classical kitchen organisation is an example of specialisation with chefs each being responsible for specific parts of a meal production which accounts for the formal and hierarchical nature of the kitchen brigade.

There are six ways in which an organisation can be departmentalised although larger organisations are likely to adopt some, if not all, of these for their various parts.

Function

This is very common because most organisations can clearly identify different functions for instance production, sales or finance departments. On a small scale in a hotel these functions are likely to be food and beverage, front office and personnel. The major advantages of this organisational breakdown are that it makes sense to the parties involved and employees can easily understand it and second that it recognises the specialist nature of different functions and so takes advantage of specialisation. It does have disadvantages, however. First, middle management are specialists and may therefore not develop the all-round management expertise that would facilitate their promotion to a higher level. Second, decision-making or problem-solving affecting two or more functions can only be resolved by a higher level manager or executive. Lastly, difficulties arise when the organisation diversifies, that is to say develops different products, sells different services and satisfies the demands of new markets.

Task 10.2   Organisational design of an industrial catering unit

From the list of staff below and the sketch-plan of the unit design an appropriate organisation structure.

Situation: staff restaurant in office block — contract caterer

The staff

Lil Aitken	43	M	East London	Management waitress
Clara Barber	30	M	West Indian	Counterhand/tea trolley

Betty Booth	44	M	North London	Head cook
Colin Drummond	21	S	North London	2nd management chef
Maxine Francis	46	M	West Indian	Counterhand/tea trolley
Neil Greenwood	63	W	East London	Stillroom
Eddie Hedges	41	S	East London	Head kitchen porter
Mabel Howell	39	M	East London	Management waitress
Sharon Hughes	18	S	Welsh	Kitchen assistant
Helen Jennings	18	S	Welsh	Counterhand
Patrick O'Donnell	31	S	Irish	Kitchen porter
Isabell Payne	50	M	South London	Control clerk
Robert Phillips	19	S	North London	Assistant manager
Jane Pierce	52	M	South London	Counterhand (head)
Maisie Pointer	27	S	West Indian	Counterhand/tea trolley
John Read	51	S	Irish/East London	Kitchen porter
John Roberts	26	S	Scottish	Tea room porter
Jane Savage	46	S	East London	Kitchen assistant
Claire Sharp	29	M	East London	Counterhand/tea trolley
Chris Stapleton	39	M	South London	Storekeeper
Roy Sutton	24	M	North Kent	Manager
Mary Thatcher	48	M	North London	Dining rooms supervisor

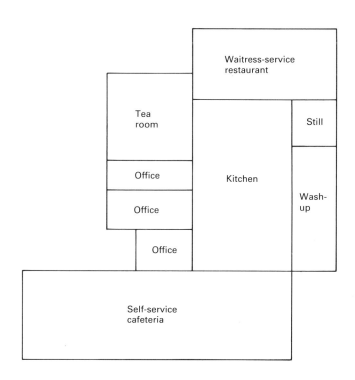

Product

With growth and diversification it is usual for organisations to group their activities according to the different products they are selling thereby creating smaller and more effective units. For instance, it is not unusual for large hotel companies to have corporate decisions based on the type and grade of their hotels.

Case example 10.1   Organisation of a hotel group

Trusthouse Forte Hotels Limited, an operating company within Trusthouse Forte plc, organises its activities into six 'brands' according to product type.

(1) Exclusive

A collection of top class hotels in the UK and abroad with that certain something extra, e.g. Grosvenor House, London; Compleat Angler, Marlowe; George V, Paris.

(2) London and International

A selection of good class hotels situated in London or abroad.

(3) Forte

Mainly four-star hotels situated outside London, such as the Albany Hotels and the Wessex at Winchester.

(4) Post Houses

This 'brand' which is exclusive to THF has a division of its own and is continuing to expand.

(5) Family

A collection of more economical mainly 3-star hotels, situated in the country and in resorts which cater specifically for the needs of the family.

(6) Inns

A mixture of large and small hotels ranging from 2-star to 4-star, but all having a historical background, such as the Hurtmore at Peaslake or the Lion in Shrewsbury, offering the traditional attributes of an inn.

Each of the above brands will have its own operations director responsible for the brand and a number of area directors responsible for a particular area.

Geography

In very large organisations where operations or units are spread over a wide area an organisation may have almost similar divisions producing the same product or service, but separated on a regional basis to help interaction and communication between management.

Case example 10.2   National Health Service

The NHS is an excellent example of an organisation that is based on geographical sub-divisions. A large-scale reorganisation in 1974 saw the creation of a three-tier system:

1. Regional Health Authorities.
2. Area Health Authorities.
3. District Health Authorities.

There was also an increase in functional management, i.e. the hospital catering officer became accountable to the district catering officer rather than the hospital administrator.
   Following a great deal of criticism of this 1974 structure the organisation was modified in 1982 and 1983 by dissolving one tier of the hierarchy — the AHAs. Thus, each District Health Authority will serve a population of around 200 000 with about 12 DHAs in each Regional Health Authority. At the same time the new emphasis on local management has reversed the decision of functional chains of command so that 'wherever possible staff working within units in non-clinical support functions (catering, domestic services, etc.) should be accountable to the unit administrator'.

Customer

Each department of an organisation is based on a particular category of customer that is being served. The sales function is often departmentalised in this way. For example, the former sales department of Grand Metropolitan Hotels had sales forces assigned to sell any Grand Metropolitan hotel to various customer groups such as tour operators, function and conference organisers, and mini-holidays.

Process and/or equipment

This is primarily relevant to industries employing mass production techniques and where several processes or production lines are taking place. For instance in steelmaking there are divisions based on producing pig-iron, making steel and manufacturing finished products.

Time

In non-stop operations both in manufacturing and hotel and catering, since management cannot manage continuously over 24 hours, the operation is broken down into separate shifts. It is very common for hotels, for instance, to have a night manager and completely separate night staff.

Case exercise 10.1   Universal Hotels

The company comprises 13 hotels located throughout the UK. The company was set up as a subsidiary of the Universal Investment Corporation, who decided to invest in hotel properties that also offered some cash flow. The hotel group has grown up slowly as and when the right sort of properties came onto the market. The company has been content to achieve fairly low levels of profitability, so long as the value of the property and its site have been increasing in value. Bill Shire, the managing director of the hotel division, was an estate manager appointed by the parent company to pursue this investment policy. His main concern has been therefore to ensure the upkeep of the properties and protect the company's investment. So long as the hotels have achieved a reasonable growth in real business each year, they have been allowed to establish their own management policies. Shire has used external stock takers and auditors to report on the effectiveness of each manager, and on the rare occasions that a discrepancy has been identified he has replaced the hotel's manager. Shire maintained only a very small head office management team, comprising a controller and an administrations manager. The former was responsible for producing monthly operating statements for each hotel, identifying their revenue, wages, direct and overhead costs. The administrations manager was responsible for recruiting head office clerical staff, the payment of all salaried staff in the company and purchasing major items of equipment (see Fig. 10.3).

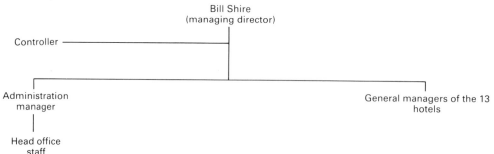

Figure 10.3   *Organisation structure of Universal Hotels.*

Bill Shire is about to retire from the company and a new managing director has to be appointed. The board of the parent company have decided that the new person should have a proven record of hotel management, since they have decided to substantially increase the hotels' profitability, the return on capital investment declining as property values remain static. The new managing director will be charged with reorganising the hotel group, if necessary by selling existing hotels and acquiring others.

From the information you have been given (Table 10.1), draw up an organisation chart for the 'new' company.

Table 10.1 *Details of the hotels in the Universal group*

Name of hotel	Star rating	No. of beds	Occupancy rate (percentage)	Type of restaurant	Function facilities	Date built	Location
White Hart	**	48	45	Restaurant	—	1735	Nottingham
Black Swan	**	140	60	Restaurant	200	1819	Leicester
Huelins	**	28	70	Restaurant	60	1787	London
Sussex	***	90	55	Restaurant Buttery	125	1816	Brighton
Empire	***	110	68	Restaurant	270	1936	Bristol
Kings	***	90	71	Restaurant	110	1907	Hull
Five Bells	***	37	42	Restaurant	—	1845	Henley
Marquis of Bath	*	40	86	Coffee shop	—	1976	Northampton
Greys	**	102	69	Restaurant	85	1973	London
Dragon	**	93	72	Restaurant Buttery	50	1966	Cardiff
Dukes Arms	****	78	51	Restaurant Coffee shop	180	1853	Carlisle
Golden Lion	****	175	70	Restaurant Coffee shop	90	1843	Edinburgh
Parliament	****	200	83	Restaurant Coffee shop	300	1972	London

10.6 CENTRALISATION v. DECENTRALISATION

A natural consequence of increasing the number of levels of management, specialisation of the workforce and departmentalisation of the organisation is a tendency towards decentralisation — control by top level executives is reduced. The extent to which an organisation is decentralised or not can be seen as part of a continuum. It is not unusual during the lifetime of a firm for it to go through cycles of centralisation and decentralisation, which is probably true of Trusthouse Forte over the last 20 years. There are various factors that help to identify the extent of a firm's decentralisation.

1. Do lower level management make a larger number of decisions?
2. How important are these decisions? For instance, can they authorise capital expenditure?
3. Do these decisions affect several functions?
4. How frequently are these decisions checked by senior management?

It does not seem to matter if firms are centralised or decentralised, but decentralisation is likely to exist in the following circumstances:

1. An organisation is broken down into divisions by product departmentalisation.
2. The organisation has grown up through the merger of several firms.
3. There is a wide spread of geographical location of operations.
4. The organisation is very large.
5. The nature of the business activity is fast-moving and frequently changing.

There are also organisational benefits that accrue from a policy of decentralisation.

1. Strain on executives is reduced allowing them to fulfil their main roles of long-term planners and policy-makers.
2. Problems can be resolved more quickly by the manager on the spot, so that the firm can react rapidly to changes in the marketplace and demand for its product.
3. The morale of middle managers is improved.
4. The additional responsibility for middle managers is a good grounding for their potential promotion to an executive level.

However, there is some resistance to pursuing decentralisation at all costs for a number of reasons.

1. There is a loss of control over the whole enterprise.
2. It is possible for one division of an organisation to be operating to the detriment of another.
3. There may be an amount of duplication of effort particularly on the administrative and personnel side.
4. The decentralised organisation may be unable to take advantage of nationally or centrally negotiated contracts or agreements with such people as suppliers or trade unions.
5. Divisions of the firm may grow to guard their independence jealously and be reluctant to request the services of head office specialists and staff management.

As we shall see later in the chapter there is no clear indication as to which end of the continuum is desirable for the hotel and catering industry.

10.7 THEORIES OF ORGANISATION

So far we have been primarily concerned with fairly simple and practical aspects of organisation structure and design. As much as possible we have tried to avoid a particular theoretical stance, since a very great number of theories and approaches have been developed in this field. We shall briefly review the four major contributions to place what we have said so far in context and to enable us to go on to analyse organisations in the hotel and catering industry.

The earliest contribution to organisation theory is that developed by the school of scientific management. We have already considered some of the work of F.W. Taylor and Henri Fayol, two of the founding fathers of the movement. Their classical approach focused on the division of labour, proper lines of command, legitimate power and authority, standardisation and explicit rules and procedures. These characteristics also form the basis of Max Weber's concept of 'bureaucratic' organisation with its hierarchical and impersonal structures. Indeed most modern industrial concerns are based to some extent on these bureaucratic lines and even today rely quite heavily upon assumptions about the workforce such as a sense of duty, economic self-interest and hard work that Weber identified.

In the mid-1930s this classical approach was challenged by the human relations school of management, largely prompted by the work of Elton Mayo. He had shown that an organisation was more than just a set of individual 'man–machine systems', but was in fact a complex social system where people's hopes and fears had been largely ignored, where levels of productivity were established by the social norms of groups, where the non-economic rewards of friendship and interpersonal interaction were as important as remuneration and where the workforce was made up, not of individuals, but of many groups and sub-groups not identified by the formal organisation structure. This view has consequently been supported by much of the work done by behavioural scientists such as Maslow, Likert, McGregor and Herzberg whose work we have already considered. Of particular note is the work of Chris Argyris who argued that the psychological health of workers is essential to the organisation. He argued that the psychologically healthy individual will be 'predisposed towards relative independence, activeness, use of their important abilities and control over their immediate world'.[5] In his view this is 'not congruent with the requirements of formal organisation which tends to require agents to work in situations where they are dependent, passive, use few and unimportant abilities, etc.' It was at this stage that ideas of motivation, job satisfaction, group dynamics and participative leadership styles were introduced into organisations and it is this approach which is probably most frequently found in industry today.

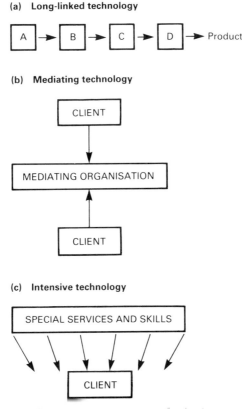

(a) **Long-linked technology**

A → B → C → D → Product

(b) **Mediating technology**

CLIENT

MEDIATING ORGANISATION

CLIENT

(c) **Intensive technology**

SPECIAL SERVICES AND SKILLS

CLIENT

Figure 10.4 *Thompson's three types of technology.*

A third approach to organisations is that of systems theory. Developed from biological research it analyses business organisations in a similar way to the examination of living organisms. As such it does not concern itself with whether or not the workforce is difficult to control or possible to control, rather the workforce is merely adaptive to and interactive with its environment. Thus effective organisation stems from the proper match of the human being and the environment.

One result of systems analysis is an emphasis that the best type of organisation structure depends upon or is contingent upon the type of environment. Within the same organisation one division may require a formal and rigid structure whilst in another part an open informal structure may work best. It is this contingency approach — the fourth and final approach to organisation theory — that we shall now consider. A great deal of work and research has gone into developing contingency models of organisation structure. In essence what has been done is to look at various aspects of organisation structure such as span of control, organisational levels, line and staff hierarchies, extent of centralisation, and to relate these to suitable organisational criteria such as output, job satisfaction, staff turnover, grievances, or lack of them and so on.

'The overwhelming conclusion was that there was no one best structure'.[6] Thus research moves to looking at the particular task undertaken by an organisation which might lead to identifying a specific suitable structure. For instance, Thompson[7] has identified three different technologies (see Fig. 10.4). The long link technology is typical of manufacturing industry using mass production techniques; the mediating technology describes organisations providing services of acting as a go-between between two parties such as estate agents, travel agents and transport firms; and the intensive technology describes organisations providing a wide variety of services such as a hotel.

This approach emphasises that organisations will differ according to their technology or what they do and attempts to provide a system of classifying these differences.

An alternative classification has been developed by Perrow[8] who emphasises the variability (number of exceptions) of inputs and materials, and the degree to which there are well established techniques to deal with these inputs (analysable v. unanalysable technology). (See Fig. 10.5.)

Technology	Exceptional cases	
	Few	Many
Unanalysable	Craft	Non-routine
Analysable	Routine	Engineering

Figure 10.5   *Perrow's classification of organisations.*

As the matrix shows, he identifies four types of technologies.

(a)   In craft industries one person makes the whole product in the same way each time, e.g. a chef.

(b)   In non-routine technology individuals have their own approach towards a large number of different tasks or problems. The duty manager in a hotel is in this sort of situation.

(c)   Routine technology is the typical mass production situation and an example from the hotel and catering industry would be a fast-food store.

(d)   The engineering technology does not refer solely to the manufacturing of products, merely to the fact that a clear approach is adopted to a wide variety of situations. An example here would be receptionists in a hotel who have a series of standardised procedures dealing with a variety of customers' bookings and registrations.

The implications for organisation structure supported by research[9] are that companies dealing with many exceptional cases must have greater flexibility and less hierarchical control, the more analysable the task the more control and close supervision is possible; so that in highly routine operations a classical approach may be appropriate.

A third well-known contingency theory is the analysis adopted by Joan Woodward[10] who identified three types of industrial firm. Process production is continuous manufacturing of highly standardised goods with long production runs which anticipate demand; unit or small batch production is the manufacture of customer built products according to demand and finally large batch production is midway between the other two, involving medium size runs, manufacturing some products to order and some in anticipation of demand. Figure 10.6 summarises the differences she found between the two extremes of technology.

	Process	Unit
Labour cost	Low	High
Decision-making	High level policy committees	Unilateral decision-maker
Levels of management	Many	Fairest
Shape	Tall	Flat
Span of control	Narrow	Large
Ratio of managers to employees	1:8	1:23

Figure 10.6   *Summary of organisation differences (after Woodward).*

The study by Burns and Stalker[11] was based on very similar ideas and dealt with an organisation's ability to cope with change. They identified two extremes of organisation; mechanistic with a rigidly prescribed managerial system, well-defined tasks and hierarchical arrangement rather like Weber's bureaucracy, and second, organic organisations which were more flexible, encouraged horizontal communication and allowed individual scope. They claim that the mechanistic organisation is suitable for stable conditions while the organic organisation is more suited to coping with uncertain environmental conditions.

Finally, Lawrence and Lorsch[12] also consider the extent to which an organisation is faced with a changing or a stable environment, but they analyse the internal structure of the organisation by the extent of its differentiation and integration. A highly differentiated organisation will be composed of many different types of people doing many different jobs in departments with different goals. For effective co-ordination and co-operation such an organisation must be integrated in some way by using such things as committees, flow charts and liaison officers. They suggest that organisations in highly unstable environments must adopt greater differentiation and hence integration.

10.8 ORGANISATION THEORY AND THE HOTEL AND CATERING INDUSTRY

The overwhelming evidence seems to suggest that much of the work that has been done so far has little or no application in the hotel and catering industry. Philip Nailon[13] attempts to answer the question 'To what extent do the organisations encountered in this industry correspond to the findings of the researchers and writers on management?'. His basic conclusion is that from Weber onwards, most theories have helped to provide an increased understanding of the industry, but that no one theory is applied in the industry or successfully suggests the 'ideal' structure. Boas Shamir[14] is particular critical of contingency models of organisations and he states 'the hotel organisation does not conform to any of the ideal types described by Thompson and Perrow'. He believes that most of the models, including all those we have mentioned so far, are far too simple to cope with the complexities of the hotel industry and he suggests that a more detailed identification of how organisations are structured within the constraints of their environment, task and technology is necessary.

Some aspects of hotel and catering operations have been identified in Chapter 1, but we emphasise four major areas, namely the heterogeneous and fluctuating nature of the demand; the conflict between the business side and the service nature of the operation (one concerned primarily with maintaining profitability and administrative convenience, the other concerned with caring for its guests); the highly differentiated nature of the hotel operations providing many different but interdependent products and services; and lastly the high status that customers in the industry hold and their capability of controlling the behaviour of staff so reducing control by management. Shamir summarises this by saying that 'the high dependence of hotels on their customers, the relative heterogeneity, unpredictability, sensitivity and reactivity of these customers, plus the diversified, personal and immediate nature of the services that have to be provided by hotels, all present hotels with two major demands — a demand for flexibility on the one hand and a demand for a high degree of control and co-ordination on the other.'

Based on what we know of the industry, the contingency theories we have examined can be used to make predictions about the way hotels should be organised. Burns and Stalker would suggest an organic structure to handle the many exceptions and respond to the differing pressures where tasks cannot be easily defined or controlled, and service is of a personal nature. Lawrence and Lorsch would propose a highly differentiated structure with a high need for integration and therefore the appearance of formal integrating mechanisms. Thompson would expect them to be differentiated in terms of the type of customer rather than by their various functions, with each department having a high degree of autonomy. Perrow would see hotels having many exceptions, but relatively established methods, which would lead to an adaptable but centralised structure.

On looking at organisation structures within hotels, we find an emphasis on a mechanistic or bureaucratic format, such as the classical kitchen brigade. This structure is based on tradition, with a breakdown of the operation into specialist occupational areas. It is also influenced by the need for a formal framework within which the uncertainty and instability of the guest input can be handled — all staff know their respective roles and positions and therefore the basis of their reactions to customers' requests. The structure is also effective in depersonalising the roles of the staff through the wearing of uniforms, the ritualised nature of much interaction and the effect of specialisation, which means that each member of staff serves a large number of customers. This will reduce the potential anxiety of customers and staff in the very personal nature of this replacement for their normal home environment. Reviewing our expectations from the contingency theories, hotel structures tend to be mechanistic and not organic as Burns and Stalker would suggest; they are highly differentiated as Lawrence and Lorsch might predict, but have few formal integrating mechanisms; they are organised by functions and not by customer, as Thompson would suggest; and with only a limited amount of the centralisation that Perrow would expect. This would seem to make it difficult for hotels to cope with the nature of their business (assuming that the contingency theories are valid) if it were not for the fact that underlying the formal facade of the organisation is an informal framework that makes operations easier. This includes the large percentage of communication which is verbal and direct (the telephone, and face-to-face interaction are the most widely used means of communication between departments); the ability of the hotel to respond to extra demand through the employment of casual staff or the redeployment of its live-in staff; and the small but significant number of staff who cross departmental boundaries, namely management trainees, receptionists who act as cashiers, and duty management.

10.9 DESIGNING THE CONSUMER SERVICE ORGANISATION

So far we have tended to suggest that not a great deal of thought has gone into organising hotel and catering operations and that there is no 'best' structure. However, at least one attempt has been made to describe what such a consumer service organisation structure should be like. We should point out that this approach is based on US business practice and tends to concern itself with the US food service industry. Sasser et al.[15] would suggest the following.

1. Because operations are usually explicit and easy to replicate they are subject to standardisation and detailed job descriptions thereby facilitating the staffing of units.
2. Because of the need for interaction with the public, staff must be employed on the basis of their interpersonal skills, so that the organisation should provide a 'hassle-free environment'.
3. The role of first-line management should be divided into two functions: the first leaves the manager with little discretion in decision making since it is the administration of standardised operating procedures outlined above; the second

demands a great deal of management expertise since it is the management of people who are often low skilled and highly mobile.

4. One consequence of the above is that organisation structure should have several levels with a narrow span of control and people managers at all but the highest levels.

5. Because standardisation reduces the opportunity for innovatory management, motivation should be derived from the opportunities for promotion and monetary incentives often in the form of bonuses for meeting or exceeding predetermined targets.

6. Because of the structures outlined above apart from people management all other functions such as finance, sales, marketing and purchasing can be totally centralised. This is seen to have advantages of cost savings and economies of scale.

Case example 10.3   McDonald's

In many respects, McDonald's, as the market leader in fast food in the UK is the prototypical example of a consumer service organisation. This case study can only deal with the firm very briefly, but a review of the catering press will provide many articles that help to illustrate this point. McDonald's is big business. By January 1984, they will have opened 135 fast food stores since 1976, each costing between £500 000 and £1 million. Their larger stores will serve over 20 000 customers a week and employ nearly 100 staff. And, in seven years of UK operation, McDonald's have never closed a single store through lack of turnover or low profitability.

The basis of this business success is control. Every aspect of the operation is considered in order to reduce costs, because of the low profit margin and the price-conscious nature of the market. For instance, fluorescent lights and air-conditioning units are timed to come on sequentially in each store to reduce energy usage, timers and thermostats monitor food production, clearly defined operational standards are laid down, staff are rostered to start and finish their shifts strictly according to forecasted demand and the financial management on a daily basis includes the analysis of each item sold, sales per operative, sales per till, average spend and so on. All pricing decisions are determined centrally, along with rates of pay, advertising and merchandising budgets and so on. Staff are employed on an above-average rate of pay and receive various bonuses often connected with sales output. They receive regular training sessions in-house, using detailed training manuals and video presentations developed at head office. Staff tend to move around within the store doing different jobs, but the basic organisation structure within the company is as shown in Fig. 10.7.

10.10 CONCLUSION

This chapter is very different from the other chapters in that it does not concentrate on people and their behaviour. It introduces the idea that there are many other factors that affect hotel and catering operations than just the workforce and the consumer — such factors as the size of the organisation, its location, its technology and so on. It also illustrates that the particular standpoint of this book which is broadly the 'human relations' approach, is (in terms of organisation theory) outmoded and old-fashioned. However, we leave it to the reader to decide the extent to which the things we have

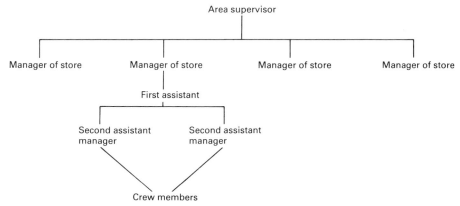

Figure 10.7 *Organisational chart from McDonald's.*

outlined contribute to our understanding of organisations. What must be emphasised is that organisations are changing all the time. The larger catering companies in the UK are notorious for their reorganisations which seem to occur almost every six months. Such reorganisations are usually prompted by people at or near the top of the hierarchy as they jostle for positional status and responsibility, but they obviously also have repercussions for all the people working for the company concerned. We suggest that you consider what the effect might be upon staff motivation, group effectiveness and interpersonal relationships in such dynamic and rapidly changing environments.

REFERENCES

1. Capey, J.G. & Carr, N.E. (1982) *People and Work Organizations*. Eastbourne: Holt, Rinehart and Winston.
2. Handy, C.B. (1976) *Understanding Organisations*. Harmondsworth: Penguin.
3. Woodward, J. (1965) *Industrial Organization: Theory and Practice*. Oxford: Oxford University Press.
4. Dyer, W. (1979) Caring and power, *California Management Review*.
5. Argyris, C. (1960) *Understanding Organisational Behaviour*. London: Tavistock.
6. Mitchell, T.R. (1982) *People in Organizations*. London: McGraw-Hill.
7. Thompson, J.D. (1967) *Organizations in Action*. London: McGraw-Hill.
8. Perrow, C. (1970) *Organisational Analysis*. London: Tavistock.
9. Magnusen, K.O. (1973) *Perspectives on Organizational Design*. New York: Columbia University Press.
10. Woodward, J. (1965) op. cit.
11. Burns, T. & Stalker, A.M. (1961) *The Management of Innovation*. London: Tavistock.
12. Lawrence, P.R. & Lorsch, J.W. *Organization and Environment*. Harvard: Harvard University Press.
13. Nailon, P. (1977) A theory of organisation in the hotel and catering industry. *HCIMA Journal*, **61**.
14. Shamir, B. (1978) Between bureaucracy and hospitality. *Journal of Management Studies*, 15.
15. Sasser, W.F. (1978) *Management of Service Operations*. Boston, M.A.: Allyn & Bacon.

11 The Consumer

I am a young executive. No cuffs than mine are cleaner;
I have a slimline briefcase and I use the firm's Cortina;
In every roadside hostelry from here to Burgess Hill
The maîtres d'hôtel all know me well and let me sign the bill

'Executive' by Sir John Betjeman [from *Collected Poems* with kind permission of John Murray (Publishers) Ltd]

OBJECTIVES: to identify the behaviour of consumers ... to describe those external and internal factors that affect consumer behaviour . . . to analyse the nature of the 'product' in the hotel and catering industry . . . to relate the human relations approach to influencing consumer behaviour

11.1 INTRODUCTION

THIS book recognises the fact that people, as workers and consumers, are fundamental to the hotel and catering industry. Until now, we have tended to look at aspects of people from the point of view of managing and organising the workforce and the role of human relations in making managers more effective. The reason for this is that by virtue of the relationship of employer–employee, the human relations approach has more direct implications on this aspect than can be applied to the vendor–customer relationship. But we cannot ignore the consumers and much of what we have discussed so far is generally relevant to the hotel guest or restaurant customer, for consumer study includes such issues as perception, motivation, decision-making and communication. What has to be made clear is that the major difference between a person who is a worker and those who are customers is the context in which they behave and not the way in which they behave. For instance, if we accept Maslow's concept of a motivation hierarchy, the type of factors that affect how hard a person works will be the same that affect which products they purchase.

11.2 A MODEL OF CONSUMER BEHAVIOUR

The human relations approach we have adopted throughout this book has been to examine and attempt to understand why people behave in the way that they do, and then to apply this knowledge to management principles. We therefore need to adopt

176

a model of consumer behaviour that will enlighten and inform. Much of the early work on the subject adopted what has been called the 'distributive approach' which did not examine the process through which a consumer went, merely the outcome of this process and possible reasons for the behaviour: for instance, people who buy Porsches will be young, rich and single. Modern research has developed a more integrated and comprehensive approach that is centred in the 'decision process' and various experts have developed models, such as Nicosia, Howard-Sleth and the consumer decision process model of Engel, Blackwell and Kollat (see Fig. 11.1). We have adopted the latter model as a basis for discussion due to the comprehensive nature of the model, and the emphasis it places on the decision-making process and some influences in that process that we have discussed in previous chapters.

The model shows two main factors affecting consumer choice. The first of these is consumers' information about the products available and their own experience. Information is derived from the media in various forms, such as marketing and advertising, to which the consumers are exposed and is processed through gaining their attention into a place in the consumer's memory. Experience is derived from previous purchase decisions. These two aspects tend to influence the early stages of the consumer decision-making process. The second major factor is consumers themselves, the environmental influences upon them and their internal make-up, and it is these with which we shall be particularly concerned.

Consumer decision-making

The model is based around the concept of making a choice, i.e. to buy a particular product. Consumers follow five stages (similar to those discussed in Chapter 8).

Problem recognition

A problem for consumers exists when they perceive a difference between what they would *like* to have and what they *actually* have. This may result from internal stimulation in order to satisfy a basic need, for example hunger will cause a person to purchase food. Or the stimulation may be caused externally by the person receiving information that suggests they have a need to satisfy, as for instance passing an ice-cream van that stimulates the feeling of 'hunger' and hence a purchase. But it must be understood that not every problem that is recognised will be satisfied if only because of circumstances such as not having enough money.

Search

Once the problem is established, the consumer 'searches' for information to establish if they have all the information they need before making a purchase. This may just necessitate thinking, but it may also involve going to look around showrooms, reading catalogues, talking to sales staff and so on. Many of our purchase decisions are routine and based on habit, either due to established brand loyalty or due to the relative low cost of a purchase. In these cases, the search and process stages are unnecessary since

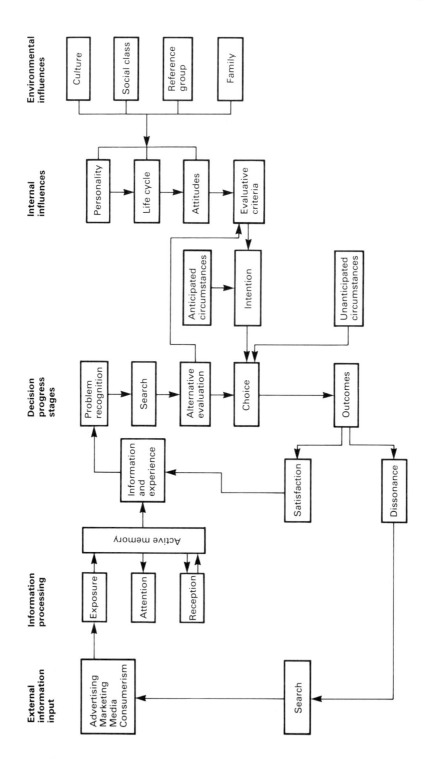

for a regularly bought product there is no need to go over the same ground each time once it has been established that the particular product, such as Signal toothpaste, the *Telegraph* newspaper on McDonald's hamburger, is the one preferred.

Alternative evaluation

At this stage consumers look around for the alternatives and are strongly influenced by external and internal drives and by the information about the world and its products that they have processed. We shall be examining these influences in more detail later in this chapter.

Choice

The logical outcome of evaluating is to make a choice and to purchase a particular product (or not) and whom to buy it from. Even at this stage, however, a sudden change in circumstances can prevent actual purchase, and it may have to be deferred to a later date.

Outcome

Once purchased, the product will result in satisfaction or dissonance both of which will have implications for further decision-making.

11.3 ENVIRONMENTAL INFLUENCES ON CONSUMER BEHAVIOUR

As we have seen, individuals' behaviour depends partly on the environment in which they live. With reference to consumerism, we can identify four groups that will affect a person's purchasing and consumption activities.

(a) Culture

Culture is the common means and procedures adopted by a large group of people that enable them to cope with the environment in which they live. This can be achieved through abstract concepts such as shared values, organised religion, accepted attitudes and common personality types or through the artifacts of a culture, those objects that the culture uses to meet its various needs such as tools, communication media and clothing. It is generally agreed that understanding consumer behaviour is greatly helped by understanding the fundamental characteristics of such cultures. Five cultural dimensions can be identified.

Transmission

Culture is passed on or transmitted from one generation to the next, primarily through the family but also through other groups and institutions such as schools, churches, the neighbourhood and media. This does not mean to say that each successive generation will be identical to its predecessors, but that culturally the similarities between each generation will be much greater than the changes that can be seen.

Adaptation

In the past cultural change was very slow, but recently the change and evolution of cultures has been considerably accelerated by advanced communication techniques and technological developments.

Acquisition

Culture is learned throughout life, but particularly when young. This provides people with a reference framework that enables them to respond appropriately to given circumstances; for instance, someone brought up in an Islamic society or a teetotal family is likely to refrain from consuming alcohol.

Gratification

One of the most important functions of culture is to satisfy the needs of those people who belong to that particular culture. Those beliefs and habits that no longer serve the common need will fade and new trends will evolve. This is particularly true of consummer items. For instance in ninteenth-century Britain, oysters and stout were very popular; their modern equivalent might be hamburgers and lager.

Participation

The notable thing about culture is that a very large number of people hold the same views and exhibit the same behaviour patterns as each other. In particular our culture will affect how we get along with others, what we eat and drink, how we dress and how we earn a living.

However, within these large societies, there also exist sub-groups or subcultures, that may have a greater or lesser impact upon the individual than the main cultural influences. Such subcultures can be based on clearly identifiable characteristics such as nationality (some British towns have large communities of Polish immigrants or Irish nationals); religion (likewise Orthodox Jews, Baptists, Presbyterians and so on tend to live in specific localities); geographical (clearly in England each part of the country has its own identity, notably Yorkshire and Cornwall); and race (which results in clear subcultures of communities with West Indian, Asian and Chinese backgrounds).

(b) Social class

The 'class system' has for many years been seen as a 'bad thing' and many people believe that we should move towards creating a classless society. Others are equally convinced that there will always be those that have and those that have not, so that a class structure of some sort is inevitable. Whatever the arguments for and against class, it is apparent at the moment that consumer behaviour is affected by a person's perceived position in the class structure, notably with regard to the quality and style of clothes worn, the type of house lived in, the nature of leisure activities, attitude towards purchasing on credit, where people shop and how long they spend on the 'search' activity of the purchasing process. There are many ways that a person's class position may be established, but the usual indicators are occupation, prestige, income and wealth. In Britain the Government produces statistics based on the socioeconomic groupings as shown in Table 11.1.

Table 11.1   *Socioeconomic groups in Britain*

Group	Examples of the group
A	Higher managerial, administrative or professional
B	Intermediate managerial, administrative or professional
C1	Supervisory, clerical, junior managerial or professional
C2	Skilled manual workers
D	Semi-skilled and unskilled manual workers
E	State pensioners, widows, casual and lowest-grade earners, unemployed

Of importance in Britain is the fact that fundamental changes in society are gradually affecting this socioeconomic breakdown: these include the increasing economic power of women; a progressively older population profile; the shift from manufacturing industries to service industries; the growth of leisure time; and an increase in the time spent on education.

(c) Social groups

We have already examined groups in some detail in Chapter 7, and how they are formed and interact, and our definition of a group is valid in terms of consumer behaviour. However, from a consumer behaviour perspective, groups have three main implications.

Socialisation

Membership of a group tends to result in the individual adopting the known behaviour patterns of the group. This process is called socialisation and is particularly important in developing people's attitudes.

Group norms

As well as influencing attitudes, the group also causes individuals to behave according to certain 'rules', either explicitly or implicitly as illustrated on p.112.

Self-concept

Thirdly, the group will influence the individual's perception of themselves and those around them.

A major problem, however, results from the fact that a consumer is likely to belong to more than one group which has a greater or lesser effect upon consumer behaviour. Groups that are influential in affecting purchasing decisions are called 'reference groups'. At the same time there are products that are purchased with little or no influence from reference groups at all. For instance, research[1] has found that products such as cars, cigarettes and beer are strongly influenced by reference groups, whereas consumers make individual choices with regard to soup, canned peaches and radios.

(d) Family

In most societies, individuals are cared for and nurtured by the 'family' which in simple terms comprises father and mother and offspring who live together. This very special 'group' has quite obviously a tremendous impact upon individuals' personalities, their evaluative criteria and attitudes, and probably is far more important than the larger social systems discussed so far of culture, subculture, social class and reference groups. From a marketing point of view, the family is often seen as a unit which goes through a similar, though more complex, decision-making process to that of individuals.

In practice, however, it has been found that usually one member of the family tends to make the consumer decisions; this is usually the husband in male-dominated cultures, but need not be so, as the product being purchased will also have an effect on the family's strategy for selection. Thus Davis and Rigaux[2] found that insurance and cars for the family were predominantly purchased by the husbands; whereas wives tended to decide what cleaning products or food to purchase. Some products the couple purchased together, notably holidays and housing; and lastly, either spouse would make decisions about alcoholic beverages or garden tools. It is also now recognised that other members of the family, i.e. the children, may also influence adult choices. US research has shown that in 80 per cent of cases where families chose to eat in a fast-food store, children had played some part in the original idea to eat out, in discussing alternative places to do so and selecting the preferred unit.[3]

11.4 INTERNAL FACTORS AFFECTING CONSUMER BEHAVIOUR

As well as those four environmental aspects which can influence the behaviour of a consumer, there are four aspects of the consumers themselves we need to be familiar with to have a clearer indication of how they make their purchase decisions.

(a) Personality

As we have seen there are many different views of personality, but we are particularly concerned that 'personality is a consistent pattern of response to external stimuli'.[4] The Freudian view has greatly influenced research into consumer motivation which is supposedly unconscious and based almost exclusively on sexual drive, so that men might be said to purchase fast cars as a substitute mistress or smoke pungent cigars to reinforce their masculinity. More recently, as a reaction to these Freudian hypotheses, social psychologists reject the theory that behaviour is biologically determined and relate personality to social variables, based on such factors as the striving for superiority, freedom from loneliness, security, satisfying human relationship and coping with anxiety. Some have suggested that three personality types can be identified in consumer terms; the complaint person wants to be appreciated, wanted, loved and included in the activities of others; the aggressive person seeks success, prestige and the admiration of others; and the detached person seeks freedom from obligations, independence and self-sufficiency. This has had some significance with how to market certain products, aftershave, for instance. The compliant male will wear any aftershave, the aggressive male will purchase the most distinctive brand and the detached male will not use aftershave at all. Lastly, the trait-factor theory discussed on p.23 has also been used to look into consumer behaviour, to attempt to find a link between certain personality types and assorted consumer behaviours such as purchase, risk-taking, attitude change, media choice, product choice and so on. Although consumer analysts would like to think that consumption patterns are an expression of a consumer's personality, research and personality testing do not produce any evidence that there is any link between personality and brand selection, although in some cases personality will be reflected in the broad category of product purchases.

(b) Life style

Life style refers to the patterns in which people live and spend money and time. There is a great deal of overlap here as explained by Block and Roering (op. cit.): 'life styles are learned by individuals as the result of many influences such as culture, social class, reference groups and the family. More specifically life styles are derivatives of consumers' personal values systems and personalities'. This influence on consumer purchases is usually investigated by a questionnaire similar to a Likert scale that asks people to strongly agree, agree, disagree, strongly disagree, or express no opinion about their activities, interests and opinions.

(c) Attitudes

Most people have an intuitive understanding of what an attitude is. However, in the area of consumer behaviour, a great deal of research and theorising has gone into investigating why people hold attitudes and several quite complex models are suggested, including the classic psychological model (see p.27), multi-attribute model, expectancy-value model, attribute adequacy model and so on. We cannot here discuss these in detail, but we shall look at how marketing strategies attempt to change consumer attitudes. Katz has suggested that attitudes have four functions.

1. Adjustment — people tend to adapt their attitudes to reflect the behaviour of friends and associates.
2. Ego-defensive — attitudes protect people from damaging their egos.
3. Value expressive — such attitudes show other people the values held by the individual.
4. Knowledge — attitudes provide consistency and stability in the way an individual perceives the world.

These functions are very closely related to self-concept so that there is a tendency for attitudes to be consistent over time, thereby rejecting any information that is inconsistent. Marketing attempts to change attitudes by means such as having a credible communicator, allowing intelligent consumers to make up their own mind by advertising in an unstructured way, using humour to gain attention and reduce the ego-defensiveness of consumers, and repeating the message often.

Task 11.1

Attempt to identify television adverts that as part of their approach use the ideas mentioned above.

(d) Evaluation criteria

It has been found that various consumer groups use substantially different criteria in assessing any given product. Such evaluative criteria are a group of features or performance characteristics that are valued by the consumer. Such criteria arise out of accumulating information and experience, and personal motives, although these in turn are shaped by an individual's personality, life style and cultural norms.

Task 11.2

Ask three different 'types' of consumer, such as teenager, young married person and a middle-aged person, on what basis they choose a restaurant.

Case example 11.1   Chinese takeaways

A survey of 30 Chinese takeaways in five major cities in the north of England sampled 304 customers. The results of the survey were analysed and broken down according to the age of the buyers (See Table 11.2).
    There are limitations affecting the results, but the most significant point is that age is obviously not the most appropriate means of analysing the market segment attracted to Chinese takeaways. It may well be that an analysis according to occupation, level of income, family status, life style or even attitudes would have shown up the importance of different factors affecting consumer choice of these products.

| Table 11.2 *Comparison of factors emerging for the three buyers' age groups investigated.*

Buyers' age groups	Factor A	Factor B	Factor C	Factor D
Age group I (16 to 29 years old)	Convenience of shop location (28.4%)	Gastronomy (17.7%)	Convenient to serve (12.7%)	Preservability for later consumption (9.8%)
Age group II (30 to 44 years old)	Convenience of shop location (25.9%)	Gastronomy (14.6%)	Convenient to serve (12.4%)	Good quality product (11.0%)
Age group III	Convenience of shop location (29.0%)	Gastronomy (14.6%)	Good quality product(s) (12.2%)	Adequate for serving (7.8%)

N = 304 respondents

Note: The percentages in brackets represent the relative importance attached to the various factors, as perceived by the different segments of customers of Chinese takeaway foods.

Source: HCIMA Journal, August 1979

11.5 IMPLICATIONS FOR SELLING TO THE CONSUMER

The purpose of advertising, promotion, and active selling is to stimulate the problem identification stage of consumer decision making and influence the search and evaluative stages. In order to do this effectively the product must be advertised or promoted to the appropriate group of consumers. This approach is called market segmentation — 'the subdividing of a market into distinct and increasingly homogeneous subgroups of customers, where any group can conceivably be selected as a target market to be met with a distinct marketing mix'.[5] Thus holidays are increasingly being sold to specific market segments — single people under 30, married couples with children, and married couples with grown-up children.

Task 11.3

Try to think of two or three holiday or travel firms that specifically cater for each of these three subgroups.

The basis on which segmentation takes place may be on any one factor or combination of factors described previously, although social class or socioeconomic factors are particularly influential, not least in determining which media to use to reach the appropriate market. Increasingly, however, segmentation is determined by 'life style' identifying groups who behave in a broadly consistent manner, have shared interests, share certain values and opinions and are probably coincident demographically.[6] Research has also gone into the use of personality as a marketing tool. Much of the dissatisfaction with personality information resulted from the use of standardised inventories unrelated to consumer behaviour. This had led to the construction of 'consumption-related personality inventories' which are designed to identify those traits of value to the marketing expert.

As well as identifying the consumer more specifically, consumer research has also considered the role of perception in the purchase decision. Much of the advertising and selling that takes place attempts to modify the consumer's perception of the product in a variety of ways. For instance, packaging is important — packets are designed to appear as if they contain more than they actually do and printed in an attractive way. Compare the packaging of a takeaway meal from a typical Indian restaurant with that from a fast-food store. Despite the fact that the fast-food meal is cheaper, its packaging is much more distinctive and expensive looking. Likewise, the product size is often not made clear to prevent close comparisons with similar products, so that, for instance, hamburgers are 'regular' and 'giant'. Interestingly, the licensed trade is one of the few instances where the product must be sold in specified sizes laid down by Parliament; most other industries are not subject to such regulations. Colour is another example of modifying consumers' attitude through perception. In foodstuffs, for instance, yellow colouring has been added to margarine to make it appear more like butter and the red colour of meat can be enhanced by the use of special lighting.

11.6 IMPLICATIONS FOR THE HOTEL AND CATERING INDUSTRY

This discussion of consumer behaviour has been only an outline of current thinking on the subject and heavily emphasises the contribution of the behavioural sciences to understanding the purchase decision-making process. For a fuller exposition of marketing techniques in the industry there are many alternative sources. However, we will illustrate the sort of contribution that our approach can make by looking at two specific instances of the consumer process — selecting a restaurant to eat out at and the influence of consumers in the market positioning strategy of hotels and hospitality firms.

The effect on consumer choice of restaurant advertising

There are many different types of restaurant operating in the non-captive market sector of the industry. Powers[7] identifies at least 16 distinct styles of US restaurants ranging from haute cuisine and nightclub to low-price steak house and fast food, most of which have their equivalent in the United Kingdom. For most of these advertising is particularly important since a restaurant meal is an 'experience good', that is to say consumers have no way of telling whether the meal meets their requirements until they have actually experienced it. It is generally accepted that market segmentation on the basis of such factors as sex, age, income and so on, will tend to determine the general type of restaurant a consumer will choose to eat in. What is needed is a model of how consumers choose between restaurants of a similar type and from this one can identify how best to advertise a particular restaurant. Robert Lewis believes that 'benefit segmentation' will do just this.[8] The difficulty arises when attempting to measure and compare such elusive qualities as consumers' perceptions and intentions, and the extent to which an attribute of the restaurant is seen to provide a benefit to customers.

The research by Lewis attempts to answer three questions: What is the joint effect of the benefits sought by the consumer? How does the relative importance of these benefits vary by restaurant type? How do consumers process advertising information in selecting a restaurant? He identified five main variables — food quality, menu variety, price, atmosphere, and convenience — that tended to be used by restaurants to advertise their product and he sought to establish their relative importance with three distinct restaurant types — family/popular (casual, relatively fast service, high turn-over); atmosphere (distinct theme, slightly up-market); gourmet (unhurried service, formal style and high-class menu).

Task 11.4

From our brief description of these three types of restaurants suggest examples that might be found in Britain. Note that the models proposed by Lewis may not apply to consumers in Britain, although there is no evidence to suggest that they do not.

From the detailed analysis of these findings, Lewis tentatively proposed three models of consumer choice.

Conjunctive model

This view of consumer behaviour rates all the factors affecting choice more or less equally. A restaurant must meet or exceed a minimum standard in each of these areas to attract custom. Consumers using family/popular restaurants are predicted to behave in this way. Therefore restaurateurs in this sector must ensure that all factors are well balanced and no single factor particularly promoted.

Compensatory expectancy value model

The consumer in this model weighs up the good points and the bad points about a number of restaurants and selects that restaurant where the good points most outweigh the bad. In the case of atmosphere, consumers regard wide menu variety as a negative influence so that this must be compensated for by the other factors. The restaurateur must therefore advertise what the consumer perceives as the restaurant's good points.

Disjunctive model

In this case, the consumer chooses between restaurants on the basis of only one or two particular attributes. Thus in the case of gourmet restaurants quality of the food and to a lesser extent menu variety are the most significant factors affecting choice. The best way to advertise a gourmet restaurant then, is to stress how good the food is and the wide choice of dishes available.

If we look back at our model of consumer behaviour (Fig. 11.1) what we are suggesting is that all those factors on the right-hand side of the decision-making process (social class, personality and life style) will tend to determine the general style of restaurant a consumer chooses. Those factors on the left-hand side (the information displayed through the media, its acceptance and retention) will influence the specific choice of restaurant within the appropriate category. What Lewis is saying is that catching the consumer's attention and ensuring retention are more likely if the true benefits, as perceived by the consumer, are advertised.

Creating a favourable image for a hotel

The following is adapted from another article by Lewis[9] that looks at images and image-making in the hotel industry. In order to know how to market a hotel effectively an image must be created which accords with consumers' perceptions of the attributes of the hotel when compared with other hotels. These perceptions may be radically different from the property's physical characteristics and this distinction is especially important to hotel marketers. The purchase decision for services is affected by several factors.

1. The hotel product (i.e. services) is intangible; it is often difficult to determine which attributes are important to consumers' purchase decisions. Indeed the consumers themselves, since they cannot experience the service before making the decision, find it difficult to decide which hotel to use.
2. Since every hotel offers a wide range of services the consumers' risk in the purchase decision is high.
3. The service provided is easily duplicated by competing hotels so that consumers cannot always distinguish between them.

Thus consumers compare intangible services only subjectively, finding it difficult to assign a monetary value and consuming them only passively. However, whereas the impact of tangible products is generally short term, services generally have a long-term cognitive and affective impact on consumer perception. Consumers will not buy a service, no matter what its intangible attributes are, until a certain minimum threshold of tangible attributes has been reached. In fact, a halo effect is possible: the existence of certain tangible characteristics is assumed to signify that a certain level of quality (an abstraction) also exists. To emphasise the concrete in advertising is to fail to differentiate oneself from one's competitors, while to compound the abstraction is to dilute the reality one wishes to represent. Thus hotel marketers should focus on enhancing and differentiating the unit's abstract realities through the manipulation of tangible clues.

In a later article Lewis suggests that a similar analysis is applicable to other sectors of the hospitality industry.

Task 11.5

From the advertising slogans below select those which you believe accord with Lewis's ideas. Identify the tangible benefit being sold and the image being created.
(a) 'Yours faithfully': a slogan used by Trusthouse Forte.
(b) 'Southern Sun Hotels — you can feel the warmth': a slogan used by a South African hotel company.
(c) 'Nothing tops the QE2': advertisement for business people going to New York.

(d) 'Wimpy is the home of the hamburger — the greatest burger under the bun': fast food chain advertisement.
(e) 'Malaysian Airways — we'll treat you like gold': airline advertisement.

11.7 CONCLUSION

This chapter has attempted to show that understanding consumer behaviour contributes greatly to the efficient management of hotel and catering operations. It identifies what motivates consumers, both consciously and sub-consciously, and attempts to show how their decision-making processes can be influenced. The extent to which the hotel and catering industry has been effective in this is very much a matter of opinion. John Burgess argues that the UK hotel sector has for the last 100 years tended to reflect the culture of the late nineteenth century, when the prevalent view of service was to ritualise and formalise the event, reduce interpersonal behaviour and create a subordinate status for staff. He goes on to say that 'organisations which now wish to reflect current society expectations and introduce hospitality must tackle established cultural traditions'.[10] He suggests that it is much more acceptable today for closer interpersonal interaction, as we have emphasised throughout this book, and he suggests that managers must become less concerned with administrative detail and start to perform a more 'public host role'. In many respects for everyone working in the industry there is the paradox that customers or consumers are referred to as 'guests' but not treated like them. Mr Smith is No. 120 according to his room number, Mr Jones and Mr Brown are the ICI contingent according to whom they work for. The industry is concerned with providing a service, but plays down the fact that its real purpose is to make a profit. We advocate by developing social and interpersonal skills much of the hospitality and service element can be put back into the industry, at no extra cost, but that guests' potential satisfaction and hence profitability will be greatly enhanced.

REFERENCES

1. Davis, H.L. & Rigaux, B.P. (1974) Perceptions of marital roles in decision process. *Journal of Consumer Reaearch*, **1**.
2. Group influence in marketing and public relationships. (1956) Foundation for Research on Human Behaviour.
3. Block, C. & Roering, J. (1979) *Essentials of Consumer Behaviour*. Hinsdale, IL: Dryden Press.
4. Soganzic, A. (1977) Family decision-making: husband, wife and children. *Advances in Consumer Research*, **4**.
5. Cannon, T. (1980) *Basic Marketing*. Eastbourne: Holt, Rinehart and Winston.
6. Kotler, P. (1980) *Marketing Management*. London: Prentice Hall.
7. Powers, T.F. Food service in 1985. *Cornell HRA Quarterly*.
8. Lewis, R.C. (1980) Benefit segmentation for restaurant advertising that works. *Cornell HRA Quarterly*.
9. Lewis, R.C. (1982) Positioning analysis for hospitality firms. *Hospitality Management*, 1 (2).
10. Burgess, J. (1982) Perspectives in attitude change and hospitality. In *International Hospitality Management*, 1(1).

12 The Management of Human Relations

They bring me roast, they bring me boiled,
But all in vain they woo me;
The waiters softly mutter 'foiled!'
The chef, poor man, looks gloomy.

P.G. Wodehouse

OBJECTIVES: to provide instances of the contribution of the behavioural sciences to the hotel and catering industry . . . to outline the necessity of an integrated approach to human relations

Introduction

THIS book is not about personnel management in the hotel and catering industry. It does not discuss in any detail the nature of personnel work and the techniques applied to personnel functions. That is not to say, however, that this book is not of special value to personnel managers for, as these case studies tend to indicate, when management have a staff problem they call in the personnel experts. This is because such problems are not seen as human relations problems, for which all management staff should be responsible, but as problems with training, job satisfaction, customer–employee relations and so on. This book should go some way towards identifying the role that all managers have in getting the best out of staff, both individually and collectively. Although many of the case studies clearly identify the personnel function, at least one shows that this function is unnecessary if managers are all skilled in interpersonal behaviour and the five functions of management identified in Chapter 9.

These case studies have a two-fold purpose. First, they are concerned with people, both staff and customers, showing a wide variety of problems and possible solutions to those problems. But they are not 'perfect' case studies in that they have been specifically written for this book to test understanding or illustrate particular points. They are in the main real-life, practical accounts of more or less everyday occurrences and procedures in the hotel and catering industry. The solutions adopted and advocated in the studies are not 'perfect' either, but at least they have the merit of satisfying the requirements of the people concerned at that moment in time. The second purpose then of the studies is to give you the opportunity to apply what you have learnt so far to such everyday problems and to critically evaluate the effectiveness of policies adopted in a wide range of establishments. In each instance there is a brief introduction to the study, reference is made to the original work from which the study was drawn, and then during and at the end of the study questions related to specific aspects of human relations are asked.

Case example 12.1   Two approaches to reducing high staff turnover

The case study compares suggestions for reducing staff turnover levels of 200 to 300 per cent in fast-food restaurants in the UK with the approach to 'supervisory turnover of 64 per cent in fast-food style restaurants in North America'.

Finding and keeping staff[1]

High employee turnover is created by improper hiring and training. Keeping your employee turnover to a minimum begins at the selection stage.

It starts in fact from the advertisement for staff. A handwritten notice stuck on the window saying 'Help Wanted' does not give an impression of a professional company. A magazine or newspaper advertisement creates a better impression, and therefore attracts better people.

When the employee arrives for the interview she or he should not be kept waiting for 15 minutes while the manager dashes around. The manager should plan and prepare for the interview.

When interviewing it is important to look for these ten basic qualities: availability, punctuality, wages, appearance and hygiene, physical ability, initiative, team spirit, willingness to be trained, honesty, attitude.

A little pre-planning helps eliminate impulsive hiring, and can help you to hire the right people for your restaurant. Having taken care to recruit the correct people it is important to ensure that all employees are properly trained.

Good managers will face their responsibilities and train the employees that work in their restaurants. They will make them feel involved in the operation and its success. They will also ensure good communications between all management and staff.

All successful members of a restaurant management team must be able to train their hourly employees.

Training involves people — that means managers *and* employees. A feeling of empathy, understanding and co-operation must filter down from the manager, and a feeling of respect, loyalty and co-operation must filter up from the employees.

A training program is only as good as managers make it. If they do not believe in it or enforce it, they cannot expect employees to believe in it and follow it.

Criticism is only one side of the coin, praise is the other. The manager must know how to offer both, since one is as necessary as the other if training is to be successful.

It is never safe to assume that any employee is trained when hired, even if they have previous experience in food service. All managers have, or should have, their own systems for work, and each new employee should be trained to follow these systems, unlearning if necessary previous work patterns.

The natural fast-food employee is a myth. While it is certainly true that some people, by virtue of their personalities and attitudes, adapt themselves more easily to food service than others, basic training in various methods and procedures is vital in presenting a uniform image by all employees to the customers. Training is managers' responsibility: they may delegate portions of the training to someone else, but the end results are a combination of what managers do and what they have trained others to do.

A key area of training is, of course, motivation. In fact you cannot motivate anybody. All a manager can do is create an atmosphere in which people can motivate themselves. This is sometimes easier said than done, but it must be achieved in order to gain good results in the end.

How can you do it?

1. Make coming to work a pleasure so your people can enjoy it.
2. Develop a trust in your people. Let them know you expect a good job.
3. Keep your standards constant.

It is important to build the will to work. Create a desire to do a good job — the first time! Teach your staff the importance of the job at hand in relation to the total picture. Always reward people for a job well done — even if only with a thank you.

It is very important for the manager to set an example; a self-motivated manager sets the pace. Encourage people to take a pride in their work, however mundane the task. Try and make them want to be the best in the company.

It is crucial to set realistic goals for your staff. High goals provide a challenge. Low goals are reached too soon and lose their excitement. Unreasonable goals discourage any effort at all!

Avoid these demotivations:
1. Never criticise one employee in front of another.
2. Never belittle an employee — nobody likes to think someone regards them as 'stupid'.
3. Never play 'favourites'.
4. Never show up an employee — this takes away dignity and self-respect.
5. Never lower your personal standards.

If you use these basics to increase motivation you will have employees who will assume greater responsibilities, work with greater enthusiasm and will correct their own mistakes.

It has been discovered that a programme of 'job enrichment' can aid motivation.

For example, a dishwasher who is given the responsibility for ordering the supplies he or she needs, and documenting the costs, watches the costs of cleaning materials much better than one who is just supplied with cleaning materials as they run out.

Everyone in the food service business wants to increase productivity. Whilst the significance of staff training cannot be overstated, the layout of the restaurant also plays a key role in keeping productivity levels up. Correct working levels, uncramped working areas and efficient lighting are all important.

Distances between heavily used equipment such as freezer to fryer should be kept to a minimum. Employees should have everything they need at their fingertips. Crossover should be avoided whenever possible.

In the customer areas there should be enough space to eliminate bottlenecks that can hamper speed of service.

As far as equipment is concerned the major innovations of the past few years such as chain driven broilers, high production coffee machines, self-filtering fryers, computerised fryers, portion control beverage dispensers and front-of-the-house minicomputers have all been designed to increase productivity.

But, remember that rundown, broken equipment does nothing to increase productivity. It has the reverse effect.

You cannot expect an employee to be motivated while trying to do a job on ineffective equipment.

Foodex slows revolving door turnover

Dr George Bryniawsky, Vice-President Human Resources at Foodex Inc. says, 'Our training is geared to increase the tenure of our employees so that they'll be able to cope with the demands of personal and professional decision-making. We don't kid ourselves that every part-time staff member will want to spend his or her life in the food service industry. We do, however, offer our people alternatives. If you want a career in this industry, we'll train and develop you. If you just want a job in this industry, we'll train you for that job. We don't put a gun to people's heads.'

The human element has a high profile in Foodex operations and unlike some of the hamburger chains, where all the food is timed or computer con-trolled, the decision-making must be the responsibility of the individual. A broilerman, for example, may be cooking 40 different orders on the same grill, with four different cuts of meat and all to be cooked to different specifi-cations.

Training is an on-going process at Foodex and begins from the moment a staff member is hired. The first step is the Hourly Employee Training Pro-gram, which begins with an orientation of the new employee to either Frank Vetere's or Ponderosa Steak House operations. Employees are gradually introduced to different work stations and an attempt is made to reinforce previously-learned skills. Each location is provided with an audiovisual pres-entation on each work station and employee progress is monitored through quizzes and station evaluations. Management at each location is respon-sible for training of hourly workers, while assistance can be sought from the training department whenever necessary.

Next step is the Prep Cook Certificate Program (PCCP) at Vetere's, and the Broiler Certification Program at Ponderosa. The PCCP is designed for food preparation personnel and cooks. Sanitation, safety, receiving, storage and food preparation are dealt with in a 96-hour program conducted by the executive manager from information in the Vetere's Operations Manual. The Broiler Certification Program, similarly, is conducted by the executive man-ager for the food preparation personnel and broiler cooks. Again, 96 hours of instruction cover such subjects as meat rotation, equipment maintenance, sanitation, receiving, storage and food preparation. On completion of the program, a certificate is granted.

These programs are held in conjunction with community colleges. 'We've been co-operating very solidly with the community colleges. I think we were one of the main proponents of the George Brown College supervisory train-ing program. In fact, we held the graduation for them at one of our restaur-ants.'

At Vetere's, waiters and waitresses take a three-hour seminar 'It's up to me', which is designed to improve sales and customer service skills. The program combines role-playing, films, workshops and lectures.

On completion of the PCCP or Broiler Certification Program, employees can apply for the next step on their way to a career with Foodex — the Key Personnel Program. This assumes that they know the company policies and procedures on each and every station of the restaurant and have demonstrated proficiency in such things as ordering, customer relations, training and dealing with customer complaints. Candidates for key employee status must pass what Bryniawski says is a stiff exam. Once the employee has passed, he or she will sit on an advisory committee to management and receive a salary adjustment.

Once they have been recognised as key personnel, employees may be selected by management to go through the Swing Managers Training Program. This is an introduction to the duties and responsibilities of a manager and deals with customer service, quality assurance and opening and closing procedures. Swing managers must qualify by completing an exam and evaluation from their manager. Once certified, the employees operate as a swing manager until such time as they are ready to become managers. If accepted, the employee enters a program called FIRST (Foodex Individual Restaurant Supervisory Training) which is a 90-day program of on-the-job training at regional offices.

At the regional offices, new assistant managers share experiences, discuss and solve problems and test new ideas while under the direction of a qualified instructor. The bill of fare includes video tapes, sound/slide programs, role playing, problem-solving, lectures, workshops, discussion groups, and structured experiences. On-the-job training allows the new assistant manager to apply new skills and ideas.

Up to this point, the employee has not been exposed to any theory — it has all been practical, job-oriented instruction. Six months after passing FIRST, the assistant manager returns to the regional office to participate in another program labelled 'FAST' (Foodex Advanced Skills Training). FAST is all theory and held in-classroom. It teaches management information exclusively and begins with leadership and time management.

'We look at the individual to establish his style of leadership,' says Bryniawsky, 'Why does he function the way he functions? And, with classroom discussion, the individual begins to find out about himself. They undergo training on leadership, power, motivation, problem-solving, employee selection, staff training, communications, employee relations, time management and decision-making. The average age of incoming managers is about 23.'

Training is a fact of life at Foodex and fits nicely with the chain's day-to-day operations. The company has taken a professional approach to development of its human resources and Bryniawsky has been rewarded with turnover figures that are better than he hoped for.

Question 12.1(a)

Compare the approach to interviewing here with that suggested in Chapter 9. What is the basic difference between this approach and that which we advocated?

Question 12.1(b)

Does Kubarycz tend towards Pell's or Boella's viewpoint with regard to social skills training? (See Chapter 6.)

Compare the above approach to that reported by Dan Wilton.[2]

Question 12.1(c)

Decide which of those motivation theories outlined in Chapter 4 Foodex appears to believe in.

Question 12.1(d)

Would you say that Foodex is an example of scientific management, the human relations school or of the systems approach?

Question 12.1(e)

Identify statements in both case studies that advocate

(a) Ad hoc training.
(b) On-the-job training.
(c) Off-the-job training.

(See Chapter 9.)

Case example 12.2   Can you also train the customer?

This short study is concerned with the operation of a new style of restaurant in the UK, opened by a well-known figure in the food service industry, Bob Payton. Payton's success is founded very much on his own particular style and individual flair. As well as looking at the role of the consumer, it is also interesting to compare his approach with that of Bryniawsky in the previous case study.

The following is part of a report that appeared in the HCITB's publication *Service*.[3]

The Chicago Rib Shack

When Bob Payton opened his Chicago Rib Shack, he had two training problems — to make sure the staff knew their job and to educate the customer in choosing and eating American-style spare ribs.

The middle-aged gentleman in the restaurant looked like any other of the thousands of others who were taking lunch about that time in London. In his dark grey suit, gold wire-rimmed spectacles and bald head he could have been the local bank manager, he al district in a department head from Harrods, just across the road.

The fact that he was wearing a plastic bib and eating spare ribs with his hands did not seem to worry him unduly even though Bob Payton has to admit it looked 'a little bizarre'. The other customers, all well-dressed, were similarly bibbed and tuckered.

The new restaurant seats 200 and employs 75 staff, about 30 to a shift. Service is fairly formal and a few staff from the Pizza Pie restaurant have moved to more senior jobs at the Rib Shack. Though most of the staff are new, many are experienced in catering and some of them have worked in leading London restaurants.

The restaurant manager is Mike Gottlieb, who trained the staff and wrote the training manuals. His problem was not only to be sure that the staff knew their job, but to ensure that the customer was educated into the restaurant's rather unusual menu and style of eating.

'There has to be constant supervision of the customer', says Gottlieb. 'Much of the initial training was geared towards this objective. One of the most important tasks of the waiting staff is to explain exactly what each item consists of and how it has been prepared and the training programme has concentrated on this.'

'We've had to teach the staff to sell the menu but we've also had to teach them not to encourage customers to over-order. The dishes are strange to first-time diners and they don't know how to order so it's the waiter's job to take them through the menu.'

Most of the waiting staff were only engaged seven days before the restaurant opened and training was entirely on the job and is completely on-going. Both Bob Payton and Gottlieb are present at each service and are constantly issuing instructions throughout the service, never letting the supervision and control slip.

Such close supervision is typical of Payton's personal, single-minded approach to his restaurants. Before each service period, he and Gottlieb get all of the staff together for a training session when they point out the mistakes they spotted during the previous service period. Payton always stands up and has the staff sit — that way, he says, they know who's the boss. He knows exactly what he wants. He's tough, doesn't pull his punches and pitches straight into them.

'I noticed a lot of Coke bottles in the bins last night. They go in the racks provided. You don't throw Coke bottles away — they cost 10p each.'

'I heard a customer ask: "Why are there no toothpicks?" He should have been offered them. That's your responsibility.'

'Try to sell the onion loaf. It's delicious and nobody has had it before. And suggest to people that they may like to try the "Other Bits" as a side dish to the ribs. They aren't really meant as a starter anyway, as everything goes together.'

'But English people like to have a starter,' one waitress interjects.

'This isn't an English restaurant,' replies Payton tartly, 'People are coming here to do what we do in America. We sell ribs and chicken which are barbecued. So we don't serve mustard with our beef sandwiches.'

These sessions last for five to ten minutes at a time and the staff get an opportunity to make their own suggestions.

Payton doesn't miss out on the sales angle either. He emphasises that starters and desserts need to be sold to diners so that they sound tempting.

'It's no good saying "Would you like the dessert?" he tells them. 'You've got to suggest that they try our delicious pecan pie. Or tell them what's on the menu and ask them if they would like to try something.'

Payton and Gottlieb expect a high standard from their staff and the regular training sessions are designed to motivate them and maintain standards. Both of them eat in the restaurant every day and watch the service like hawks, leaving nothing to chance.

'I seem to have got a bit of a reputation for hire and fire,' admits Gottlieb, 'that's probably true to a certain extent, particularly during anyone's first three months. If a waiter isn't performing up to standard, I'm not very sympathetic. But anybody who stays with us for three months has got a job for life.'

Staff/customer ratio in the Rib Shack is high because staff have to supervise the customers so closely, much more than they would need to do in a normal restaurant.

How did Payton and Gottlieb choose the English staff for such an American way of service?

'We like people who smile a lot,' says Gottlieb, 'But we don't tell all and sundry "to have a nice day". That sounds phony over here. We do greet all of the customers though because verbal contact, from the moment they come in, is very important.'

The greeter's job is to take the customers to the table and, only if the restaurant is very busy, to suggest they have a drink at the bar.

Payton tells his staff to refuse to accept parties of more than eight, and this is only one of Payton's house rules. 'No credit cards' and 'No pipes or cigars' also apply to the Rib Shack. Dealing with customers who insist on their right to smoke a pipe or cigar is also part of the training of the staff.

How does Payton equate this with his philosophy of running a restaurant as if he is inviting guests to his own home?

'There's only one star in the restaurant,' he told a waitress. 'And you know who that is.'

'You, I suppose,' said the waitress.

'No,' said Payton, 'it's the food.'

Question 12.2(a)

Attempt to evaluate Bob Payton's leadership style (see Chapter 8).

Question 12.2(b)

In your opinion, will the British consumer be attracted to this style of restaurant? Give your reasons (see Chapter 11).

Case example 12.3   A theoretical approach to customer satisfaction

Although wherever possible we have supported our statements or opinions about a topic area with research evidence, we have attempted as much as possible to adopt a common sense and practical approach to human relations. Apart from this case study, all the other studies are down to earth and look at how particular individuals and organisations tackle their real-life problems. This study,[4] however, is more theoretical in its approach, but has been included here since it is seen as a major contribution to synthesising your understanding of behavioural aspects of the industry.

Improving employee service levels

A major source of satisfaction for customers of hospitality operations is the service employees provide. In order for employees to be trained to perform activities which provide customer satisfaction, it is necessary for the hospitality manager to determine what service actions bring about satisfaction.

Customers' satisfaction is brought about by such things as a good employee attitude and customer orientation. Because customers' satisfaction and a good attitude are very difficult to define, there is a tendency for hospitality managers to talk in generalities and use unmeasurable and sometimes meaningless terms. What is needed is a way to design jobs and encourage behaviour that provides customers with satisfaction.

In any service operation it is difficult to measure how pleased or displeased a customer is, but unless managers are aware of what pleases their customers it is very difficult to ensure that employees will do those things that bring about satisfaction. For example, most customers like to be greeted by a friendly waitress. But what is friendly? Friendly is a subjective term with different meanings for different people, so to tell a waitress to be friendly is not a very effective description of desired behaviour. However, for most people, a smile is a component of friendly service. A smile is something that is measurable and can be demonstrated and thus understood by employees.

Efforts to develop employee behaviour which leads to customer satisfaction can be condensed into a three-stage process:

1. Identifying components of customer satisfaction.
2. Developing a vehicle for evaluating the amount or level of satisfaction provided by an employee.
3. Providing feedback to employees through the evaluation process.

Identifying components of customer satisfaction

Customer satisfaction is ultimately exhibited through continuing patronage. Thus a hotel or restaurant that is profitable, with a reasonable amount of repeat business, can be fairly certain that whatever it is that employees are doing is providing satisfaction. However, unless satisfaction-producing behaviour is identified so that new employees can be indoctrinated, the repeat business picture can change as managers and employees leave and new personnel change the training and behaviour expectations.

The customer is the primary information source for identifying components of satisfaction.

Many hotels and restaurants make attempts at determining components of customer satisfaction through a variety of methods, most of which are informal, or at best, statistically unreliable. One of the most popular methods is to place a questionnaire in the guest room or on the patron's table in the restaurant. Designed properly, questionnaires can provide valuable information (McCleary and Wilson 1981). Unfortunately, most questionnaires used in service operations broach only the questions of whether guests were satisfied or not, and ignore attempts to determine sources of satisfaction. For example, a questionnaire picked up recently at a Days Inn asked 'How would you describe the attitude of the employees toward you?' Response possibilities include good, fair, and poor, with a place for a checkmark by each response. A response to any of the possible answers is almost meaningless from a possible development standpoint. While completed questionnaires which consistently indicate a response of poor provide management with a warning signal, they give no indication as to what is wrong with employee attitudes.

Another way managers gather information regarding customer satisfaction is to wander through the establishment and talk informally with guests. This method of obtaining feedback at least provides two-way communication, but there is also a tendency to get less than truthful responses from many people, because they are reluctant to criticise specific employees for fear of 'getting them into trouble'. Or if guests are particularly pleased, it is difficult for a manager not trained in interviewing techniques to ask questions which identify specific actions which provide the pleasure.

A perceptive manager can gain insight by simply observing employees in action. By watching guest response during interactions with employees, a manager can get a feel for what individuals do to make guests happy. Indeed, many managers have excellent records of hiring good employees based on a 'gut feeling' developed through years of experience. However, unless the manager does all the hiring and training, much of the responsibility for personnel will be delegated. Thus, people responsible for training must be made aware of actions which provide satisfaction so that this information can be passed on to employees.

The task facing a hospitality manager, then, is to gather information in a systematic manner that accurately identifies sources of satisfaction which can be translated to employee training and effectiveness. To accomplish this task, the first step is to develop a sound data-gathering instrument.

Designing an instrument for developing customer-satisfying behaviour

An instrument constructed for use in a fast-food restaurant which is reliable and valid for that restaurant's customers and employees will not contain the same degree of reliability and validity for a hotel or fine dining restaurant. In fact, an instrument constructed for a hotel in Chicago will not provide the same degree of accuracy for another hotel in the chain which is located in San Francisco, although it is likely that one instrument could be used chain-wide with only minor modifications if there is a great deal of similarity between the two properties.

The first step necessary to construct the data-gathering instrument is to generate a large pool of experimental items. These items should be generated to reflect opinions of managers, employees and clientele of the property so that comparisons can be made among the group regarding perceptions of the importance of items which constitute satisfaction. The inclusion of the three groups becomes important in helping to point out misconceptions on the part of employees and management as to what customers consider to be good service and accentuates differences which can be focused on in training. Information for item generation can be gathered through focus group and/or personal interviews conducted separately for each of the three categories of respondents. The interviews might centre around the theme of comparing the best and worst service encountered in an establishment of the type in question. The interviewees' responses should be coded so that they can be content-analysed by the respondent group, question by question.

The second step consists of evaluating the items generated in step one. Here again it would be highly beneficial to include representative samples from employees and management as well as from clientele, for the reasons mentioned previously. Evaluation is conducted by directing the respondent to reply to a standard series of questions for each evaluative item. These questions, while having the same content, are worded somewhat differently for the employee and management groups than for the clientele group. For example, the management and employee groups may be asked to respond to the following series of questions for each proposed evaluation item:

1. Does this item present information which could be used to improve your service? (YES/NO)
2. If you were to construct an evaluation instrument would you include this item? (YES/NO)
3. Would you need additional information to interpret the response to this item? (YES/NO)
4. Do you believe clientele can accurately evaluate you on this item? (YES/NO)

The clientele group will respond to a parallel set of questions for each trial item. The questions, however, might be phrased as follows:

1. Do you believe this item is relevant for appraising the described service? (YES/NO)
2. If you were to construct a questionnaire for gathering information about service, would you include this item? (YES/NO)
3. Would you want to qualify your response to this item? (YES/NO)
4. Do you believe you have enough information and/or are competent to evaluate those aspects of service referred to by this item? (YES/NO)

Although the completed instrument will probably not contain all of the items being evaluated in step two, it will not contain any additional items.

Finally, clientele will also be asked to respond to a global item designed to assess overall satisfaction with employees' service delivery. This global item might be formulated as the following question:

Would you please rate your overall satisfaction with the service provided by the employees of —— hotel.

1. Very satisfied
2. Satisfied
3. Neither satisfied nor dissatisfied (neutral)
4. Dissatisfied
5. Very dissatisfied

The reasons for including the global question are twofold. The first reason revolves around the validity issue. The instrument would demonstrate con-current validity if the clientele were responding to both the individual items and the global item in a similar fashion.

The second reason for using a global question is consistent with the reasoning used for having sample members respond to individual evaluative questions. The responses provide a comparison of the overall service level before and after incorporating the use of the service rating instrument in the company's training program.

The third and final step in constructing an evaluation instrument involves analysing the data gathered in step two and selecting items to be included in the final instrument. Selected items must be examined to determine if they need to be qualified in any way in order to be understandable and to be sure that items can be used for meaningful evaluation. Even if clients feel items are important, the items should not be included unless they are in a measurable state which will contribute to the management decision process. An evaluation instrument can then be developed from the information generated in the three step process presented above.

The final instrument should be pretested on a group of managers for readability, clarity and comprehensiveness. It is also necessary to determine if the changes that were made have enhanced the final instrument. The results from this final pretest may be incorporated in the finished instrument.

Measuring employees' performance

After management has developed a valid and reliable instrument and has used this instrument to identify specific employee behaviours desired by guests, the gathered information can be used for assessing individual employee performance. Each item generated from the data-gathering instrument will be measurable, and together these items will measure components of attitude and customer orientation.

To clarify what a typical evaluation may contain, Fig. 12.1 presents an example of some measurable items which might be generated for front desk performance during check-in.

The items in Fig. 12.1 are all measurable simply by observing what a clerk does while checking in a guest and noting the level of performance on an employee rating form.

Measurable items like those in Fig. 12.1 can be set up for all areas of the hotel and restaurant and for each phase of service where employees interact with customers. While it is recognised that different customers will desire somewhat different behaviours, the process of gathering information on a mean desired level of behaviour at least provide management with a base for measuring performance. This process, of course, will not and should not take away the individual employee's ability to insert his/her own personality into the employee/guest interaction. The attempt here is to lend an element of objectivity and measurability to an otherwise totally subjective process of measuring employee performance.

The assumption behind measuring employees' performance is that there is a correlation between high behavioural performance ratings and consumer satisfaction. Thus, the level of customer satisfaction should also be monitored to determine if in fact satisfaction has been improved. This can be accomplished by using the original items generated to determine satisfaction for developing a questionnaire administered to a sample of guests from time to time.

Improving employees' performance

The ability of employees to exhibit customer satisfying behaviour depends not only on their own motivation but also on the property's ability to manage, and a commitment to developing an atmosphere conducive to providing customer service. For example, because some of the items in Fig. 12.1 are not toally within the control of the employee, managers must understand the importance of designing work situations which make it possible for employees to perform activities which provide satisfaction. In a situation where there are not enough desk clerks on duty or there are too few terminals, employees will not be able to meet the ideal point for check-in time through no fault of their own. Unless management responds by providing necessary resources, designing customer-oriented jobs, and then rewarding employees based on the performance of behaviour which provides satisfaction, the whole process of evaluation becomes frustrating and non-productive. It is counterproductive to tell a waiter that he must spend extra time selling wine to a table and then evaluate him on how many customers are served in a given time period.

I. Guest was greeted with a smile		Yes ____ No ____
II. Guest's reservation was located within thirty seconds	Comment	Yes ____ No ____
	Actual time	
III. Guest's name was repeated three times during check-in		Yes ____ No ____
	Actual number	
IV. Guest was given directions to the elevators		Yes ____ No ____
	Comment	
V. Guest was given directions to guest's room		Yes ____ No ____
	Comment	
VI. Desk clerk was able to answer guest's questions regarding hotel		Yes ____ No ____
	Comment	
VII. Total check-in time was under three minutes		Yes ____ No ____
	Comment	
VIII. Guest was dismissed with a smile		Yes ____ No ____
	Comment	
IX. Guest was wished an enjoyable stay		Yes ____ No ____
	Comment	

Figure 12.1

Once it has been determined what actions provide satisfaction, employees must be told of the desired actions and trained in their performance. This is much easier when specific behaviours can be communicated and demonstrated than when phrases like 'develop a good attitude' are used. In addition, employee rating forms can be used periodically in an appraisal interview to point out specific reasons (such as a failure to repeat the guest's name) for the rating received by the employee. The use of videotape can be a valuable aid in demonstrating performances such as how to check-in people efficiently, and also in capturing more subjective behaviour in handling guests. This can be accomplished by taping outstanding employees in specific situations to use as a model.

Question 12.3(a)

Look at Fig. 12.1. What is the danger inherent in training staff to satisfy such a checklist? How might this danger be reduced? (see Chapter 6).

Question 12.3(b)

How do you think staff will react to being 'measured' by inventories such as those shown in Fig. 12.1?

Question 12.3(c)

Assume that such evaluation was to be introduced into a hotel for the first time. Identify from the study how any staff resistance to this change might be reduced (see Chapter 9).

Case example 12.4   Developing a management team in a large hotel

This case study is adapted from an article about the implementation of 'management by objectives'. Whilst MBO is outside the scope of this book, what is particularly interesting is the style of management found in this particular hotel and how Blundell[5] and his colleagues successfully changed the structure and style of the team.

The case study begins with some problem areas: 'Delegate — of course I delegate. Listen — I have all my heads of department in my office every single morning and tell them exactly what to do. That's delegation'.

The above statement was made by a general manager of a large hotel and more disturbingly still, he really believed he had a progressive approach towards modern management.

The hotel has more than 500 rooms. The general manager, Pete, is in his first chief executive post, although he has held positions of responsibility in other hotels within the chain. He had been in this post for six months when the authors discussed with him some of the problems which, in his view, existed.

Training could achieve little for his team, all they needed was to work harder. Okay, a training programme could be introduced but it had to get the staff to work harder. He personally would not participate as it might indicate a weakness, in him, in the eyes of his subordinates (implied in conversation). He had no real authority as head office controlled all decisions. Head office was always breathing down his neck for reports which left little time to do any real jobs around the hotel. His first six months had been lonely and he had had no real informal contact with his subordinate managers.

After this preliminary encounter interviews and discussion groups were held on a very informal basis with senior and junior management and supervisory staff. Our general consensus was that:

1. Communications at all levels were counterproductive and often destructive.
2. No information regarding performance was readily available.
3. The general manager never really got into contact with people.
4. Too much checking up was done — this undermined personal pride in work.
5. Managers were not motivating juniors or staff so morale was low.
6. Every little problem was passed up through the organisation and ultimately to head office, so no manager held any real authority.

7. No room for ideas or innovation existed — 'follow the book is best' seemed to be the general view.

From our findings, it became quite clear that there was a need to change the overall style of the chief executive which alternated between autocrat and compromiser in its effect upon the group's behavioural style. High impact on the group would be necessary to stimulate the flow of positive thinking in producing an innovative and creative team.

The original organisational chart of top management in the hotel was as follows:

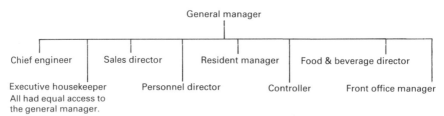

All had equal access to the general manager.

During the training sessions these eight managers were given a 'change attitude' questionnaire, consisting of questions such as those shown below.

TEAM MANAGEMENT ANALYSIS

Analyse your team by rating it from 1–7 on the scale below. This questionnaire will form the basis of a group discussion.

		1	2	3	4	5	6	7	
1	Degree of mutual trust. High suspicion	3		1		1		3	High trust
2	Degree of mutual support. Each participates for self only		3	2		1	1	1	Genuine concern for each other
3	Communications. Guarded and cautious	1	1	1	3	1			Open and authentic
4	Team objectives. Not understood by team	1		1	3	2	1		Clearly understood by team
	Team is negative towards objectives		2	1	2	3			Team is committed to objectives
5	Handling conflicts within team. We deny, avoid or suppress conflicts			1	1	1	3	2	We confront conflicts and "work them through"
6	Utilisation of team resources. Our abilities, knowledge and experience are not utilised by the team	2	2	1	1			2	Our abilities, knowledge and experience are fully utilised by the team

7 Control methods.

Control is imposed on us.	1 2		2 3		We control

8 Organisation environment.

Restrictive, pressure toward conformity	1 3 2 2		Free, supportive, respect for individual differences

The results of these 80 questions resulted in scores that showed a wide range of attitudes towards the effective management of the hotel.

Attitude	No. of group with attitude
Sabotage	2
Slow down	
Protests	1
Apathy	3
Indifference	1
Acceptance	
Support	
Co-ordination	
Commitment	1

The team also answered a questionnaire on delegation as shown below:

HOW MANAGEMENT FUNCTIONS AS AN EFFECTIVE TEAM

Yes				No			1	Do management meetings develop into a 'one way street' of instructions handed down by the chief executive?
3 2	1	0	1	2 3				
3 2				2				

Yes				No			2	There is a strong feeling that all decisions are 'sold' to the group but the group has little influence upon the decision making process.
3 2	1	0	1	2 3				
2 3		1	1					

Yes				No			3	Can management meetings be characterised as 'subordinates accepting management ideas after discussion'?
3 2	1	0	1	2 3				
1	2	3	1					

Yes				No			4	Decisions, based upon the chief executive's or senior managers' points of view, are presented to subordinates and are changed as a result of the views of the group or specialists within the group.
3 2	1	0	1	2 3				
	4	2	1					

Yes				No			5	Management meetings from a continuous review of subordinates' functions, presented by each individual as an appraisal of his or her positive contribution to departmental effectiveness.
3 2	1	0	1	2 3				
	1	5	1					

Yes				No			6	Do ideas develop from subordinates' well-constructed 'cases' which contribute to the effectiveness of the position and not the indiv idual?
3 2	1	0	1	2 3				

Question 12.4(a)

Speculate as to the style of leadership of Pete (see Chapter 8). As a result of this and other activities the manager developed a new organisational chart.

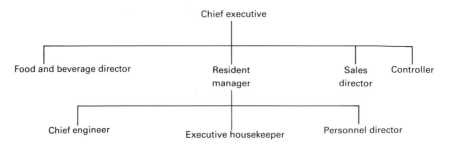

Question 12.4(b)

Speculate why the organisation was modified in this way (see Chapter 10). Following this re-organisation, a pilot scheme was introduced utilising the management by objectives approach. After six months, a further re-organisation took place.

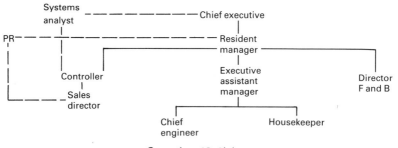

Question 12.4(c)

Compare the first chart with this new one. What span of management existed and now exists from the viewpoint of the chief executive? What effect has this had upon the number of management levels? (See Chapter 10).

Question 12.4(d)

What sort of activities and functions is the chief executive likely to be concerned with within the new organisation and what responsibilities has he delegated? (See Chapter 9).

Question 12.4(e)

The new chart shows no personnel director. Why do you think this might be? (See Chapter 10).

Case example 12.5   Multi-skilling in hotel and catering industry

The previous case study identified at the management level a need for the clear demarcation of responsibility and high degree of mutual trust. This case study suggests that at the lower levels trust is still essential but that the division of labour into particular job categories is counterproductive. It is based on a study[6] that has had a major impact, if a somewhat controversial one, upon the attitudes towards staff deployment. Mars, Mitchell and Bryant advocate the idea of the multi-skilling of staff. As the study shows the idea is not as outrageous as it first appears and has been implemented in many other circumstances. For instance, Tovey does it in his world-renowned Miller-Howe hotel, fast-food operators do so as a norm, and on a much smaller scale one of the authors practised the concept in his own restaurant quite successfully for two years.

'One of the major difficulties faced by many organisations in this industry is that they possess a high degree of division of labour. This is particularly characteristic of the traditionally hierarchical organisation within large hotels. This division of labour results in low productivity since each group of workers tends to perform only a limited range of specified tasks. It is, however, feasible, given the services that a hotel normally provides, for one worker to perform several tasks. Put at its simplest, a chambermaid can, for instance, also operate as a waitress. Such a degree of multi-skilling essentially breaks down traditional hierarchical structures. Instead of being based on official occupational grades, rewards can be related to skill levels. Multi-skilling also has the advantage of increasing possibilities for incentives and promotion.'

As support for this viewpoint, they cite the example of the *Hotel Aeropolitan* which is the pseudonym for one of the large hotels at Heathrow.

'Hotel Aeropolitan is a 400 bedroom hotel built at a major airport by a multi-national conglomerate company, which had newly moved into the UK hotel industry. Its management soon realised that if the hotel was to be viable it needed to maintain a high level of consistent service. In order to keep its staff, the hotel had to pay wage rates which were high because of prevailing rates set by other jobs in and around the airport, and because of competition from other hotels in the area. But how could the hotel achieve its aims with high wages and with the normal low productivity of hotel workers?

The solution, management decided, was to embark on a deliberate campaign to recruit local workers who had not worked in a hotel before and to train them to perform multiple tasks. This policy, it was predicted, would increase productivity and job satisfaction. The company would then be able to pay its workers higher wages than other hotels in the area. This policy was in fact implemented and, as predicted, met with success, at least initially. Labour turnover, for example was far less than is normally experienced in hotel operations, particularly new ones, and was certainly way below that of other hotels in the area. The initial success, however, created some snags and difficulties.

The scheme's major difficulty arose because traditional hotel workers from outside the local labour market, who had been drawn to the hotel by the prospect of higher wages, were not readily able to adapt to working with the new 'type' of staff. Moreover, these traditional workers did not fully appreciate the changes in the socio-technical system. They expected to find individual contract making and the structure of the total reward system similar to those they had previously experienced. They failed to realise that the purpose of multi-skilling was, in part, to give senior management greater control over the total reward system and to centralise and regulate all aspects of payment. Many of these traditional staff were highly skilled which exacerbated the division between them and the newly hired, multi-skilled 'types' who had no previous experience of the industry. Conflict between these two groups led to a temporary increase in labour turnover, and the whole basis of raising productivity through multi-skilling was set back until management was able to regain control of the total reward system. This it did both by more selective recruitment (and training) from the local labour market, and by reinforcing its policy of eschewing individual contracts.

The scheme as it has subsequently developed appears to be an overall success. The level of service has been consistently maintained at a distinctively high standard; labour turnover has been considerably reduced and remains low compared with that of other hotels in the same area.

> Investment in the training of manpower.
> Investment in technical resources.
> A brand new hotel and specifically designed to exploit the most modern equipment available.
> New hotels and newly created hotel industries.'

They also record the effect of a similar policy of multi-skilling at a smaller unit which they call *Le Pays du Nord.*

'One of the major problems facing most small restaurants and particularly those at this end of the quality market is the frequently high and often sudden turnover of its staff.

For such a restaurant to lose its chefs can be extremely serious. Realising that good staff and particularly good chefs tend to be ambitious and that ambitious staff tend to leave a small restaurant, this owner decided to control such movements by scheduling them. To this end he made explicit arrangements with higher grade and larger and more prestigious restaurants so that his chefs are able to see their posts with him as part of a logical progression which leads from first chef in 'Le Pays du Nord' to third chef at, say, the Café Royal. When a chef leaves now he tends to leave by arrangement and at a time mutually convenient; sudden, unplanned and disruptive departures are thus minimised and mutual trust is increased.

Whereas many restaurants employ socially marginal workers particularly in posts as cleaners and kitchen hands, this restaurateur recruits most of his staff from temporarily unemployed actresses and actors who work for him between their highly paid jobs on the stage or in television. For these people he offers a degree of what can be called transient job security in that he is prepared to carry, if necessary, an extra hand.

At the same time he practises multi-skilling by encouraging mobility throughout all of the restaurant's operations. One ambitious cleaner, for instance, had been eased through most jobs in the restaurant and had ended up as second chef. By developing such multi-skilling the restaurateur achieves not only flexibility in the deployment of his staff but also higher productivity which allows him to pay higher than prevailing wage rates.

All pressures towards the making of individual contracts and the rivalries that these provoke are eschewed and the total system of rewards is essentially visible and legitimate. As a result both of this and of multi-skilling, group cohesion is well marked amongst the staff. But this cohesion is consciously and continuously built upon by the proprietor's offering of collective recognition for target achievements; he offers small acknowledgements of chocolates or cigarettes if the restaurant is particularly busy for instance, and also by such arrangements as allowing staff to cover for each others' absences if they so desire.

Whereas other establishments suffer a crisis if sudden staff shortages occur, this proprietor is able to shuffle his staff to cover a shortage in almost any area.

As a result of these strategies the ad hoc and short-term tactical adaptations that are such a feature of this industry have largely been eradicated.

One important practice, much appreciated by this owner and his staff, is the opportunity offered for information sharing — that is, information passing through staff in contact with customers to the owner. This not only allows managerial decision making to be shared, but also for it to be informed from a base in reality. Consequently, the staff see a widening of their role as this affects the actual operation of the restaurant. Many useful revisions have, as a result, been made to decor, table layout and to times of opening as well as on the choice and price of available dishes, the needs for which could not have been known without this kind of participative communication which is now highly systematised.

The method is essentially simple. Waitresses ask their customers to arrange a number of cards in order of their preferences and this allows the proprietor to see which aspects of his services are rated highly and to find out customer preferences on a range of questions and specialised packs which ask for information on specific areas.

One unanticipated result of the operation of this system has been the appreciation of it expressed by customers. They repeatedly say how unusual it is to come across a restaurant whose staff really do show they care what customer preferences are and who are actually prepared to change aspects of the organisation in order to improve the level of service. Certainly the loyalty and regularity of its customers is a strong indication of this restaurant's success.'

Question 12.5(a)

Suggest which of the theories of motivation the concept of multi-skilling is based on (see Chapter 4).

Question 12.5(b)

The concept appears to be sound, but it does not appear to be common practice in many sectors of the industry. Suggest reasons why this is so (see Chapters 7 and 9).

Case example 12.6   Implementing change in a large hotel

This last case study is an account of the installation of computer technology and the repercussions of this in the Penta Hotel, London (now the Forum Hotel).'

Booking in the future of a giant hotel

A novel application of new technology in a fast-growing service industry can be found at Grand Metropolitan's London Penta Hotel in West London. One of the largest hotels to be built in Europe since the last war, the London Penta tower block dominates the Cromwell Road area of West London. With beds for 1,859 guests the Penta employs over 500 people.

Opened in June 1973, the Penta was designed to cater for the rapidly-growing tourist trade in London but by the early 1970s the problems associated with running such a mammoth hotel were beginning to appear. The sheer size of the building made such problems as locating vacant rooms, making reservations and keeping track of guests and their accounts increasingly difficult.

A particular problem was the volume of paperwork, which kept the NCR 42 accounting machines busy 24 hours a day, leading to rapid deterioration and frequent mechanical breakdowns. These difficulties led to problems in tracing and 'interpreting' customers' bills and to long queues of waiting guests at reception. The resulting dissatisfaction experienced by guests and staff made life tedious for all concerned.

In 1975, when the hotel's accounting machines were due for replacement, the management decided to investigate the possibilities of an alternative system. The rapid development of integrated computerised systems had opened the way to such an alternative.

The first stage was the transfer of the guest accounting and location systems from paper to computer. The second stage, which came in 1980, was the fully integrated system, adding advanced reservations, availability analysis and special events booking facilities.

The new system allows reception to see at a glance which rooms are free, who is occupying each room and when they are due to leave. The housekeeping staff can dial the computer via the telephone system to let reception know as soon as a room is ready for occupancy. The vacancy list is therefore constantly being updated.

In addition, the accounting staff can print out the guests' accounts, with all bills up to date, at a moment's notice. Advance reservations, such as travel agents' block bookings, can be put straight on to the computer and reservations staff can find out easily whether rooms will be free or not. This facility allows the hotel to accomplish much better long-term planning.

The system also allows direct crediting and bad debt reporting of companies which have accounts with the hotel, and there are various analytical functions such as marketing analysis, availability analysis and banqueting analysis.

As soon as the hotel envisaged change to a computerised system the management began to consult staff and inform them of the proposals. From the start, the process of change and consultation was seen as a function of the training department, not the personnel department. The main objective was to win staff confidence and co-operation and the training sessions presented the ideal opportunity to use existing avenues of communication with staff. Although the London Penta recognises the GMWU hotel and catering union, the union did not negotiate about the new system with management.

All members of staff were told about the new system, even those not directly affected by the change; what the computer could do, why it was being introduced and how it would cut costs. Most importantly, management stressed that there would be no job losses, and that job interest would increase, not decrease.

The training officer ran special training sessions with mixed staff groups, consisting of various grades and skills, to acquaint them with the system, build co-operation between grades, and discover any teething troubles. Training sessions were a useful medium for winning staff over to the new system and, as enthusiasm grew, the management asked them how they wished to effect the changeover, in one go or over a period of time.

The staff chose to 'go live' overnight and arranged the shift systems themseves to cover the event. Once it was in operation, the next six weeks were used as an evaluation period, with staff filling in forms to report any problems.

While the new system has automated many previously manual jobs, there has been no job loss. There were, and still are, 18 staff in reception. However, there is no doubt that the nature of jobs and 'job interest' has changed. Reception and cashier duties are now much more integrated, and a guest's problems or inquiries can now be dealt with by one employee, rather than the customer being shunted from desk to desk.

At the same time, the accounting staff have had much of the drudgery of accounts ledger work removed, leaving them free to concentrate on particular problems. Similarly, advance reservations work has become less time-consuming and routine.

The reception staff are part of the hotel's job-evaluated pay structure. While old-fashioned typewriters and accounting machines have gone, keyboard skills are still required, and those who did not have this skill have had to learn. This, in turn, has led to regradings and more pay for these staff, and has opened up new career possibilities.

The other staff affected by the new system are the housekeeping staff. The turnround of rooms in a hotel is most important — an unprepared vacant room is money lost — so the new system is designed to ensure that supplies of fresh linen, for example, are sent to the right floor in the right quantities at the right time.

Chambermaids can signal the computer as soon as a room is ready and supervisors can signal the room vacant as soon as they have checked it out.

The chambermaids work to a simple work measurement system. They must achieve at least 65 points per day, with extra points paid at bonus rate. Each day, a chambermaid is given her room numbers with the points per room (four for a single, five for a double and six for a triple) from the computer print-out. The computer keeps a check on how many points have been achieved.

The housekeeping staff have their own VDU which they can use to delete rooms taken out of service through damage, for instance.

Question 12.6(a)

Identify what, if any, are the likely courses of staff unrest about the introduction of this technology (see Chapter 9).

Question 12.6(b)

Identify what aspects of the new system contribute to the motivation of typical reception staff and housekeeping staff (see Chapter 4).

Question 12.6(c)

Suggest what advantages management might cite for installing the system (see Chapters 5 and 8).

Question 12.6(d)

Compare the Penta Hotel's approach to implementing change to that advocated in Chapter 9. What, if any, are the differences?

REFERENCES

1. Kubarycz, N. (1982) Finding and keeping staff. *Fast Food*, May.
2. Wilton, D. (1983) Foodex slows revolving door turnover. *Canadian Hotel and Restaurant*, January.
3. *Service*, April/May 1982. HCITB.
4. McCleary, K. & Weaver P. (1982) Improving employee service levels through identifying sources of customer satisfaction. *Hospitality Management*, **1** (2).
5. Blundell, S. (1977) Implementing MBO in the hotel industry. *HCIMA Review*, **2**(3).
6. Mars, G., Mitchell, P. & Bryant, D. (1979) *Manpower Problems in the Hotel and Catering Industry*. Farnborough: Saxon House.
7. White, G. (1980) Booking in the future of a giant hotel. *Employment Gazette*.

Index